Fourteenth-Century
English Poetry

Fourteenth-Century English Poetry

Contexts and Readings

ELIZABETH SALTER

Clarendon Press · Oxford
1983

Oxford University Press, Walton Street, Oxford OX2 6DP

London Glasgow New York Toronto
Delhi Bombay Calcutta Madras Karachi
Kuala Lumpur Singapore Hong Kong Tokyo
Nairobi Dar es Salaam Cape Town
Melbourne Auckland

and associated companies in
Beirut Berlin Ibadan Mexico City Nicosia

Oxford is a trade mark of Oxford University Press

Published in the United States
by Oxford University Press, New York

British Library Cataloguing in Publication Data

Salter, Elizabeth
 Fourteenth-century poetry,
 1. English poetry—History and criticism
 I. Title
 821'.009 PR502
 ISBN 0-19-811186-X

Library of Congress Cataloging in Publication Data
Salter, Elizabeth.
 Fourteenth-century English poetry.
 Bibliography: p.
 Includes index.
 1. English poetry--Middle English, 1100-1500--History
and criticism. 2. Chaucer, Geoffrey, d. 1400--Criticism
and interpretation. 3. Langland, William, 1330?-1400?
Piers the Plowman. I. Title.
PR311.S26 1983 821'.1'09 83-4098

ISBN 0-19-811186-X

Typeset by DMB (Typesetting), Oxford
and printed in Great Britain by
Hazell Watson and Viney Ltd.,
Aylesbury, Bucks

Preface

Elizabeth Salter began this book about 1972. It grew out of her dissatisfaction and impatience with the inert and unexamined assumptions that constituted much of the literary history of the period, and was originally conceived as a comprehensive account of the literary, social, and historical context of English poetry in the fourteenth century. The first three chapters here are written according to that original conception. As the work developed, the concentration grew more close upon Chaucer and Langland, and the later chapters therefore demonstrate a shift of emphasis. The last two chapters, particularly, on Chaucer, are interpretative accounts of the *Parlement of Foules* and the *Knight's Tale* that are squarely within a critical tradition of 'close reading', though inspired throughout by a sense of context—in this case, literary context. The book as a whole is something of a pilgrimage, from literature to history and back to literature.

The author herself was constantly revising the book. About four years before her death in 1980 she embarked on a total re-writing of the opening chapters, in which, inevitably, she found herself writing the history of twelfth- and thirteenth-century literary culture as the preliminary to the study of the fourteenth. Two chapters were completed, and a third drafted, but subject, chronology, and mode of approach made it impossible for us to work these into the design of the existing book. We hope to bring out this late work in a separate publication. For the rest, we have worked with a complete and author-corrected typescript of the first three and last two chapters, in which all that was needed was the filling out of the annotation in certain cases. Chapter 4 is the only one in which we have had to make any editorial intervention, in effect by bringing together a section on alliterative poetry in general and another on Langland which seemed destined to be united. For this purpose we have supplied a brief paragraph of transition.

There has been no attempt to update the annotation, except by referring to Elizabeth Salter's own late writings, where she explored in depth some of the issues raised in these chapters; however, a supplement to the Bibliography is provided, in which important recent books and articles, relevant to the subject but brought out too late to be mentioned in the notes to the text, are listed.

We should like to thank the friends who have helped with specific enquiries, and who have encouraged us in our determination to bring this book to publication. We should like to thank, too, the Oxford University Press and its officers for their helpfulness and courtesy. The work is not as its author would have wished it to be, but we are sure that lovers of medieval literature will be glad to see the mature writing of one of its most gifted critics and exponents.

DEREK PEARSALL
NICOLETTE ZEEMAN

Contents

Abbreviations

BJRL	*Bulletin of the John Rylands Library*
DNB	*Dictionary of National Biography*
E & S	*Essays and Studies*
EETS, OS, ES	Early English Text Society, Original Series, Extra Series
EHR	*English Historical Review*
ELN	*English Language Notes*
ES	*English Studies*
EStn	*Englische Studien*
JEGP	*Journal of English and Germanic Philology*
JWCI	*Journal of the Warburg and Courtauld Institutes*
LSE	*Leeds Studies in English*
MÆ	*Medium Ævum*
MED	*Middle English Dictionary*
MLN	*Modern Language Notes*
MLR	*Modern Language Review*
MP	*Modern Philology*
MS	*Mediaeval Studies*
Neoph.	*Neophilologus*
NM	*Neuphilologische Mitteilungen*
NQ	*Notes and Queries*
n.s.	new series
OED	*Oxford English Dictionary*
PBA	*Proceedings of the British Academy*
PL	*Patrologia Latina*, ed. J.-P. Migne
PMLA	*Publications of the Modern Language Association of America*
RES	*Review of English Studies*
SATF	*Société des anciens textes français*
SP	*Studies in Philology*
STS	Scottish Text Society
TRHS	*Transactions of the Royal Historical Society*

1 Introductory: standards

Medieval English poetry belongs to those centuries in which romanesque art passed into gothic: to read it is, in a very real sense, to read the English medieval world—the problems it raises and the rewards it offers are complex, rich, and imprecise. No later age has ever utilized poetry quite so naturally and so relentlessly. It was a universal medium; reduced to its simplest form in the vernacular languages of Europe, it was a necessity for those who had to learn by ear, as a verbal equivalent to learning by eye, from images in stained-glass, wall-painting, and sculpture. But no later age has been, at the same time, so minutely conscious of the art of poetry, so sensitive to exquisite decorative effects. The whole range of medieval life—inner and outer—was expressed in poetry: it served practical needs and refined appetites with equal enthusiasm and fidelity.

Consequently, the difficulties of handling it are formidable. It is both high art, and doggerel; like the life of medieval man, it moves rapidly between meanness and magnificence. There is no simple way to judge it, and its contacts with us are unpredictable. Turning the pages of a volume of medieval lyrics, we can expect to find a sense of familiarity quickly followed by a sense of total alienation. The startling directness and economy of a thirteenth-century song in praise of summer may be entirely to modern taste: a fifteenth-century drunkard's song may capture perfectly for us the absurd and delightful solemnity of the situation:

> D ... dronken—
> dronken, dronken, y-dronken—
> ... dronken is tabart atte wyne.
> hay ... suster, walter, peter,
> ʒe dronke al depe,
> ant ichulle eke!
> stondet alle stille—

> stille, stille, stille—
> stondet alle stille—
> stille as any ston;
> trippe a lutel wit þi fot,
> ant let þi body go![1]

But we shall most likely remain cold to the attractions of a rhymed version of the Ten Commandments:

> Have on god in worship,
> Ne nem thou his name in idelschipe
> Wite wel thine haliday ...[2]

And this can be our experience of reading the work of major poets too: the vigorous and compassionate idealism of Langland, the sliding ironies of Chaucer are easy to admire. It is not so easy to accept the fact that they are interleaved or juxtaposed with stiff, abstract allegory, or gestured rhetoric. The artificial *Man of Law's Tale* has a place in the Canterbury sequence, and Langland dryly versifies the Ten Commandments into a flat, allegorical map immediately after presenting the seven deadly sins in a deeply-dimensioned landscape of vice.[3]

But selection and praise of the poetry which immediately appeals to us involves us in half-truths. The first whole truth to be faced is the plain fact of what medieval English poetry is. For its span is remarkable; at one extreme, simple, mnemonic calendar poems, recording country activities through the months of the year: at the other, the encrusted verse narratives of the 'alliterative revival' of the fourteenth century, and the subtler verbal harmonies of *Troilus and Criseyde*. Between these extremes, a mass of writing, lyric, didactic, dramatic, moving—often imperceptibly—from entertainment to edification and satisfying the demands of an amorphous public: illiterate, sophisticated, learned. Perhaps the hardest thing for us to accept is the integral part played by medieval verse in the ordinary business of life. Not only chivalric narratives, love-themes, fabliaux, and fables but history, religious instruction, medical and dietary information, political comment, complaint, and satire were all conveyed in verse, not prose, for the greater part of the medieval period.[4] Poetry covered nearly all genres, including those which we would now describe as the popular novel, journalism, and political propaganda. A collection of medieval poems need have no stronger claims upon our attention—or indeed, upon that of its own age—than a collection of present-day magazine articles. The *Treatise for Laundresses*, by John Lydgate, monk of Bury St. Edmunds in the earlier fifteenth century, is technically, poetry. But these matters go into poetic form mainly so that they may be more easily summarized and remembered; there is only a faint and uncertain hint of amusement at the incongruity of the theme:

> Of wyn away the moles may ye wesshe
> In mylk whyt; the fletyng oyly spott
> Wyth lye of beenes make hit clene and fresshe.
> Wasshe with wyn the fervent inkes blot ...[5]

Similarly, the anonymous author of a fourteenth-century rhymed sermon, intended to be delivered in the person of the High Priest, Caiaphas,[6] no doubt regarded verse form as a useful means of attracting and holding the attention of a motley audience, in the open air, on a Feast Day.

This universal coverage by verse is vitally important to recognize, for it may change our expectations of what we are to find in a collection of medieval verse. It instructs us about the close relationship of function and form, and disposes us to look for something nearer to *Hymns Ancient and Modern* than for the religious poetry of Donne or Herbert when we first encounter what editors still optimistically call 'medieval lyrics'. It also helps us to understand why major poets such as Langland and Chaucer, for all their great skill in the arts of composition, did not feel they had betrayed their 'art' when they treated verse in a familiar, business-like way, asking it sometimes to act as an efficient carrier of information rather than as an instrument of the imagination. Verse was, at once, the goddess and the maid-of-all-work.

The difficulty, then, is to know where literary preoccupations end, and historical take over. How comprehensive a view of medieval verse are we bound to take? Lydgate's *Treatise for Laundresses* need not delay us long, but it is possible that we could be too hasty in weeding out what is unworthy of our attention. In the case of a poem such as *Piers Plowman*, a totally evaluative reading, based on modern aesthetic criteria, may perform a crucial kind of surgery upon it, and endanger the life of the whole organism. From some points of view, anything that is in verse form is relevant to generalizations about medieval poetry; Ernst Curtius gave authority to this 'documentary' approach:

> For our investigation there is no distinction between respectable and reviled elements of tradition. The whole stock must be taken together ... Only then can we see Antiquity without bias, and re-evaluate the Middle Ages. Only then can we gauge how the modern literatures continue the tradition and how they differ from it.[7]

In such a context, the most pedestrian Middle English romance or rhymed prayer of penitence is significant. Indeed, its very obvious inadequacy as imaginative literature may reveal, if we are interested to inquire, a cultural situation of great interest; it may prompt thought about the relationship of poet and public, about the forces—religious, social, and educational—which affect the poet's choice or rejection of image, epithet, and metrical structure. The total implications of a particular poem may be extremely wide. So, the fact that some medieval verse is terse, almost to the point of poverty, need not always prove lack of inventiveness. It may indicate that the writers are using a sort of short-hand notation for a powerful emotional statement, which may be difficult—though not impossible—for us to read back. A brief poem such as

> Foweles in þe frith,
> þe fisses in þe flod,
> And i mon waxe wod.
> Mulch sorw I walke with
> for beste of bon and blod.[8]

has a musical accompaniment which, if not expressive in a modern sense, strengthens the slender thread of words. But it is, also, a series of brief references to a complex body of assumptions about the nature and experience of refined and unrequited love, and its place in the created universe.

This can lead us to other branches of the arts: we know how the visual imagery of stained glass, wall-painting, and sculptured column was designed—sometimes in co-operation with words,[9] and sometimes in lieu of them—to stimulate and vivify the imagination of medieval man. A fourteenth-century preacher tells us:

I say boldly that ther ben mony thousand of pepul that couth not ymagen in her hert how Crist was don on the rood but as thai lerne hit be si3t of ymages and payntours.[10]

The barest treatment of the Passion, or of death, for instance, could rely upon an instant supply of strong and vivid associations, which were daily reinforced by the sight of brilliant or sombre tableaux of life and death in parish churches, cathedrals, and the halls of the nobility:

> If man him biðocte
> inderlike and ofte
> hu arde is te fore
> fro bedde te flore,
> hu reuful is te flitte
> fro flore te pitte,
> fro pitte te pine
> ðat nevre sal fine,
> i wene non sinne
> sulde his herte winnen.[11]

One version of these lines appeared in fifteenth-century mural inscriptions in a chapel in Stratford-upon-Avon.[12] A fourteenth-century manor house in Northamptonshire, Longthorpe Tower, still displays to us, in its wall-painting of life and youth confronted by death, how medieval man ensured that he 'meditated inwardly and continuously' about his humbling last journey.[13]

The frail hold that some of these medieval poems have, of necessity, upon our imagination, is well demonstrated by the well-known thirteenth-century 'Sunset on Calvary' quatrain:

> Nou goth sonne under wod, —
> me reweth, marie, þi faire Rode.
> Nou goþ sonne under tre, —
> me reweþ, marie, þi sone and þe.[14]

The original life of this poem is only partly restored to it when we try to conjure up a possible time and place for its composition—

from what cloister-garth in what green valley that sunset was seen in the evening hour of meditation ...[15]

The dramatic moment of vision, when the imagined religious scene is fused with a particular English sunset of the thirteenth century— 'the sinking of the sun behind some lonely forest ...'[16] —is only one element in the whole significance of the poem for us. Its particular context in St. Edmund of Canterbury's *Speculum Ecclesiae* shows us how it draws its essential power from the lines quoted immediately before it:

> Ne vus amerveillez mie,
> Que io su brunecte e haslée,
> Car le solail me ad descolurêe[17]

They, in turn, are based upon *Canticles*, i.15, 'Quia sol decoloravit me'. The 'sun' which has stained the Virgin's face is also her 'son': she is suffused with fading sunlight, grief, and reflected divinity. No doubt a medieval poet, and his readers, would have been familiar with the 'sun shining through glass' as an image of the Incarnation.[18] And familiar, too, with the picturing of the Virgin shafted by sunlight, reading, or kneeling in a Gothic oratory.[19] But when we engage in activities of this kind—looking *behind* a lyric to its original frame of reference, insisting upon a build-up of all possible sorts of meaning—we are trying to understand rather than judge. Definition is more in our minds than assessment. There may be objections to making 'no distinction between respectable and reviled elements of tradition', and some may feel in sympathy with the plain question 'whether or not the poem is a good poem'.[20] The dangers of such a question for the study of medieval literature begin to be clear when we go on to read that our only responsibility to these poems is to see 'which of them still work, are still effective. We ought to ask ourselves whether anything happens when we read them ... if nothing happens, there is nothing to discuss.'[21]

It is true that to be contented with the role of literary annalist is a retreat from difficulties. But we should hardly have made much progress with understanding and appreciating early Celtic evangelist portraits, twelfth-century Catalan wall-painting, or, indeed, with the first experimental work of Picasso if we had assumed, on first encounter, that 'if nothing happens, there is nothing to discuss'. For the foundations upon which such art is based differ radically from those most familiar to us. Few would now find any problems in recognizing and accepting the principles underlying Netherlandish landscape painting of the seventeenth century, English portrait painting of the Gainsborough or Reynolds era, or French impressionist painting of the nineteenth century. But a Romanesque madonna, a Henry Moore warrior, a late Gothic tomb canopy may possibly evoke little positive response—initially, at least. Here our sensibility has to be aided by basic knowledge about alien principles, functions, and conditions. In this, art criticism seems to be far more advanced than literary criticism: difficulty of access is accepted as a challenge to discover, not a reason for capitulation. Modern artists have been decisive here; looking to the art of the pre-Renaissance centuries for inspiration, they have not tried to minimize, but to stress and use the differences they observe. Moore's rejection of the 'happy fixed finality', the 'resolved world' of much classical and Renaissance art in favour of the 'disturbed world' of more primitive art forms— African, Mexican, medieval European—is symptomatic.[22] And, indeed, a full response to the art of Picasso, Braque, or Moore requires the same preliminary readjustment of critical attitude as we have to make when first coming upon the massive painted evangelist figures of the twelfth century, with their total disregard for 'normal' spatial harmonies, and their totally 'unrealistic' colour range.[23]

Willingness to respond to an entirely new kind of artistic stimulus is important: 'good' or 'inferior' we have also to be concerned with—but we must inquire into the original principles and criteria of the art or literature we study. This is of particular relevance to some kinds of medieval wall-painting.

An important purpose of country church wall-paintings was didactic ... this purpose was still served by means of clarity in composition, and vigour in execution ... (they) might be described as 'crude, but instinct with life and significance' ... Condemnation for inappropriate reasons of the average medieval wall-painting is roughly equivalent to condemnation of really good modern 'poster' design, on the ground that the latter lacks the 'finish' peculiar to a portrait miniature on ivory.[24]

The 'average medieval wall-painting' is very close in aim and method to the average medieval religious poem: as the equivalent—in Tristram's terms—of modern poster design, they have a right not to be summarily dismissed. It may be that even within the special conditions of their art they are inferior, but they deserve serious attention before judgement. And it may be that a more flexible attitude to the relationship between understanding and assessing will extend for us our own range of sensibility. The proof of this is easy to find in branches of the visual arts: it would be an unsophisticated and limited approach to an eleventh-century ivory plaque which criticized its 'flattened' perspectives in the light of later medieval carving of the fifteenth century, with its exploitation of deep 'scientific' perspective.[25] The advantages of using vanishing-point perspective are clear, but is also true that a fixed and unvarying viewpoint has its disadvantages for the artist. In our own day, Braque tells us why:

Scientific perspective ... makes it impossible for an artist to convey a full experience of space, since it forces the objects in a picture to disappear away from the beholder, instead of bringing them within his reach, as painting should.[26]

If it is possible to learn how to look freshly and appreciatively at the crowded surfaces of early ivory panels, in which everything is brought within reach, and nothing distanced, it is surely also possible to learn how to make radical and rewarding changes in our view of earlier forms of literature.

So, a fair reading of a poem such as *Troilus and Criseyde* should take into account the question of viewpoint, which affected medieval literature as well as medieval art in a very significant way. The lack of fixed viewpoint in *Troilus* makes it a rather disorderly poem, if we are judging it by later narrative standards: it makes up for this by great tonal richness:

... the author felt little pressure to maintain a single attitude to his subject or a consistent tone to the reader ... instead of homogeneity there was heterogeneity of tone and attitude ...[27]

In this case, clearly, we should be at fault if we regarded the very variable attitudes taken up by Chaucer towards his materials, his characters, and his readers as the product of carelessness alone, or if we pretended that such variability does not exist. The experience of reading *Troilus and Criseyde* is not that of watching the unfolding of an 'argument': the peculiar pleasure it offers is that of viewing a fixed narrative from many different points of vantage and of persuasion, not all of which are rationally compatible. The effort to realize this is no greater than the effort to realize similar characteristics in European art of Chaucer's day. No one has yet suggested that the *Flight into Egypt* by the Master of the *Grandes Heures de Rohan*[28] is a primitive or defective piece of book-painting because it presents that most urgent of journeys from a number of viewpoints, human and divine.

Rather than limit the number of medieval English poems which may be expected to interest and move us, we should, surely, wish to extend that number. But here some conscious effort is needed; few medieval poems have any chance of becoming 'something experienced ... contemporary with the reader'[29] if we are not first disposed to prepare ourselves for a new range of experience. There is, in fact, no single and simple way of dealing with medieval English poetry, no rapid way of deciding whether or not it is good or bad—unless we are satisfied to confine our reading to a safe area of compositions which approximate, in various recognized ways, to the kind of literature we are more familiar with. If we are not to provide ourselves with a narrow and entirely predictable range of enjoyment, we have to arbitrate between our own literary tastes, as they have been shaped by post-Renaissance poetry, and our obligations to those of the past. This need not lay too much stress upon a sense of duty, but upon imaginative curiosity—a desire to widen more our reach in poetry.

There are medieval poems which need only the barest introduction to us. A good deal of Chaucer's writing can be quite naturally associated with dramatic and narrative literature nearer our own time. His rapid and racy fabliau poems, with their economy of setting, their grace and energy of dialogue, remind us of qualities we admire in short stories and dramatic scripts. Similarly, we do not have to be persuaded into responding to the savage beauty of the winter landscapes of *Sir Gawain and the Green Knight*, nor to the predicament of man, alternately suffering and escaping their rigours, on horseback or in castle bedchamber:

> Bot wylde wedereȝ of the worlde wakned þeroute,
> Clowdes kesten kenly þe colde to þe erþe,

> Wyth ny3e innoghe of þe norþe, þe naked to tene;
> þe snawe snitered ful snart, þat snayped þe wylde;
> þe werbelande wynde wapped fro þe hy3e,
> And drof uche dale ful of dryftes ful grete.
> þe leude lystened ful wel þat le3 in his bedde.[30]

For this we have been prepared by later romantic poets' nostalgic, and often exquisite, pictures of that medieval world—by Keats' chilling evocation of death in 'icy hoods and mails', and of love, warmth, and civilization beleaguered by the vast hostile storms of the universe.

But there is very little in later literature which will help us to feel totally and immediately at home in Chaucer's courtly elegy for Blanche of Lancaster, the *Book of the Duchess*, or in the *Gawain*-poet's elegy, *Pearl*. Both resist us with alien forms of thought and emotion, momentarily involving us in familiar sights and experiences. The sad, graceful arabesques of love described by Chaucer's Man in Black are only briefly disturbed by recognizable lines of pain:

> 'Allas, sir, how? what may that be?'
> 'She ys ded!' 'Nay!' 'Yis, be my trouthe!'
> 'Is that youre los? Be God, hyt ys routhe!'[31]

The severe rituals of patience, demonstrated in so pure a form by the dream-maiden in *Pearl*, are only briefly interrupted by a vision of the rewards of patience, in the familiar terms of setting sun and rising moon:

> Ry3t as þe maynful mone con rys
> Er þenne þe day-glem dryve al doun,
> So sodanly on a wonder wyse
> I wat3 war of a prosessyoun ...[32]

Both are uncompromisingly medieval poems, based firmly upon assumptions about death and love and suffering which are no longer universally acceptable. To compare them unfavourably with *In Memoriam*, or *Thyrsis*, is equivalent to comparing Uccello's *Rout of San Romano* with Picasso's *Guernica*, or an early Flemish *Martyrdom of St Sebastian* with Goya's bitter indictment of murder by firing-squad. The earlier paintings and poems are not primitive versions of the later, but differently formulated as patterns of grief and consolation.[33]

A sympathetic awareness of 'difference' can, of course, enrich our responses to works which may already be comprehensible in modern terms. Our delight in the winter landscapes of *Sir Gawain and the Green Knight* is not reduced if we learn that, in addition to being sensuous and energetic descriptions, they are also 'functional in the strict rhetorical sense'.[34] There is a special kind of beauty to be discovered in the winter scene which opens part IV of the poem. It is impressive, immediately, for its visual and tactile power—the snow-scenes in James Thomson's *Winter*, the *Winter-Piece* of Ambrose Phillips are not better done, although they are more extensive. But we can also see it, in its traditional medieval context, as 'a rhetorical amplification of Gawain's state of mind'.[35] This cannot be written off as a piece of historical information only. The strong dramatic impact of the whole poem cannot be fully explained without reference to the close formal connection, recognized by poet and audience, between 'inner and outer weather'.[36]

In this way we can often use scholarly findings to vivify, not simply to chart more accurately, the meaning of a medieval poem. Our first response to the snow-flurried, mountainous landscapes of *Sir Gawain* draws upon attitudes to man and nature quite unknown to the medieval poet. For all that, it is not a response to be dismissed, but rather to be supplemented and enriched, just as our first response to the opening ten lines of the *Canterbury Tales*—'a breath of uncontaminate spring-ride'[37]—can be both enlarged and sharpened to take in the religious and semi-scientific allusions Chaucer carefully provided for the full appreciation of his readers.

The need and the reward for a various and flexible approach to medieval poetry can be made clear by examining our reactions to some shorter religious verses of the fifteenth century. The mortality lyric, *Farewell, this World is but a Cherry Fair*[38] begins with such dramatic force that we might be tempted to compare it with a seventeenth-century lyric:

> Ffare well, this world! I take my leve for evere,
> I am arested to apere at goddes face.

This is not inferior to Donne's

> This is my play's last scene; here heavens appoint
> My pilgrimage's last mile; and my race,
> Idly yet quickly run, hath this last pace;[39]

And, as the poem continues, the drama is sustained; the poet briefly but vividly re-creates for us the moment when death appears before seignorial life, and summons it:

> Today I sat full ryall in a cheyere,
> Tyll sotell deth knokyd at my gate,
> And on-avysed he seyd to me, chek-mate!

and the drop from fear to despair, as the voices of the world come distantly to the grave:

> Speke softe, ye folk, for I am leyd aslepe!
> I have my dreme, in trust is moche treson.

But rueful acceptance of a desperate situation does not blur the image of man, whether in his pride of life, or in his confrontation with death, grave, and judgement. There is even a kind of dignity in the way the stricken soul addresses God:

> O myghtyfull god, þu knowest that I had levere
> Than all this world, to have oone houre space
> To make a-sythe for all my grete trespace.
> My hert, alas! is brokyne for that sorowe ...

The first three stanzas of the poem are remarkable for their record of a human dilemma: 'ffram dethes hold, feyne wold I make a lepe'. Fear, shock, resignation, sound, and silence register precisely and poignantly. But it becomes clear, as the fourth stanza proceeds, that the poem is not to reach its climax, or to end, in this mode. A dramatic presentation of a crisis of terror—

> lo! how sotell he maketh a devors,
> and wormys to fede, he hath here leyd my cors—

is not its real point. As it moves towards the conclusion, repentance, submission, and reconciliation are expressed in a flat, contrasting mode of quiet statement:

> This febyll world, so fals and so unstable,
> Promoteth his lovers for a lytell while ...
> Experyence cawsith me þe trowth to compile,
> Thynkyng this, to late alas! that I began ...

We lose what the opening lines may have encouraged us to expect—the sense of an undaunted personal involvement with a great problem. In the poetry of Donne, or of Herbert, such involvement often means the most strenuous and sustained wrestling with difficult issues, with faith, fear, contrition, to the very last line or word. The poem is almost totally concerned to record, and even to give the illusion of reliving, a desperate crisis. Resolution is sometimes the final gasp of a drowning man—

> I have a sin of fear, that when I have spun
> My last thread, I shall perish on the shore;
> But swear by thyself that at my death ...[40]

and sometimes hardly enters into the poem—

> Ah, my dear God! though I am clean forgot,
> Let me not love thee if I love thee not.[41]

In contrast, the medieval poet uses the drama of death's summons, and of man's struggle for breath and for a reprieve of 'oone houre space' as a prelude only to his real theme— man's monstrous neglect of the way to salvation, and the redemptive mercy of God. The dramatic illusion of a poem which is an immediate record of a spiritual crisis is unhesitatingly abandoned for the sake of emphatic statement:

> Experyence cawsith me þe trowth to compile ...

No doubt Herbert and Donne were equally certain of the 'trowth' which their poems appear to skirt, probe, and mistake before coming to joyful acclamation: their postponement of the moment of clarification is, in many ways, an artifice, designed to enrich the poems imaginatively, not to gauge for us the extent of their personal despair. But the medieval poet makes no attempt to conceal that the 'drama' of the first three stanzas was only a means to a predetermined, essentially didactic end:

> Beati mortui qui in domino moriuntur
> Humiliatus sum vermis.

The change from English to Latin reinforces the stability of the poem: the flickering, restless emotions of an individual are transmuted into the grave substance of an inscription.

We might say that this writer of the fifteenth century deliberately, and regrettably, checks an impulse towards vivid, dramatic language, and then we might give our approval to

part of the poem only. The change of tone at the beginning of
the fourth stanza—

> This febyll world, so fals and so unstable ...

would, in this kind of appraisal, mark the limit of the reader's
patience with a poet who so sternly controlled his dramatic
talents. To find purely religious justification for his procedure
should not force us into an unwilling admiration. But it might
suggest a different kind of response to the movement of the
poem. The possibility of an imaginative life buried in the poem
is worth some attention.

To begin with, the original medieval pattern of emphasis has
to be restored to the poem: an authoritative statement 'Beati
mortui qui in domino moriuntur' is to be illustrated and proved
upon us by means of an exemplary human experience. In the
description of this experience, poet-persona and reader are first
subjected to a rapid and confusing stream of emotions—pride,
fear, regret, even panic—as the soul draws painfully away from
bodily allegiances. But all of these are simply preliminaries,
and their urgent expression marks out an area of instability.
What succeeds to this may, indeed, appear to us, on first
acquaintance, as a diminution of vigour—

> Experyence cawsith me þe trowth to compile ...

To the medieval poet and his reader it would be the welcome
sign of a steadying focus of attention. The grave, sonorous
language of the last stanza resolves, in a different mode, the
excited questioning and exclamation of the opening stanzas. It
can be seen, in its own religious and imaginative terms, as a
completion of the explorative movements initiated by the
poem. But it completes them not by travelling with dramatic
verisimilitude from fear and regret to certainty, but by decisive
removal to a different plane of significance. The restless poet-
persona becomes, abruptly, his own sternest mentor, backed
by authority. The graph of the poem is not familiar to us, nor,
on a first reading, particularly attractive to us—tracing as it
does a substitution of devotional acquiescence for imaginative
arousal, rather than a complex relationship between them.

It is, however, a common graph in medieval religious poetry.
In the dream-elegy, *Pearl*, for instance, the doubts and strugg-

lings of the bereaved dreamer are not resolved from within their own dramatic world, but from the realm of unassailable spiritual logic. The *Pearl* maiden refuses to enter into any relationship with the dreamer and his problems; she simply brings him face to face with the dazzling edifice of truth. The vision she obtains for him of the New Jerusalem, set high on its glittering battlements, is symbolic of many things, but in one important way it symbolizes the eternal truth which the human mind can only recognize and accept, never penetrate. So, the dreamer's attempt to *experience* that vision is rash, and is harshly dealt with:

> Of raas þaȝ I were rasch and ronk,
> ȝet rapely þerinne I watȝ restayed.
> For, ryȝt as I sparred unto þe bonc,
> þat brathþe out of my drem me brayde.
> þen wakned I in þat erber wlonk ...[42]

In the *Cherry Fair* poem, the withdrawal from the human scene and from human responses may still be judged sudden and unsubtle—but only if we lay our main emphasis upon the opening dramatic predicament. It may equally well be judged appropriate and decisive, if we allow the point of the poem to be contained in 'Beati qui moriuntur ...'. And this need not deny an imaginative drive to the poem, nor the possibility of our own imaginative response; the imagination is not barred, but given special direction, according to devotional needs. By later aesthetic standards, this lyric has a limited range of appeal; like *Pearl*, and many other works of its age, it juxtaposes drama and dogma, or utilizes drama for overtly dogmatic ends. Medieval standards, so often concerned with functional decorum, would applaud that very openness of procedure which we might be inclined to think crude. Power, not elegance, was here the criterion. It would be a pity, however, if we could not take any interest or pleasure in the discovery of this 'double life' of a work from the past. The building of aesthetic laws upon a base of devotional necessity is frequent enough in the plastic and pictorial arts, where equivalent kinds of distortion and disunity are readily accepted for their power, not for their beauty. The enlarged, compulsive eyes, the unnaturally elongated and expressive hands of Christ and his Saints in

Byzantine painting and mosaic; the strange contrasts of style and mode in some of the twelfth-century sculpture of Chartres, realism and formalism boldly paired; examples easily come to mind.[43]

There are, of course, many times when attentiveness to alien patterns and assumptions in medieval art, as in poetry, go unrewarded. A good number of verse compositions in the Middle Ages were totally uninterested in dramatic or imaginative responses, and, even within their own limited didactic range, reached a very low standard indeed. No amount of patient 'restoration' can give back to them what they never possessed. When we have satisfied ourselves about their nature and function, such poems must be valued for their documentary value. The lengthy versified instructions made by a father for his son in the early fifteenth century calls itself a 'treatise', not a poem:

> Fore-thi, my gud sone, understande,
> And tak this tretys oft in hand,
> And set weil thar-one thi entent,
> Quhill thow art yhonge and Innocent[44]

Its easy, undemanding use of a short verse couplet is not artistically significant, but only a mark of the author's desire to be understood and remembered:

> For here ar wrytin, in lytill space,
> Sum thingis that may help and sped.
>
> (ll. 1948-9)

Again, a poem which begins

> Ther ben iij poyntis of myscheff
> That arun confusion to many man,
> Weche that werkyn the soule gret gryff,
> I schall hem telle ʒou as I can.[45]

is not likely to yield much to us, however many adjustments and enlargements of our receptive field we may prepare for. Many of these medieval works never go, and would have seen no reason to go, beyond their stated informative limits. Relying for their effectiveness upon their readers' belief in the absolute truth of what they say, they need not search for vivacity of presentation.

And here we can never exaggerate the influence of a known public, with demands and shortcomings precisely calculable by the poet. John Audelay, an Augustine Canon, and a prolific verse writer of the earlier fifteenth century, tells us that his poetry was made 'Ad honorem domini nostri Jhesu Christi. Et ad exemplum aliorum in monasterio de Haghmon.'[46] The range and the tenor of his verse are predictable, but not, for all that, to be despised. His personal situation—he was blind, deaf and ailing—is put at the service of the community: 'timor mortis' is, for him, a pressing theme—

> Lade, helpe! Ihesu merce!
> *Timor mortis conturbat me ...*
> Fore blyndnes is a heve þyng,
> And to be def þer-with only,
> To lese my lyȝt and my heryng;[47]

But it is made to yield consolation:

> Lerne þis lesson of blynd Awdlay;
> When bale is hyest þen bot may be ...
> Say *passio Christi conforta me.*
>
> (ll. 43-4, 46)

His warmth of feeling for the innocence of the child—an emotion more unusual in his age than we might think possible—

> He wot never wat is envy;
> He wol uche mon fard wele him by;
> He covetis noȝt unlaufully,
> Fore chere stons is his tresoure ...[48]

is not indulged, but turned to useful account in his numerous Nativity lyrics, celebrating

> ... þis freschele Floure,
> Houe fayre He was in His coloure,
> And hou sote in His savour ...[49]

The stability of his best verse, perfectly shaping emotion to the celebrative language of the Church, is, in its modest way, impressive. His short piece, *De Amore Dei*, is reminiscent of Herbert in balanced moods of reconciliation and praise:

> I have a love is heven Kyng;
> I love His love fore ever more.

> Fore love is love and ever schal be,
>> And love has bene ore we were bore;
> Fore love he askys no noþer fe,
>> But love aʒayn; he kepis no more;
>> I say here-fore.[50]

This is poetry in which subject-matter and treatment are intimately related to the needs of others: it is centrifugally driven. But all medieval poets, from Chaucer to the most obscure romance versifier, were actively concerned with the adjustment of personal feeling and imaginative invention to established forms and functions. The discriminating, as opposed to the selective, reader will want to know more of these delicate processes of adjustment, which vary so much from poet to poet, yet are essentially 'medieval' in impetus and direction. A vague and excited impression of similarity between the protestations of Chaucer's Troilus to the dawning day—

> O cruel day, accusour of the joie
> That nyght and love han stole and faste iwryen,
> Acorsed be thi comyng into Troye ...[51]

and Donne's

> Busy old fool, unruly Sun,
> Why dost thou thus,
> Through windows and through curtains call on us?

may be good advertisement for the Middle Ages, but it takes no account of very subtle and important differences of modulation. The audacious leap of Donne's reasoning in the closing lines of his poem

> This bed thy centre is, these walls thy sphere ...

is forecast in the dramatic licence of his opening lines. The greater formality of Troilus's language and syntax points to a situation in which such a triumphant volte-face could never be made. For the medieval poet, even within the fiction of his poem, time cannot be defeated: a day, and the sun, remain acknowledged enemies of love to the last:

> Therwith ful soore he syghte, and thus he seyde ...
>> (iii. 1471)

2   Conditions and Status

The heavy conditioning of all medieval English poetry by social, political, and religious factors is a plain historical truth. Nowhere is this conditioning more clearly demonstrable than in its uncertain and changing status over the period. It would not be an exaggeration to say that the ambiguous position of the English language as a literary medium affected most medieval English literature, from the twelfth to the fifteenth century. In long perspective, the literary role of English was not securely defined until the sixteenth century—or perhaps we should say 'redefined', for it had been secure enough before the Norman Conquest of England. But the Conquest was of particular significance for English poetry. Unlike art, and architecture, and unlike certain kinds of vernacular prose—all of which were able to assimilate new materials and forms without grave internal damage—vernacular poetry was seriously disturbed by the linguistic changes which followed the introduction of a second spoken and written language into the country.

Alliterative verse did survive the Conquest, and, indeed, we can be fairly sure that it maintained an independent life of its own in certain western areas of England. It survived, however, at the expense of a good part of its original subtlety, and, if we are to judge from the variety of alliterative verse forms in vigorous existence in the thirteenth and fourteenth centuries, it was quick to co-operate with other very different kinds of poetic composition. The earliest alliterative verse of the Middle English centuries is a rougher and looser art form than that of *Beowulf* or the *Seafarer*, and is often equally remarkable for its attempts to compromise with a French-based verse system as for its strong adherence to older 'Germanic' ways of making poetry. It would be unfair, when reading and judging the only long alliterative poem between 1066 and 1350, Laȝamon's *Brut*, to discount the frequent enlivening and quickening influence of

French rhymed verse upon the traditional Germanic line:

> Wher beoð mine þeines, wher beoð mine sweines,
> wher beoð mine kempes and mine kene men?
> Eorneð and eaerneð and al þis lond bearneð,
> and alle þa men slaeð þe ʒe cumeð neh.
> and heore children and heore wif werpeð in-to þe waeteren,
> and brekeð heore walles and berneð heore halles,
> seaelleð heore tures and swaleð heore bures ...[1]

In any case, even if we can believe in the healthy existence of alliterative verse, as an oral form with occasional written witness throughout these transitional years, we have to admit that its literary status was precarious. Laʒamon's poem, a verse-history of the Britons, had, according to manuscript evidence, a very limited circulation.[2] His main sources—Geoffrey of Monmouth's *Historia Regum Britonum* and the French verse chronicle by Wace, 'Frenchis clerc', had a very wide circulation.[3] But then the same can be observed of the only large-scale English rhymed verse contemporary with the *Brut*—the debate poem, the *Owl and the Nightingale*. Here an English poet shows himself thoroughly at home with a continental verse form: his rhymed couplets are easy and strong. Again, his work exists in isolation. It has no antecedents and no descendants in English, although it has a rich surround in Latin and French.[4] Even the complimentary way in which the debate between Owl and Nightingale is referred, at the close of the poem, to a clerical authority is strongly reminiscent of Anglo-French poems of the time: the romance *Ipomedon*, for instance, written in the late twelfth century by the Norman-Welsh clerk Hue de Rotelande, refers courteously to a 'canon of Hereford' who 'knows the gloss on this text'.[5] In fact, it gives the impression of having been written for some small circle of friends and patrons, to whom the use of English—natural as it may have been for *spoken* purposes—appeared interestingly novel for a serious literary project. For whereas the flourishing life of English as a spoken language, and as a prose medium of great technical and emotive power, is unquestionable,[6] its poetic life is more difficult to reconstruct for this earlier Middle English period. During the Norman and Angevin reigns, and well into the thirteenth century, we can see how the prestige, the public, and the whole cultural context of poetry in English has been put into question: the Conquest had ensured that its incentives were no longer clearly defined.

The old generalization about the use of English for literature directed towards the lower classes, French for the middle and upper classes, and Latin for the learned is an inadequate account of a complex linguistic situation. If, after 1066, English was rapidly learnt by the new rulers, French must also have become increasingly accessible to the English.[7] The writing of a lively and accomplished verse-play, the *Jeu d'Adam*, in England at about 1140 suggests mixed audiences, Norman and Saxon: fragments of bilingual plays and bilingual lyrics can be found from the twelfth and thirteenth centuries. The most authoritative account of Anglo-French literature emphasizes that it was not narrowly confined to any particular class or genre, but ranged widely, taking in verse-chronicle, romance, lyric, as well as saints' life and didactic treatise.[8] It clearly catered for many different levels of society—royalty, minor aristocracy, clerks, parish priests, and, through them, perhaps, the most lowly congregations. The response to the decree of the Fourth Lateran Council, in 1215, that more instruction should be provided for the laity in the vernacular, was the production of works in Anglo-French, as well as in English.[9] Both languages were able, apparently, to serve widely divergent needs: both literatures often had common aims.

But the dependence of English upon Anglo-French, for source-material and for art-forms, must be recognized. English poetry, during these first centuries of the Conquest, was faced with abundant evidence of the growing fame of French poetry, both at home and abroad. If religious plays in Anglo-French were being performed in English churches, on a higher artistic level—and perhaps in an English abbey—Marie de France, high-born lady and poetess, was turning the matter of Celtic Britain into elegant French couplets, and dedicating her work to an Angevin patron.[10] Twelfth-century England was decisively international in its political and cultural temper. Under Norman and Angevin rule, historians, poets, theologians, philosophers, and mathematicians moved easily between England and the Continent—and further, too: for the ties between the royal houses of England, northern France, and Norman Sicily were strong, and encouraged free interchange in many spheres of activity. Englishmen such as Adelard of Bath or John of Salisbury studied abroad, and travelled unceasingly: they wrote exclusively in Latin for a learned European, rather than narrowly English, public. English painters imitated the colours and the designs of Byzantine mosaics,[11] which they may easily have seen for themselves on visits to the Sicilian court, or which they found, at one remove, in patternbooks, brought to northern Europe along the crowded trade and pilgrimage routes. Herefordshire churches, Kilpeck and Shobdon, reflect, in their carvings, traditions of art more familiar in southern France and Spain.[12] The queen of Henry the Second, Eleanor of Aquitaine, was the acknowledged lady of some of the most famous troubadours of the time: the English poet Laȝamon knew that it was to her that Wace had dedicated his verse-history:

> a Frenchis clerc,
> Wace wes ihoten, þe wel couþe writen;
> And he hoe ȝef þare aeðelen Ælienor
> þe wes Henries quene, þes heȝes kinges.[13]

In such a setting and atmosphere, it is no wonder that English poetry was variable and erratic in quantity and quality. While maintaining itself in some of its older ways, it more often imitated new: usefully serving those who could be most conveniently instructed in English (in Biblical paraphrases, for instance, such as the early thirteenth-century *Jacob and Joseph*[14]), it is sometimes found associated with more sophisticated readers, who, far from viewing debate, lyric, or romance in English as a necessity, might have seen it as a welcome innovation, or, at least, an acceptable alternative to French. There is, in fact, no simple answer to the question of who read and wrote English poetry during the twelfth and thirteenth centuries. The *Owl and the Nightingale* (c.1200) and the romance, *Floris and Blancheflur*[15] (c.1240) point to high standards of composition, and powerful motivation, which are not confirmed by other contemporary works of similar scope and length. It may be that, for very obvious reasons, we have lost a good many secular poems in English. But gaps and silences may equally

well tell us of a situation in which both Anglo-French and
English were acceptable as literary media—the edge of greater
literary authority belonging, however, to French. What evidence we have points to the conclusion that, increasingly, as
the twelfth century passed into the thirteenth, most classes
except the very lowest (who could hardly have been in a position to exert any influence upon poetry)[16] were equally comfortable with French and English. It is a little surprising to find
Marie de France, in the twelfth century, dedicating her version
of *Saint Patrick's Purgatory* 'en romanz' (in French) to 'la simple
gent' as well as to 'seignurs',[17] if only because so much of the
rich Anglo-French literature of that century was produced for
kings and queens, members of their households, and of their
baronage.[18] But her words cannot be passed over, even at this
date, and even without exact knowledge of what she meant by
'simple gent': some kind of 'simple gent' may have watched
Anglo-French religious drama in that century. By 1200 the
interchangeability of English and Anglo-French becomes more
marked. The well-born ladies for whom the devotional guide,
the *Ancrene Wisse*,[19] was written, at the turn of the century,
understood and could read French,[20] but received their *Rule*
in English prose. Conversely, many influential religious
treatises, aimed either at a general lay public, or at less learned
parish priests, were produced first in Anglo-French, and only
later in English. The *Manuel des Pechiez*, a comprehensive verse
treatment of confession, sacraments, and prayer, put together
by an unknown Englishman, about 1260, exists in twenty-
four manuscripts. Its English translation, made by Robert
Mannyng of Bourne in 1303, comes to us in only four manuscripts.[21] High and low demanded works in the vernacular,
and the choice of English or French is not wholly predictable
from the nature of the patrons, the intended public, or the
subject-matter.

For Eleanor of Provence, mother of Edward I, John of
Howden recast his Latin poem, *Philomena*, into Anglo-French;[22]
for 'la laie gent', 'ceux que ne entendunt de letrure' ('those
who are not lettered'), an unknown cleric wrote his rhyming
sermon on Antichrist and the Fall of Man.[23] But a thirteenth-
century debate-poem, *Blancheflour et Florence*, perhaps composed

by a canon of Hereford, Elias Brichulle, speaks of an *English* original:

> Banastre en englois le fist,
> E Brykhulle cest escrit
> En franceois translata[24]

Many later thirteenth and earlier fourteenth-century miscellanies of verse mingle French and English pieces indiscriminately: two of the most famous, MSS Digby 86 and Harley 2253[25] give the impression that their compilers were 'quite as much at home in the French language as in English'.[26] There is no sense in them that French and English serve classes of readers sharply distinguished from each other by education or social standing. The bilingual, and even trilingual lyrics of Harley 2253 are both sophisticated and easy in their verbal range:

> Scripsi hec carmina in tabulis:
> Mon ostel est en mi la vile de Paris;
> may y sugge namore, so wel me is;
> ȝef hi deȝe for love of hire, duel hit ys.[27]

Bilingual fragments of religious plays also date from the turn of the thirteenth century, and it has been suggested that the English is not so much a gloss on the Anglo-French, as an alternative version, for the actor's convenience.[28]

For the thirteenth century, it is certainly true to say that 'French was a suitable medium for the instruction (and entertainment) of the laity at large ... it was universally understood. ...'[29] But so, too, was English, and it is more often as an alternative, than as a rival or competitor, that this century seems to present the role of English as a literary language. Its status was neither dominant, nor depressed: the fluent prose of the *Ancrene Riwle*, the brisk couplets of the *Owl and the Nightingale*, the practised lyrics of Harley 2253 are products of a relaxed cultural situation. Even the first translations of Anglo-French romances into English seem to bear this out. It is true that from 1240 onwards English versions of the romances originally written in the twelfth century for the 'seigneurs barons', or for lesser nobility, begin to appear. It would be a mistake, however, to over-simplify, and to imagine that the transition to English always marks the transition from high-born to lowly readers, who demand English of sheer necessity. In some cases this may have been the situation,[30] but the latest studies of individual romances seem to suggest that although the thirteenth-century audiences of romances such as *Havelok* and *Beves of Hamtoun* were probably wider, more varied than the original courtly audiences of their Anglo-French originals, they were not always drawn from classes limited to the under-standing and use of English. For the household of a rich land-owner, of a bishop, or of a London civic official, at 1250, or 1280, English and French must have been virtually inter-changeable. It is to such audiences, rather than to mixed groups of peasants and artisans, collected in the market-place, that many of the earlier verse translations were addressed.[31] A good illustration of a complex state of affairs is provided by the Fulk Fitzwarin romances: the exploits of that Shropshire family were celebrated over the thirteenth and earlier fourteenth centuries in Anglo-French couplets, Anglo-French prose, and—very probably—in English alliterative verse.[32] Noble houses such as this, with lands in the western marches, and administrative power in the city of London,[33] were well placed to span, in taste and patronage, many languages and many literary genres.

In such a situation, it needed the exertion of outside forces—local or national—to determine which of the vernacular languages would become the more significant for literature. This period, before 1350, in which English and French were held 'in solution', is difficult for us to imagine. Yet part of our difficulty is only that we have learnt from the later history of Europe—as well as from some eminent literary historians[34]—to associate national feeling and the use of a 'mother-tongue'. This associ-ation, however true of the fourteenth century, is not so before. The thirteenth saw the loss of Normandy and the consolidation of a sense of national identity, especially during the years of opposition to Henry III, and his encouragement of 'foreign' causes and of 'foreigners' in high secular and ecclesiastical office. 'Yet all of this took place at a time when England enjoyed three literary languages, and three competing cultures ... the country was loyal, patriotic, anti-Welsh, anti-Scottish, anti-French. It showed, in fact, all the essentials of national feeling, except that, so far as education allowed, it preferred Latin to French, and French to English.'[35]

The Preface to a *Life of Edward the Confessor,* dedicated before 1264 to Henry III's queen, Eleanor of Provence, speaks proudly of Henry as head of a unified people:

Now are king, now are barons and the kingdom, of a common blood of England and Normandy.[36]

The *Life* is in French verse, translated from the Latin prose of Aelred of Rievaulx: the illustrations to the text are in a style which is a rich blend of earlier English and contemporary French elements—fluid and elegant outline drawing, and warm, varied colouring. Such a manuscript, with translator and artists in co-operation, represents the 'Englishness' of the thirteenth century just as authentically as the *Owl and the Nightingale,* or *Havelok the Dane.* In the same way, the 'early English' style of architecture is developed, in the first half of the thirteenth century, as a 'national version' of European Gothic, but 'strongly tied to *Anglo-Norman* tradition'.[37]

There is, however, evidence of change over the century: perhaps what is first noticeable is a growth of self-consciousness about the existence of two vernacular languages in England. Even so, the attitudes of writers vary greatly with their education and their motives. The scholar and scientist, Roger Bacon, in his *Compendium Studii Philosophiae* of the mid-century, takes it for granted as desirable that the English speak three languages, English, French, and Latin, 'Sicut maternum in qua natus est'.[38] For a man of Bacon's learning, this is understandable: it is only noteworthy that he places English first in his list—'ut nos loquimur Anglicum, Gallicum, et Latinum'. Towards the end of the century the monastic chronicler who goes by the name of Robert of Gloucester complains, in his *Chronicle of England,* about the disuse of English, except by the lower classes:

Ich wene ther ne beth in al the world contreyes none
That ne holdeth to hor owe speche bote Engelond one ...[39]

The fact that he regards English as 'hor owe speche' is interesting, as is, indeed, the fact that he writes his *Chronicle* with Anglo-Norman precedents in mind, but in the English language. The passage loses a little of its force as evidence because of its obviously simplified statements about the exclusive use of French by the aristocracy after the Conquest: it has something of the air of a set-piece about it. Put beside other contemporary documents, it is fairly mild: like King Alfred and Roger Bacon before him, Robert of Gloucester sees the educative value of knowing more than one language:

> Vor the more that a mon can, the more wurthe he is
> (l. 7547)

At about the same time, there appear various kinds of treatises, designed to teach correct French to families of good birth. Walter of Bibbesworth designed his teaching manual for Dionysia de Munchensy, of Hemmingfield, near Chelmsford, 'pur vos enfans acune apryse de frаunceys en breves paroles'.[40] The existence of this and similar works, from the late thirteenth century onwards, suggests that while the status of French, as a spoken and written medium, was still very high, some effort was needed to keep it up, even in the households of gentlefolk.[41]

But a far more assertive, even militant, approach can be found in the Prefaces to some English romances and religious poems at the turn of the thirteenth century. If the contents of the manuscripts Digby 86 and Harley 2253 tell us of the peaceful co-existence of English and Anglo-French literature in one kind of cultural context,[42] romances such as *Arthour and Merlin* and *Richard Coeur de Lion*,[43] with their outspoken championing of the cause of English, admit us to a different world of sentiment. Their Prefaces are strongly class-conscious: French is for the 'gentilman', but not all gentlemen are capable of using it. All can understand and use English:

> Freynsche use þis gentil man
> Ac everich Inglische Inglische can
> Mani noble ich have yseiȝe
> þat no Freynsche couþe seye.
> (*Arthour and Merlin*, ll. 23-6)

The Preface to *Richard* assures its audience that

> Lewede men cune Ffrensch non,
> Among an hondryd unneþis on ...
> (ll. 23-4)

Both poems are probably the work of a Kentishman, of the late thirteenth century:[44] although we may take his most sweeping statements with some scepticism, we must be impressed with the genuine quality of his emotion. He presents, and caters for, a type of reader only just beginning to be a force in English literature—as also in English politics: the secular middle-class citizen, urban, literate or partly-literate, aspirant, yet not entirely imitative of the tastes and criteria of his social superiors. The stirring events of the sixties, when the citizens of London backed Simon de Montfort against Henry III, and helped to secure, in the *Mise of Lewes*, the dismissal of his foreign relatives and dependants, were warnings of this new force operating in a political field. It could not be long before it operated in the field of literature. Not surprisingly, when it did, it showed itself only partly satisfied with a vernacular language which was a reminder, not only of social hierarchies, but also of some 'foreign' resentments and antipathies.

These thirteenth-century Prefaces give fragmentary evidence of a most elaborate and shifting pattern of change, which is basically social and political in nature. In a minor way they, too, 'illustrate the long-term processes at work in the thirteenth century, the steady growth of a class of professional legists and clerks, the multiplication of powerful new mercantile interests, the surge of enterprise from below which fashioned the craft movement'.[45] And what they merely suggest, the fourteenth century confirmed: Robert of Gloucester's regret seems temperate beside the thoroughgoing anti-French zeal of the Franciscan, Robert Holcot. He sees the introduction of French into England as a deliberate, and dastardly, act of the Conqueror, and extends its significance into the world of moral conflict:

just as the schoolboy begins by learning French, so the youth, starting on his career in the world, by toil and study learns to tell lies.[46]

That there was a real necessity for teaching manuals not only among the lesser gentry, but also among the aristocracy, might be deduced from literary apologies such as were made in 1354 by Henry, Duke of Lancaster. He excuses the French of his devout treatise, the *Livre de Seyntz Medicines*: 'pur ceo qe jeo sui Engleis et n'ai pas moelt hauntee le franceis ...'.[47] And the incipient nationalism of the romance Prefaces is fully realized

in prefaces to religious and historical works, intended principally for a similar middle-class lay public. The author of the
early fourteenth-century verse-history of the world, the *Cursor
Mundi*, who is competing for the attention of his public with
'romans red on maneres sere / of Alisaundur e Conquerour
...',[48] already displays that 'close, emotional association of
national feeling with the vernacular'[49] which will be strengthened by later medieval poets such as Chaucer, and never
seriously challenged after the sixteenth century:

> þis ilk boc es translate
> In to Inglis tong to rede
> For the love of Inglis lede,
> Inglis lede of Ingland,
> For the commun at understand.
> Frankis rimes here I redd
> Comunlik in ilk(a) sted,
> Mast es it wroght for frankis man:
> Quat is for him na frankis can?
> Of Ingland the nacion
> Es Inglis man thar in commun:
> þe speche þat man wit mast may spede,
> Mast þarwit to speke war nede;
> Ꝫelden was for ani chance
> Praised Inglis tong in France ...
> To laud and Inglis man i spell
> That understandes þat i tell ...
>
> (232-46, 249-50)

But the takeover, by English, as the favoured literary vernacular of the fourteenth century was not a simple, forward-
driving process, ending in triumph with Chaucer and Langland.
The status won for English verse after 1350 cannot be seen as
an isolated victory, but as one manifestation of complex and
active socio-political developments. All sorts of motives and
persuasions were at work in fourteenth-century writers, impell-
ing them variously towards the defence of English, as well
as towards the continued use of French. The learned friar,
Holcot, reflects a genuine and growing conviction among professional historians of the disastrous linguistic effects of the
Norman Conquest. Glimpsed briefly in Robert of Gloucester,
it is more extensively set out in the monastic *Polychronicon*, by
Ranulph Higden, and given final shape in the late fourteenth-

century *Historia Croylandensis*.[50] But Holcot's particularly dramatic version of 'honest English and deceitful French' was no doubt prompted as much by a passion for moralizing as by extreme patriotism. It has a slightly academic flavour, and we may also note that neither Holcot nor Higden ever put enthusiasm for English to literary use: both wrote exclusively in Latin.

It would be unreasonable, however, to deny the considerable political feeling in the words of the *Cursor Mundi* Preface, as well as the practical recognition of the utility of English. The lines

> Selden was for ani chance
> Praised Inglis tong in France

remind us that the loss of Normandy, in 1204, was the beginning of a long process of withdrawal, reconciliation and ultimate rejection of a 'sense of kinship' between the two countries. The confiscation of Gascony, in 1337, and the opening of the Hundred Years' War gave latent animosities full outlet. By the time of Richard II, a fair portion of Englishmen, from the Duke of Gloucester to William Langland, were prepared to cast France as the national enemy: 'desire to secure her humiliation was to persist as a dominant factor in English foreign policy until after the end of the Middle Ages'.[51] The patriotism of the English songs of Laurence Minot, celebrating victories over the Scots and the French in the early years of Edward III's reign, raw though it may be, is a version of nationwide sentiment:

> Calays men, now mai ʒe care,
> And murning mun ʒe have to mede ...[52]

Langland's constant complaint about foreign Cardinals, and his identification of the Devil as 'proud prikere of Fraunce'[53] tap sources of resentment already plentiful in the poetry of the first half of the fourteenth century. Not only Mannyng and Minot, but a number of anonymous verse-writers express in crude but pungent English their pride in 'Inglis lede of Ingland', and their concern about corruption and exploitation.[54]

It is significant that the romances, *Arthour and Merlin* and *Richard Cœur de Lion*, with their sturdily English Prefaces, appear in the same manuscript as one of these early English complaints, *The Simonie*,[55] and that this manuscript is the first large collection of medieval verse to show a solid preference for English over French: the Auchinleck Manuscript.[56] All of its verse items are in English, and it is thought to have been produced in London, between 1330 and 1340, specifically for lay-readers and buyers of the middle-class.[57] If this is so, it confirms a very important new development in the composing and collecting of English verse: the literary tastes of certain sections of the laity are now being calculated on a commercial basis. Nothing in the Auchinleck Manuscript is exquisite—least of all the decoration; its contents are shrewdly organized to satisfy a demand for entertainment, edification, and information. Its readers have been generally described as 'middle-class', the 'bourgeoisie'; but it is useful to remind ourselves of the variety of people such a term might cover, in London, in the first half of the fourteenth century. Here, above all, in a city which in many respects was already a capital as we today might understand it, older conventions of social, political, and religious life were being reshaped. The rapid advancement of the London merchant classes, on their higher levels, into literacy; the creation of a body of professional civic administrators, drawn from lawyers and clerks; the breaking of the ecclesiastical monopoly of education, with the growth of the London Law Schools—these are only some of the many processes which helped to form a new and eager medieval reading public. To merchants, lawyers, civil servants of all kinds in London and Westminster, we must add the lower strata of the gentry—for lawyers and merchants intermarried with the minor gentry, and, indeed, shared with them their ways of life and modes of education.[58]

Historians, writing of London merchants, lawyers, and clerks in the fourteenth century, have used phrases such as 'elements which are the opposite of static'[59] and 'a quickening sense of growth'[60] to describe their roles in contemporary society. The Auchinleck collection is not an unlikely product of these active and ambitious classes: it admits the status of English as a suitable medium for verse to be read by a substantial, and influential, section of Englishmen. It conveys a sense of the utility of English, its wide intelligibility, sharpened by some growing sense of independence of, even hostility to French.

And for much English verse of the fourteenth century a similar generalization would hold good. Practical recognition of the utility, and sometimes, in the case of religious works directed towards an illiterate public, the necessity of English, spiced to varying degree with patriotic assertiveness: these are the powerful motivating forces for a large proportion of romance translators, writers of religious and satirical verse, and writers of religious lyrics. The net can be spread widest by the use of English—as is admitted by the author of one of the most popular of fourteenth-century religious poems, the *Speculum Vitae*:

> Bothe lered and lewed, olde and yonge,
> Alle understonden english tonge.[61]

But it is worth stressing that the status of English as a high art-form is irrelevant to such writers and compilers. A very different sort of statement could be made about some of the anonymous poets of the lyrics collected in that manuscript roughly contemporary with Auchinleck—Harley 2253:

> Ichot a burde in a bour ase beryl so bryht,
> Ase saphyr in selver semly on syht ...[62]

The use of English in many of the Harley poems is sophisticated and courtly. Harley 2253 was probably, like MS Digby 86, compiled by a west-country cleric: the Digby MS has strong Franciscan connections, and the Harleian collection must probably be associated with one of many religious establishments in Hereford,[63] as well as with the household of Roger Mortimer.[64] Although we know nothing in detail about the compilers of these manuscripts, we know a good deal about the kind of religious and cultural milieu in which they were set. Educated men themselves, they would be in contact with high ecclesiastics, noble benefactors, as well as with travelling scholars and minstrels. Their collections would tend to cater for the needs of others of similar taste and training—and while they would include a fair amount of verse material intended for the simple instruction of an illiterate public, they would also reflect something of the greater world of medieval learning and literature, in which English concerns were still not separable from those of Europe generally.

Consequently, it is not surprising to find that the repertoire of the Harley manuscript, if we simply consider the English material, is so varied and versatile—ranging from English 'complaint-type' poems (*On the Follies of Fashion,* the *Song of the Husbandman*) to sober informative verse (*The Harrowing of Hell, Debate of Body and Soul*), and further to graceful, elaborate love lyrics, hardly bettered by any later medieval courtly compositions. Nor that this English poetry should appear in juxtaposition with French: the compiler saw no problem in setting the English *Song of Lewes* next to the French *Lament for Simon de Montfort*. Both languages, undoubtedly, were authentic media for celebration of the life and death of the great Earl, and he could accept them as such.

The Auchinleck Manuscript shares five items with Harley 2253,[65] but none of them are the finest of what Harley has to offer. Nevertheless, many interesting points are raised by a comparison of these two manuscripts—the one specifically designed to attract and satisfy a vigorous, secular, middle-class public, the other more traditionally involved with the Church and, possibly, the aristocracy.[66] In many ways, the Auchinleck Manuscript is forward-looking: its single-minded dedication to English for the poetry of England reminds us of Chaucer, and it would be pleasing to accept the fact that Chaucer actually read and used the manuscript.[67] But this single-minded dedication has clearly not advanced the quality of the verse written in English. It has approved a convention for the future, but it has also approved a mediocre artistic standard. And, in fact, most English poetry produced for the lay middle classes of the fourteenth century is of similar quality. The shrewd and, as seems likely, professional assessment of what would satisfy—whether it was romance or religio-historical narrative—certainly enlarged the scope and reinforced the authority of English poetry, but it ensured a competent, rather than a remarkable achievement.[68] Both Chaucer and Langland probably read poems which appear in the Auchinleck Manuscript; its rough materials were of use to them: they sharpened their critical senses upon them, took basic themes and even language from them.[69] But their best poetry was

produced to different stimuli, in different cultural environ-
ments. Chaucer may have sprung from the same class of people
who enjoyed *Guy of Warwick* and *Richard Cœur de Lion* but he
had vastly improved himself, both socially and intellectually,
by the time he began his apprenticeship to poetry.[70]

It is, in fact, self-evident that an increasing demand by the
middle-class laity for English poetry of entertainment and
instruction, and an increasing willingness by secular and
religious writers alike to meet that demand could not, by themselves, have created the proper context for the magnificent
English verse of the second half of the fourteenth century. In
the same way, the growing interest of the educated laity in
history, and especially in that of antiquity, stimulated Franciscan scholars of the first half of the fourteenth century: 'it was
bound to do so, given the pupil-teacher relationship between
priest and layman. On the other hand it set a ceiling to their
achievements.'[71] This particular piece of social history—the
gradual emergence of a new multi-faceted class of readers, with
sufficient power to create their own market for poetry—had
important consequences for the stabilization of English as the
dominant literary vernacular. Its immediate artistic consequences were less dramatic: it set a ceiling to poetic endeav-
our. The ultimate attainment of a high status for English
medieval poetry had as much to do with movements in the
upper levels of society as it had with those of middle levels.

At first sight, this looks unlikely. The linguistic habits and
literary tastes of the English aristocracy during the fourteenth
century appear conservative, sometimes retrograde, beside
those of the middle classes. The prestige of literature written
in French seems to have gone unquestioned by them: their
libraries apparently contained works in Latin and French only.
Whatever they spoke, they composed and collected in French.
Thus the considerable number of books bequeathed by Guy
Beauchamp of Warwick to Bordesley Abbey in Worcestershire
in 1305 included many romances and chansons de geste, but no
English works.[72] The Earl of Salisbury, William Montacute,
seems to have been a collector of books: he owned a *Historia
Scholastica* in French—taken from the King of France, at the
battle of Poitiers (1355). It was he, apparently, who provided
the French poet of the romance of *Partenay* with at least one of

his sources—in Latin or French.[73] Likewise, there are very few English books in the large and varied library of Thomas of Woodstock, Duke of Gloucester, inventoried after his death, in 1397: the Duke of Gloucester seems to have possessed only the Gospels and a Bible in English, and a Gospel 'glossed in English'.[74] According to available records, Richard II owned no English books in 1384/5; his taste at that time was for French chansons de geste and romances[75]—although Froissart's well-known praise of his proficiency in French ('he spoke and read French very well') has been taken to mean that English was at least as natural to him as French.[76] The statement that 'Richard's court was thoroughly French in its reading'[77] is fairly supported by the evidence from Wills. Royal ladies left copies of Arthurian romance and of contemporary French verse in the 1390s: Isabella, Duchess of York, left to her son the poems of Guillaume de Machaut, and a French *Lancelot*.[78] Another substantial inventory, that of Simon Burley, who had been one of Richard's tutors in his youth, and was beheaded in 1388 by order of the Merciless Parliament, credits the knight with wide-ranging literary and devotional interests; only one out of twenty volumes, however, is in English—'j livre de Englys del Forster et del Sengler'.[79] When Henry, Duke of Lancaster, composed his *Livre de Seyntz Medicines* in 1349, he felt it obligatory to use French, not English. And as late as 1433, Joan Holand, Countess of Kent, presented an Anglo-French version of the *Ancrene Riwle* to Eleanor Cobham, second wife of Humphrey, Duke of Gloucester.[80] Besides facts such as these, the possession of '2 libros de Englysshe'—valued, it is true, at only eightpence—by two bankrupt grocers in the 1390s[81] looks rather enterprising.

We cannot, however, make absolute distinctions between the nobility and the middle classes, separating conservatism from enterprise on the crucial issue of 'French versus English'. If Henry of Lancaster spoke English, but wrote French, so too did Andrew Horn, fishmonger and Chamberlain of the City of London. He expounded Edward III's famous *Charter of Liberties* (1327) to a mass meeting at the Guildhall 'in English';[82] he copied part of Brunetto Latini's treatise on government, *Tresor*, into the *Liber Custumarum* in its original French, and he probably wrote, in Anglo-French, the *Speculum Justitiariorum*, or

Mirror of Justices, which he left to the Guildhall library, among other legal and historical volumes, in 1328/9.[83] If the Auchinleck Manuscript tells us that the middle classes were, by 1340, showing a growing preference for poetry in English, other records of the middle classes tell us that they continued to use French extensively in business transactions and personal correspondence: proclamations to citizens, communications between one town and another, and contracts with skilled artisans were all in French throughout the fourteenth century— 'at Southampton the water-bailiff's accounts were kept in French as late as 1428.'[84] In matters of business and administration, English is the exception until about 1430: only the very humblest were totally confined to English for the conduct of business and of day-to-day life in the fourteenth century. And in spite of the very impressive series of dates, from the midcentury onwards, marking official recognition of English in law courts, Parliament, and grammar-schools,[85] there is a mass of 'middle-class' evidence to support the statement that 'the French used in England was no mere accomplishment, but ... a *true vernacular*, whose roots had penetrated deeply into all classes of English society who could read or write.'[86] A carpenter's contract, no less than a queen's letters, could naturally assume French as a medium. It is interesting that although French was being taught in earlier fifteenth-century Oxford as 'illa lingua Gallica'—a phrase which puts it in a rather special and 'foreign' category—the courses offered catered for teaching French conversation to travellers and merchants, letter-writing in French, the drafting of charters, and the art of pleading in French. The *Dialogues* of William of Kingsmill,[87] which provide examples of conversational French, deal, not with travels abroad, but with travel about England, and in particular about Oxfordshire—Woodstock Fair, Abingdon, and Witney. William Caxton, who was a practical man of business, thought it worthwhile to print, as late as 1483, a *Vocabulary in French and English* intended for the use of merchants and schoolmasters.[88]

And, indeed, when we begin to find solid evidence of middle-class book-ownership, it is not of a very adventurous nature from the point of view of 'libros de Englysshe'. For many reasons Wills are not entirely satisfactory hunting-grounds, but they have something to convey. We know, for instance, from the Will of Nicholas Picot, alderman and mercer of London in the early fourteenth century, that the richer middle classes were interested in educating their sons for literary, as well as practical reasons —

> the said Nicholas and John are to study and attend school
> *donec dictare et versificare scient racionabiliter*[89]

So might Geoffrey Chaucer have been sent to school, some decades later.[90] But the books owned by London citizens in the early and mid-fourteenth century or, more accurately, perhaps, thought worthy of being bequeathed, were nearly always in Latin or French, and of sober historical, legal, or devotional worth.

In fact, it would often be difficult to distinguish between clerks, chaplains, and merchants simply in terms of the books they left. A chaplain such as John Sprot, of London, might own, in 1349, one or two volumes of special professional importance for him—the *Pars Oculi Sacerdotis*, for instance[91]—but his book of *Holy Legends* was a common enough part of the legacies of merchants. The books left by Andrew Horn, fishmonger and annalist, to the Guildhall, in 1328, are impressively but predictably serious; none are in English: 'a great book, *De Gestis Anglorum* ... another book *De Veteribus Legibus Anglie*, together with a book called *Bretoun* ... also a book compiled by Henry of Huntingdon and a book *De Statutis Anglie* ...'.[92]

Whatever the demand for collections of English works in the 1340s in London, no one was apparently leaving such manuscripts as part of valuable estate: much more common is the bequest of 'a small psalter covered with cloth of Tars'.[93] In 1349 Thomas Giles, of Fleetstreet, a citizen of some substance, left to his son Thomas, who was to be educated as a clerk, 'all his books'; his library was extensive, covering 'canon and civil law, literature (*grammatice*), dialectic, theology, as well as geometry and astronomy ...'.[94] But the Will is silent on the question of English writings, and it is unlikely that something equivalent to the Auchinleck Manuscript was meant by 'grammatice'. Other middle-class book-owners of the mid-century can be found among London pepperers, stockfishmongers and vintners:

the books concerned are biblical or liturgical. William de Thorneye, pepperer, left the *Parabola Salamonis* (the *Proverbs of Solomon*) to his son John, in 1350; John Syward left 'chalice, books and vestments' to the Church of Saint Nicholas Coldabbay, in 1349.[95] A 'psalter written in Latin and English', left by Robert de Felstede, vintner, in 1350 to John Foxton, a clerk, provides an unusual but not very explicit reference to English.[96] In fact, these early bequests allow us little room for conjecturing what differences there may have been in the reading range of merchants and clerks: the common denominator certainly seems to have been that staple educative force of the Middle Ages—the Saint's Life.

The next century preserved something of this picture of the middle classes: bequests between 1403 and 1483 are still mainly of Bibles, service-books, philosophical and historical works, with more frequent references to English writings in the field of religious prose than in that of poetry—devout or secular. Richard Rolle's translation of the *Psalter*, Walter Hilton's treatises on the religious life, and the meditative life of Christ by Nicholas Love, Carthusian Prior of Mount Grace, *The Mirror of the Blessed Life of Jesu Christ*, are very well represented.[97] This persisting reticence about English books is not, of course, peculiar to the middle classes, nor, even, to the laity in general: monastic libraries rarely list English books in their catalogues. But it is possible to see that the middle-class laity might be particularly sensitive to the problems raised by admitting ownership of English books: as the records of the Lollard movement in the later fourteenth and fifteenth centuries make clear, lay possession of such volumes could be regarded with suspicion. In the fifteenth century, many were arrested and tried on grounds of owning, reading, and teaching from English books,[98] and although the censure of the Church was directed towards English versions of the Scriptures, English versions and expositions of certain prayers in daily use, and Wycliffite tracts, the atmosphere of suspicion may easily have cautioned against mentioning any but the most orthodox and sanctioned English literature. Nicholas Love's *Mirror* was a very 'safe' bequest, having been licensed by Arundel of Canterbury in 1410 expressly as anti-Lollard propaganda.

But for a variety of reasons, some of which are clearer than others, bequests conceal as much as they reveal. John Carpenter, town clerk of London in the early fifteenth century, left a large number of books to the Guildhall at his death in 1442: none, apparently, were in English, and only two in French.[99] This is the man who commissioned English verse for City occasions from the poet and monk, John Lydgate; on his instructions, too, Lydgate's translation of the French text of the *Danse Macabre* was revised, to accompany murals for the Cloister around Pardon Churchyard, near Saint Paul's.[100] Thomas Hoccleve addressed a begging-poem to him.[101] His interest in contemporary English poetry lies hidden behind his massive bequest to the Guildhall—if, indeed, it was ever more than a professional interest in suitable verse for civic ceremonies. It is not until the later decades of the fifteenth century that we find substantial evidence of the middle classes owning a fair number of English writings. Even then it is the minor gentry rather than the merchants who have the most interesting collections; although such men were frequently and closely connected with trade, by origin and by marriage,[102] the range of their books may represent the aspirations of a section of society rather than its norm of taste and habit. Sir John Paston, for instance, who died in 1475 and represents exactly the new but soundly established gentry of the fifteenth century,[103] had a varied collection of books, drawn from Latin, French, and English poetry and prose: Chaucer and minor Chaucerian poets were represented, with Hoccleve and Lydgate, as well as the type of English metrical romance we have come across before, in the Auchinleck Manuscript—*Guy of Warwick* and *Richard Cœur de Lion*.[104] Sir Thomas Urswyck, Recorder of London, and Chief Baron of the Exchequer, left volumes of Chaucer, Mandeville, and Froissart in 1479, as well as law-books and two unspecified devotional works.[105] Sir Thomas Cumberworth, a well-known Lincolnshire book-owner, bequeathed 'the talys of Cantyrbury' in 1451 to a niece: he probably also owned a copy of Nicholas Love's *Mirror of the Blessed Life* and Hilton's *Scale of Perfection*.[106] Sir Thomas Charlton had, among goods confiscated during this same period, a *Canterbury Tales*, a 'troyles', and an English version of the *De Regimine Principum*, probably Hoccleve's.[107]

These later fifteenth-century references to the possession of English literature, and, in particular, of English poetry, by 'gentlemen' have been called by one historian 'slender finds'.[108] And it is true that the proportion of English works in any one collection is never high: it is, nevertheless, always significant. A booklist, found on one of the fly-leaves of a fourteenth-century manuscript, records a lost library of the fifteenth century, which resembles somewhat the named collections we have been considering:[109] it is still trilingual, and strongly inclined towards Saints' Lives and devotional literature generally, but it includes what we can now recognize as staple items by Chaucer, Hoccleve, and Lydgate—the 'talys of Cauntyrbury', 'Hocklyf de Regimine', and 'The pylgrymage of the Soule'. There are other sources of information about literary taste in the fifteenth century: William Caxton had noble patrons, customers, and even noble translators for his printed editions of the 1470s and 1480s. But both of his editions of the *Canterbury Tales* (1478 and 1484) were brought out at the request of 'gentlemen'.[110] It is interesting that the few books which he printed at the request of his friends among the merchant classes confirm those substantial and sober literary tastes with which we have already found them associated. Not Chaucer's poetry, but his prose version of the *De Consolatione Philosophiae* was printed for 'a singuler frende'—probably the same mercer, William Pratt, who gave Caxton a copy of the *Book of Good Manners,* in French: his translation and edition of that text (1487) was intended for 'the comyn people'.[111] The *Mirror of the World* was translated and printed 'at the request, desire, coste and dispense of Hugh Bryce', alderman of London.[112]

All of this speaks of the dominance of literature in English in the later decades of the fifteenth century, but, more specifically, of the part played by the gentry in the confirmation of a high status for English poetry. Whereas Andrew Horn's books, in 1329, and John Carpenter's, in 1444, are at best ambiguous witnesses to the cultural value placed upon English literature, John Paston's books come out decisively for the special pre-eminence of English poetry. Those of Urswyck, Cumberworth, and Charlton corroborate this. Moreover, we can at last find comment upon the changed situation. Caxton tells us about pre-Chaucerian poetry in his *Prologue* to the second edition of the *Canterbury Tales* that 'in thys royame was had rude speche and incongrue, as yet it appiereth by olde books whyche at thys day ought not to have place ne be compared emong ne to hys [Chaucer's] beauteous volumes and aournate writynges'.[113] Earlier, the copious poet, John Lydgate—whose life and works in themselves testify to the century's acceptance of the sufficiency and the potential of English poetry—had looked back to a time before Chaucer, when English poetic language was 'rude and boistous' and 'of litel reputacioun'.[114] It would be difficult, now, to state confidently what 'olde bookes' Caxton had in mind:[115] difficult, also, to be sure whether Lydgate was writing generally or specifically of that time of 'litel reputacioun' for English poetry. But their words can remind us of, and return us to, those uncertain years in the mid-fourteenth century, before the achievements of the courtly alliterative poets, and of Chaucer: a time when the middle classes were showing themselves so eager to have collections of works in English, produced for their amusement and instruction, and yet so reluctant to acknowledge, in their bequests, an 'official' status for English literature, comparable to that of Latin and French. Perhaps the Auchinleck Manuscript would have qualified as one of Caxton's 'olde bookes'; certainly for all its scope and variety, it and similar collections seem to have been held 'in litel reputacioun' by those very classes of people for which it was made. If it was ever in Chaucer's possession, he did not think it worthy of mention—and if he used it, he used it more as material for satire than for imitation.[116]

In fact, the middle class of the fourteenth century, with their practical respect for English as a useful and convenient instrument of literature, law, and government, but with their equally practical sense of its limitations, can only begin to account for the splendour of English poetry—and English prose—after 1350. Middle-class demands could guarantee a steady flow of works in the English vernacular—however little they were acknowledged in bequest form. English metrical romances, produced in such numbers from the later thirteenth century onwards, must no doubt be seen in a particular social context, catering for a 'class of social aspirants who wish to be entertained with what they consider to be the same fare, but in

English, as their social betters'.[117] It is no accident that the
first great move towards providing English versions of French
and Anglo-French romances coincided with the thrusting social
and political movements which were to change the balance of
power in London life between 1270 and 1350.[118] The solid
mass of romance translations, made between 1275 and 1340,
and the almost equally solid mass of religious translations,
similar in literary quality, and often in purport, must have a
close connection with the solid achievements of the urban
middle classes over those years.[119]

But middle-class demands could not guarantee literary
standards. If such readers 'aspired', in a literary sense, it was
not towards the greater refinement and enrichment of English
poetic language, but towards the understanding and possession
of accredited works in French—and, in some cases, Latin. The
Auchinleck Manuscript is a perfect statement of the advances,
in scope and range of material, made by English versifiers in
response to a thriving and energetic need: it is also a perfect
statement of the imaginative and stylistic limitations imposed
upon poets by the nature of that same need. The indebtedness
of Chaucer and Langland to the content and the form of Auch-
inleck-type verse—Chaucer to the rhymed romances, Langland
to *The Simonie*[120]—is an interesting possibility. But the most
important legacy of the Auchinleck and similar collections is a
habit of composition, a linguistic convention. If Chaucer's
poetry could not have existed without such collections, it could
not also have existed without the poetry of Boccaccio, Machaut,
and Graunson. Nor could it have existed without the stimulus
of a court whose king had civilized and educated tastes for the
Roman de la Rose, for the poetry of Chrétien de Troyes, and for
the exquisite book-painting of Jean Pucelle, which came to
him, in the *Belleville Breviary*, as part of the dowry of Isabella of
France.[121] The miniature, in Corpus Christi College, Cambridge, MS 61, of Chaucer reading *Troilus* to Richard and his
court, in parkland foiled by a burnished sky, and crowded with
gaudy brocades, is more than a compliment. It is a stylized
recognition of the exclusive and sophisticated milieu of Chaucer's verse. *Troilus* is, as we might expect, a connoisseur's
poem, appealing designedly to readers of learning and dis-
crimination. It is a poem for a cultural élite, headed by a king

whom we see as the patron of French and English poets—
suggesting a new work to John Gower, receiving a luxury
volume from Froissart—'it was illuminated ... with a cover of
crimson velvet with ten studs of silver gilt, and golden roses in
the middle ...'[122]—and, possibly, urging upon Chaucer the
writing of the *Legend of Good Women*. Such an élite included the
Savoyard poet, Oton de Graunson, who spent twenty years at
the English court, often employed in the service of the house
of Lancaster, and who became, in 1393, 'home lige de vie' of
the king himself. His elegant balades and dream poems were
as acceptable to and influential upon Chaucer as they were
upon Continental poets, in France and Spain.[123] Those of
Chaucer's exact English contemporaries who responded most
sensitively to the quality of his verse were laymen of substance
and importance in public life; their professional activities and,
sometimes, their family connections link them with noble
houses—even if they themselves must be called 'minor gentry'.
Sir John Clanvowe's *Book of Cupid*[124] and the delicate *Balade* of
Squire John Halsham[125] are perfect illustrations.

Something similar could be said of English religious prose,
which reached its greatest heights of elegance and expressiveness in the later fourteenth century not at all by reason of the
demand for spiritual teaching by a wide variety of people who
could not read Latin or French. They were, indeed, catered
for, but in fairly unsophisticated religious poetry: metrical
passion poems, versions of the Gospels, lyrics commemorating
the festivals and basic doctrines of the Church are all witnesses
to the serious note taken of these people and their needs. But
the finest work of Hilton, of the author of the *Cloud of Unknowing*,
and of Dame Julian of Norwich was done in highly specialized
contexts, for named or unnamed disciples of special vocation,
and in close contact with other specialist literature on the
contemplative life. The best religious prose of the century was
written for a spiritual élite.

A far larger share of responsibility for the nature of Chaucer's
work must be borne by its courtly affiliations than by its 'tap-
root'[126] in the literary and linguistic *mores* of English bourgeois
society. The fact that Chaucer's first poetic venture was a
version of the *Roman de la Rose* should remind us of the aristocratic library of his day, rather than of the Auchinleck Manu-

script. Thomas of Gloucester, Simon Burley, and King Richard himself all owned copies of the *Roman*: Gloucester's volume had been purchased from the executors of Sir Richard Sturry, who died in 1395.[127] The dream-allegory was clearly much in demand among courtly readers well known to Chaucer: Sir Richard Sturry was an old friend of his—they were associated in foreign embassies as early as 1377[128]—and Simon Burley sat with Chaucer on the same commission of the peace in 1385. The literacy and intelligence of the English nobility of the fourteenth century is no longer a question for debate. Enough evidence exists to show that the barons of Edward III were well equipped for diplomatic business, and were interested in education and cultural affairs. Henry of Derby, in the 1390s, had his sons taught Latin; we have no reason to think that this was unusual.[129] Among the families of fourteenth-century magnates are avid book-collectors—Guy Beauchamp of Warwick, Thomas of Woodstock, Duke of Gloucester, and Henry, Lord Scrope, who was executed for treason in 1415, and whose life and books bridge two centuries. There are authors too—Henry of Lancaster, father of Chaucer's Duchess Blanche, and John Montacute, third Earl of Salisbury, and devoted follower of Richard II, whose lost verses were praised by the French poetess, Christine de Pisan: 'gracieux chevalier, dit Christine, aimant dictiez, et luy-mesme gracieux dicteur'.[130] The author of a contemporary French *Chronicle* on the Deposition of Richard II speaks warmly of him as a courtly poet: 'Right well and beautifully did he also make ballades, songs, roundels and lays.'[131]

But it is more difficult to define the part played by the nobility of the fourteenth century in shaping and encouraging English poetry than it is to define the part played by the middle classes—which, if it was limited, was decisive. As we have seen, English books in noble libraries, from king to magnate, seem to have been rare: whatever was spoken in noble households, French reading-matter seems to have been favoured. John Montacute's poems were probably all in French: he is said to have loved French culture and manners.[132] Perhaps the fairest description of the literary role of the rich and powerful in England, from the thirteenth century onwards, should lay stress not so much upon the collection and fostering of literature in English as upon the provision of source-material for composition in English, and the provision of good cultural settings and stimuli for the eventual upgrading of English literature, and, in particular, of English poetry. A Worcestershire library such as that of Guy Beauchamp, ranging widely over didactic and historical treatises, epic legends, and romances could have provided French and Latin source-material for any number of English alliterative poems, written after 1350, in the west country.[133] A library from the south-east, such as Thomas of Gloucester had collected by 1397, could have offered similarly rich rewards to an aspiring poet. Aristocratic patronage of individual English works is thinly documented, but the examples we have suggest fruitful and various contacts between noble patrons and their books and poets in their service.

We know for a certainty that Humphrey Bohun, Earl of Hereford, commissioned (about 1350) the translation of *William of Palerne* from French into alliterative verse.[134] Probably other alliterative poems of the later fourteenth century had similar beginnings: the *Destruction of Troy*, an alliterative version of Guido delle Colonne's *Historia Destructionis Troiae*, promises, but fails, to reveal 'the nome of the knight þt causet it to be made and the nome of hym that translatid it...'.[135] Nothing quite so specific is known of the relationships of fourteenth-century magnates and poets as is known of the relationship of the prose-writer, John of Trevisa, and the lords of Berkeley Castle, in Gloucestershire. His impressive series of English works was translated while he was Chaplain to two successive lords of Berkeley—and at their request.[136] But English alliterative poems such as *Pearl, Sir Gawain and the Green Knight, St. Erkenwald*, and the *Morte Arthure* have to be explained as end-products of a complicated process, in which social, political, and literary forces co-operated: the collection of materials in the libraries of an increasingly literate nobility and gentry, and the growing acceptance of English for highly literary purposes, as the victories of Edward III, in mid-century, inaugurated a brief but 'glorious summer' of national unity. In particular, these and other splendidly confident poems of the second half of the century tell us of the likely interaction of two things: an aristocracy able to offer conditions and materials for the labour of poets, and a class of authors, possibly of middle-class origin, but perhaps also of minor-gentry status, in the employ of or associated closely with the aristocracy. Such men might reasonably have been well read in European literature, and sensitive to sophisticated taste, but also interested in the potential of English as an elegant and powerful literary medium.

In different literary areas, Chaucer and John of Trevisa fulfil these conditions: in them and their work we see that union of aspiration and patronage which could hope to produce literature well grounded in a stable English vernacular, but responsive to outside influence and encouragement.

Chaucer's friendships with contemporary French poets, whom he met at the English court as well as on his travels, his translations and adaptations from their works, his oblique dedications to noble patrons (the *Book of the Duchess*) and his more open references (the *Legend of Good Women*, ll. 496-7— 'And whan this book is maad, yive hit the quene / On my behalf, at Eltham or at Shene') place him quite as authentically as the links to the *Canterbury Tales*, with their slightly reductive comments upon the poet and his position in high society. It is significant that, outside the work of the *Gawain*-poet and Chaucer, the most refined and appealing dream-poem of the later fourteenth century, the *Book of Cupid*, was written by Sir John Clanvowe, courtier-knight, friend of Chaucer and Simon Burley, and employed by both John of Gaunt and the King.[137] French verse and Chaucer's minor poetry are allusively present in Clanvowe's stanzas: the courtly context is made gracefully apparent in lines such as

> Under the maple that is feire and grene,
> Before the chambre wyndow of the Quene
> At Wodestok, upon the grene lay
>
> (ll. 283-5)

From internal evidence, as well as from historical researches— not yet complete—we can reasonably conclude that the *Gawain*-poet worked similarly close to aristocratic patronage.[138] And the latest study of John Gower sees him 'in the same two worlds as Chaucer, the upper middle class society of the franklin, merchant and lawyer, and the aristocratic society of a trusted retainer in a noble household'.[139] Gower is particularly interesting, since his poetry bears witness to the congruence of old and new patterns. Writing in Latin, French, and English with equal ease, he deliberately presented his three major poems as part of a whole—a vast trilingual work of 'instructive material', in three 'books'.[140] In many ways, therefore, Gower appears as the last striking representative of that 'relaxed cultural situation' in which Latin held its position as the traditional language of serious philosophical and theological writing, and both vernacular languages were acceptable for different, distinct kinds of subject-matter. But only in the case of Gower's long English poem, the *Confessio Amantis*, is there any strong association with courtly patronage. The *Prologue* to the poem, later excised when it was re-dedicated to Henry IV, gives a convincing account of poet and patron, Gower and Richard II, talking on the royal barge— 'in Temse, whan it was flowende'.[141] From Gower's words, it seems that Richard was not averse to the idea of an *English* poem:

> And bad me doo my besynesse
> That to his hihe worthinesse
> Som newe thing I scholde boke
> That he himself it mihte loke ...

And, indeed, for all that has been said about Richard's taste for French literature, and French culture generally, there is nothing improbable in the idea that Gower's *Confessio* and Chaucer's *Troilus* would have been acceptable to him, and to his court, as vernacular works of elegance and fluency comparable with French. The fine-drawn openings of these poems and of the *Legend of Good Women*—also royally connected— mark an important occasion, to which English poetic language is now expected to rise.

The suggestion has been made that, in contrast to the *Confessio Amantis*, Gower's *Cinquante Ballades*, a decorous bouquet of love-poems in French, were written for the richer merchant classes of London—and even more specifically, for the 'Brethren of the Pui ... a religious, charitable, convivial and musical organisation', whose members met at a 'royal feast' and performed songs, celebrating the 'becoming plesaunce of virtuous ladies'.[142] Whether this particular linkage can be accepted or not—the merchant *Pui* seems to have been a feature of the earlier fourteenth century in London rather than the later—it is interesting that Gower's French *Ballades* are less up-to-date in their use of courtly French verse than the minor poems of Chaucer. As we have seen, the middle classes were by no means devoted to the use of English for literature or for business; to write for a merchant *Pui* rather than for the Court might mean less need to experiment, as well as less need to allude to fashionable Continental verse. But however we account for the *Ballades*, Gower's poetry drives us to question the simple identification of middle-class interests with the emergence of English as a prestigious literary vernacular. If, as seems probable, his massive Latin complaint poem, the *Vox Clamantis*, was written for the higher and influential levels of clerics, and his French *Mirour de l'Omme* for the educated and pious laity, the English *Confessio Amantis* was written at the suggestion of one king, and dedicated to another.

With him, as not with Chaucer, we look both back and forward: his last literary act was to gather together, in one presentation volume for Richard's successor, three kinds of work: Latin verses, the *Cinquante Ballades*, and an English poem, *In Praise of Peace*. We might be back in the world of Harley 2253. Yet the poem in which 'Gower's potential imaginative power is released fully for the first time'[143] responded to a royal desire for 'some new thing', and it was in this context that his exquisitely plain style was developed. By the last decades of the fourteenth century it was no longer entirely true that 'what counted for more than the quality or nationality of the writer was the taste, power and the riches of the patron.'[144] But they were still highly influential, and it remains true that they were responsible for much of the finest English poetry of the fourteenth century, as they were for much of the finest English art. The Wilton Diptych, the Bohun Psalters, and *Troilus and Criseyde* are products of a courtly and cultivated society, with the strongest of European affiliations. Chaucer mentions no earlier English poet or poem, but is quick to name and praise his French and Italian predecessors and contemporaries. In this he is at one with the temper and taste of the court he knew so well: the literature and the art it sponsored was subtly English, not crudely nationalistic. And we cannot remind ourselves too often that the printing of Chaucer's poetry, and the preservation and even the copying of important manuscripts of English alliterative verse were active concerns of the upper classes in the fifteenth century.[145] To them we owe *Sir Gawain and the Green Knight*, and the Thornton manuscripts: to the middle classes we owe the kind of substantial book collections with which John Carpenter strengthened the Guildhall library in 1442, and Caxton's *Book of Good Manners*, and the popular encyclopaedia, *The Mirror of the World*.[146]

To this general design, William Langland and *Piers Plowman* might seem to be clear exceptions. In his poem, some of the finest English writing of the later fourteenth century was achieved without patronage, without courtly stimulus of any kind. The audience of *Piers Plowman* was very different from that group of courtiers, set like iridescent flowers about the poet Chaucer, as he recited *Troilus* to them: it was different, too, from the audience of *Sir Gawain*, or of the *Confessio Amantis*.[147] Yet, for all the differences of approach and verse-method, *Piers Plowman* could not have been written—or at least it could not have taken its initial or final shape—without the mid-fourteenth-century revival of interest in alliterative poetry, closely associated with noble patronage, and court society, in London and in the provinces.[148] It is obvious that Langland rejected a good deal of what he must have learnt, in his early days in the west country, of this upgraded alliterative verse; we see him gradually dispensing with some of its favourite conventions, bending others to his own purposes, as he worked at the successive versions of his poem. The alliterative rhetoric of the spring-opening, with its bird-song, tumbling waters, and grassy slopes gives way to a terser statement of intention—

> And in a launde as ich lay . lenede ich and slepte[149]

The elaborate, dense descriptive techniques are often employed satirically, not seriously.[150] Moreover, Langland has, for long stretches of his poem, a more strictly utilitarian attitude to the composing of verse than any of the major poets we have been considering.[151]

But I do not think that it would have been possible for him to contemplate writing a work of such urgent import as *Piers Plowman* in English alliterative metre, had not some status been won for that verse by his older contemporaries and predecessors. Whatever his later feelings about the matter, Langland launched his poem in the best formal alliterative style and he never abandoned interest in the special verbal effects to be gained within that poetic tradition.[152] No doubt he commanded a large audience, even in the fourteenth century, mainly on account of his subject-matter: it has been called 'a national public with specialised, non-literary interests'.[153] But if some of the first recorded owners of *Piers Plowman* manuscripts were priests, others were minor gentry, and the poem would not have contained, in its last version, the C-text, so many passages of finely-wrought alliterative style if Langland had not been able to count upon the recognition, by his 'national' public, of the established and potential dignity of his chosen medium.

The fifteenth century confirms many of the patterns we have made out for the fourteenth, and introduces a variety of new. There are aristocratic poets, writing in English—the Duke of Suffolk, William de la Pole; there are aristocratic French poets, writing French verse in England, and finding willing translators for their work—Charles, Duke of Orleans, who was taken prisoner at Agincourt, and remained in luxurious captivity for 25 years.[154] There are clerkly and monastic poets, writing in English for royalty, aristocracy, and gentry, as well as for the wealthier merchant classes—the industrious John Lydgate, monk of Bury St. Edmunds, wrote for patrons of all kinds, and so did Thomas Hoccleve, Clerk of the Privy Seal.[155] The personal libraries of the aristocracy are impressive: they vary from that of Henry, Lord Scrope, which in 1415 contained a large number of service books and religious texts in French and Latin and only a small proportion in English, to that of Sir John Paston, later in the century, with its strong taste for Chaucer's poetry and for the work of his imitators. A smaller but interesting collection belonged to Sir John Fastolf, who died, in 1456, one of the richest landowners in England: here we find romance and dream-allegory—the *Romaunce of the Rose,* a *Brut* in rhyme, a *Liber de Roy Arthour*—as well as a good deal of Latin Chronicle and pseudo-science.[156] No doubt the contrast between the books of Scrope and Fastolf on the one hand, and those of John Paston on the other, is a contrast of old and new: taken together the Scrope and Fastolf volumes remind us of earlier libraries, such as that of Guy Beauchamp of Warwick.[157] But that reminder is useful in a variety of ways. John Paston was a protégé of Fastolf's, and his enthusiasm for books may have been partly stimulated by the example of Fastolf's collection. It was, indeed, the collection of no simple landowner and war-veteran, but of a shrewd and literate man, who had the *Dicts and Sayings of the Philosophers* translated into English for him,[158] and who had, as his secretary, one of the best-read and most interesting scholars of the day, William of Worcester.[159] As we have already noticed when dealing with the fourteenth century, it was not the active desire to possess books *in English* which characterized the making of the aristocratic medieval library so much as the gathering together of important and varied works in Latin and French, as source-materials and incentives for others.

In this light, the Inventory of John de Veer, thirteenth Earl of Oxford, who died in 1512/13, is doubly significant.[160] A substantial list of service books and religious texts in Latin, some with elaborate covers—'w[t] thone syde covered w[t] silver and a picktur of o[r] lorde'—is interrupted by a brief and tantalizing reference to 'a chest full of frensche and englisshe books'. The old, formal hierarchies of language die hard, but the Earl of Oxford's chest was 'full' of vernacular books.

3 Mappings

Kenneth Sisam's *Fourteenth Century Verse and Prose* provided a useful map, in which most of the main literary areas of the fourteenth century are defined. With the exception of *Piers Plowman*, which is shown spanning the whole of the central west midlands, across the home counties, to London, texts and authors are localized in a way which makes it easier to accept the Parson's reference to himself as a 'southren man', who could not manage (or appreciate?) alliterative verse,[1] or the earlier reference, by an unnamed alliterative poet, to himself as a 'westren wy', who distrusted the pleasures of life in the south of England:

> Dare never no westren wy, while this werlde lasteth,
> Send his sone southewarde to see ne to here,
> That he ne schall holden by-hynde when he hore (for) eld es...[2]

And, indeed, it is possible to point to the recognition, by fourteenth- and fifteenth-century writers, of linguistic difficulties. The scribe of Cambridge University Library MS Ii.4.9 describes his text (of Rolle) as 'translate oute of Northarn tunge into Sutherne that it schulde the bettir be understondyn of men that be of the Selve Countrie'.[3] The annotator of MS Additional 6578 (of Love's translation of the *Meditationes Vitae Christi*), from the same library, warns southern scribes to look out for northern dialectal forms: 'cave de istis verbis gude pro gode item hir pro heere in pluraliter'.[4] And we cannot overlook, even if they are themselves derivative, the statements made by Ranulph Higden in the earlier fourteenth century, and corroborated by John of Trevisa in 1387:

> þerfore hyt ys þat Mercii, þat buþ men of myddel Engelond ... undurstondeþ betre þe syde longages, Norþeron and Souþeron, þan Norþeron and Souþeron undurstondeþ eyþer oþer.[5]

We might, then, be tempted to accept, without question, what such evidence implies—that communication between the north and south of England was hampered by dialectal peculiarities, that London and the South were regarded as 'different', and dangerously so, by west country people, and that there were, understandably, distinct and separable literary areas in the fourteenth century. These areas, which have often been proposed as inviolate by critics and literary historians, divide English poetry into three main sections: alliterative verse, rhymed and unrhymed, in the counties of the west and north-west midlands, court verse, headed by Chaucer and Gower, in London and the immediate surrounds, and tail-rhyme verse centred upon East Anglia.[6]

In this pattern London contrasts strongly with provincial areas—its famous named poets set against the unknown authors of *Sir Gawain and the Green Knight*, of the *Morte Arthure*, or of *Athelston*. Critics have even been persuaded of connections between political, geographical and metrical issues: it has been suggested that the alliterative line was fostered by western magnates as yet another sign of baronial defiance of the king and court in London,[7] and that the tail-rhyme stanza, from vigorous and fast-developing East Anglia, was 'in itself a declaration of independence against the French couplet which dominated narrative poetry in the thirteenth century'.[8] Thus both alliterative and tail-rhyme verse have been seriously proposed as evidence for particularly 'English' literary movements in the fourteenth century, with strong geographical bases, and anti-French persuasions. Certainly there has been widespread tolerance of the idea that the 'alliterative revival' of the mid-fourteenth century was a 'local affair'[9] and that Chaucer found the techniques of such poetry 'completely alien'.[10] Similarly, although the centring of tail-rhyme romance in the East Anglian area has been subjected to some detailed criticism,[11] no general refutation has been attempted. Indeed, Chaucer's *Sir Thopas*, with its satirical use of the tail-rhyme stanza, has helped us to isolate this kind of verse from accepted styles of court-poetry in fourteenth-century London.

But while appreciating the usefulness of a literary map, made in the twentieth century, we should not fail to test it against a real map, made in the fourteenth century. Fortunately we have one easily available—the so-called *Gough Map*, drawn about 1360, and described by its editor as 'a map for travellers ... an official compilation for couriers and other servants of the Crown who must have frequented the fourteenth century highways'.[12] Perhaps the most striking thing about this map is the evidence it offers about communications in the fourteenth century. London is at the centre of a network of roads which spread out across the midlands to Wales and to Cheshire and Lancashire, and directly to the northern midlands, and to York. On the evidence of the map, we should naturally conclude that travel between all parts of England was extensive and well-served by its highways: 'a national system of roads radiating from the national capital'.[13] The map-maker's lack of detailed attention to hill-ranges probably indicates where his main interests lay—in means of communication. Rivers and roads assist communication, but mountains hinder it; the rivers, roads, and the towns they link are boldly and clearly drawn in.

The *Gough Map* confirms, if in a rather special way, what we gather from historians about English society in the later thirteenth and fourteenth centuries: that it was interconnected, and highly mobile. We have, for instance, fairly exact knowledge about the large-scale movement of immigrants into London between 1280 and 1350. A study of the merchant classes of medieval London tells us that 'from the earliest years of the fourteenth century, London was drawing on the entire kingdom, any large sample of names conjuring up a map of the length and breadth of England'.[14] But links between London and Yorkshire, and London, Norfolk, and Lincolnshire were particularly strong among the mercantile and professional classes.[15] The Swanland family, rich London merchants in the earlier fourteenth century, were of Yorkshire origin, with kinsmen well established in the knightly and ecclesiastical society of that county. One brother remained a clerk, and obtained a living in Yorkshire.[16] Simon Fraunceys, mercer and spicer from Pontefract, who exported and imported in Newcastle, Hull, and London, 'emerged with property in four counties, and a city estate substantial enough to buttress the fortunes of a second generation of mercers'.[17] Sir Geoffrey le Scrope, Chief Justice of the King's Bench from 1324 to 1338, and influential adviser to both the government of Queen Isabella and Roger Mortimer and that of Edward III, was a 'self-made northerner, as so many of the London lawyers were'.[18] The Yorkshire estates which he amassed were the foundations of the power of the Scropes of Masham, 'one of the great northern families of the later Middle Ages'.[19]

The family of the Kentish poet, John Gower, may have been originally of Yorkshire, coming south in the earlier fourteenth century in the service of the Strabolgis, Earl and Countess of Atholl.[20] Sometimes the move to the capital meant a severing of ties with the provinces: the poet of *Winner and Waster* implies that this was his experience of the matter. But often it was not so: Sir Geoffrey le Scrope was always actively concerned with his Yorkshire possessions, and was brought back for burial to the Yorkshire Abbey of Coverham.

Even more decisive in their effects were the migrations of Norfolk and Lincolnshire merchant classes into London, which, beginning in the later thirteenth century, became 'socially significant'[21] in the reign of Edward II. A recent historian of medieval London sees the relationship between the capital and the counties of the east and north-east in the four-teenth century as 'close and continuous', evidenced in business transactions, in family relationships, and in bequests of Lon-don wealth to religious foundations in Norfolk: 'The one clearly marked immigration trend was a flow into London from the rich, commercialized provinces of the old Danelaw, East Anglia, the east Midlands, east Lincolnshire, and southern Yorkshire ... London's trade was already oriented towards these provinces, with the Husting closing for Boston Fair, and the city fishmongers colonizing Yarmouth. ...'[22]

Many leading figures in London life of the fourteenth century were of Lincolnshire or Norfolk origin: the mercer John de Causton, for example, who exported from London, Yarmouth, and Boston, had property in Norfolk, Middlesex, and London, and at his death in 1353 made handsome bequests to the fra-ternity of Saint Anne.[23] Among the aldermen of the 1340s was William Thorneye—a pepperer, and one of the greatest im-porters of the century: he came from Lincolnshire, and endowed a chantry nave, as well as owning land in Cambridgeshire.[24] The pattern of trade, property, and piety in London and the eastern counties is repeated a score of times during this century and the next: Walter Burneye, mercer and alderman in the 1360s, left bequests to Norwich churches; John Chircheman, pepperer and alderman in the 1380s, who kept establishments in Harwich and London, endowed a chantry in Heylesdon, Norfolk.[25] And we cannot pass over without mention the most famous of Londoners whose family was ultimately of Norfolk origin—Geoffrey Chaucer.[26]

Another strong immigrant process in the fourteenth century linked the central counties of England with London. The geographical centre of England was itself an area of great change and movement during the period: it was particularly well traversed by the main roads of the *Gough Map*—the Great North Road, and Watling Street—and, as linguists have stressed, its dialect was more easily accessible than that of other parts of England. The influence of this dialect upon London English, and the important contribution it made to the nature of the standard written English eventually established from London are marks of the close links between the counties of Leicestershire, Bedfordshire, and Northamptonshire and the capital.[27]

It is not difficult to see that the cultural implications of these immigrant patterns are very various. The central counties of England, for instance, in the fourteenth century, are more likely to aid communications between the south-east and the distant lands of the west and north-west, and even between the south and the north, than to act as any solid barrier to communication. The wide acceptability of their language is one important aspect of this. A substantial number of texts, originally composed in the north or north-east of England, come to us in manuscripts using the homogeneous language of the central midlands—texts as influential as the *English Psalter* of the Yorkshireman, Richard Rolle, the *Scale of Perfection* of Walter Hilton, Canon of Thurgarton, Nottinghamshire, and the *Mirror of the Blessed Life of Jesu Christ* by the Prior of Mount Grace, Yorkshire, Nicholas Love.[28] It was a written language as familiar in Somerset and Dorset as it was in Leicester or London: the later version of the Lollard Bible, and nearly all of Wiclif's sermons circulated in it. So what emerges from a co-ordination of sociological and dialectal facts is not so much a map as a 'flow-chart', recording movements of people and literature, which may be concentrated in particular geographical areas, but never precisely contained within them.

This is illustrated again when we consider the theory that the tail-rhyme romances not only 'represent a "school" as definite as that of the West-Midlands', but can also be 'located with certainty'.[29] The dangers of ignoring a whole complex of economic, social, and religious factors are clear when we find that East Anglia, and especially Norfolk, is categorically stated to be the 'home' of tail-rhyme verse. The location of a 'tail-rhyme centre'[30] in this area, and the connected theories of 'East-Anglian training' and the development of a 'heroic style' in Norfolk[31] can only be based on part of the total evidence available. And, in fact, the view of East Anglian society which helps these theories is extremely narrow: as we have seen, business and family relationships in the east of England span, with ease, Newcastle, Hull, Boston, Yarmouth, and London. The connections between East Anglia and London, and especially Norfolk and London, are 'close and continuous'. There is little in what historians tell us to support the idea of the 'isolation' of East Anglia, 'more marked in the Middle Ages', nor of the 'self-centred' nature of this part of England.[32] On the vexed question of metre alone, it is impossible to make rigid demarcations. Perhaps the tail-rhyme stanza, with its interesting combination of couplet and short line, was only widely used for *narrative* purposes by poets of the eastern side of England. But it was well established as a narrative measure in French verse: one of the liveliest verse-chronicles of the late fourteenth century, on the *Deposition of Richard II*, was written in a variety of tail-rhyme—perhaps by a French courtier knight, or perhaps by a Welsh bishop.[33] And it was already well known as a lyric measure in English, exhibiting some of the same characteristics as it does in the romance narratives. Lyrics from the earlier fourteenth-century manuscript collection, Harley 2253, show the same tendency to heavy alliteration in the short line as do the tail-rhyme romances.[34] While the source of the measure, and its provenance—in a variety of forms—are still matters for debate, it is not really possible to make a totally convincing case for the peculiarly English, and peculiarly East Anglian, nature of tail-rhyme verse.

The spread of the poems, as shown by the manuscripts, accords far better with what we already know of those 'close and continuous relationships' between the capital and the whole of eastern England. Some of the best of the tail-rhyme romances (*Horn Childe, Amis and Amiloun, Guy of Warwick*, the *King of Tars*) occur in the early Auchinleck Manuscript, which has been shown to be the product of a London bookshop of the 1330s or 1340s.[35] Whatever the original place of composition of poems such as *Amis and Amiloun*,[36] at a date not long after composition it was being presented to a London public, among others of its kind. If the Auchinleck tail-rhyme romances are indeed 'the fountain-head of the style',[37] they were first 'published' authoritatively in a London setting. At the opposite end of the time-scale, the Thornton manuscripts contain good texts of other tail-rhyme poems (*Octavian, Isumbras, Eglamour*, the *Erl of Tolous*, the *Sege of Melayne*, and *Rowland and Ottuell*), but have been just as conclusively assigned to fifteenth-century Yorkshire.[38] By 1390, at least one tail-rhyme romance was included in a west midland collection: the *King of Tars* in the Vernon manuscript (Bodleian MS Eng. Poet. a. I). And although many of the tail-rhyme romances survive in the dialect of the north-east midlands, Thomas Chestre wrote his tail-rhyme romance, *Sir Launfal*, somewhere in the south-east of England during the later fourteenth century.[39] The unknown poet who, at about the same time, adapted Hue de Rotelande's Anglo-French romance *Ipomédon* into tail-rhyme, and who came from somewhere in either Lancashire or the north-east,[40] marks out more northerly limits for the use of the stanza. Clearly, one significant point to make about this verse in tail-rhyme is its easy and rapid spread as a popular narrative form throughout all areas of the east of England during the fourteenth century: in one, and perhaps two cases, it is found in more westerly contexts. It reinforces what we already know of the live connections between East Anglia and London, rather than defining East Anglia as a distinctive 'literary area'. The vigorous tail-rhyme romance of *Athelston*, written towards the end of the fourteenth century, reveals in its author an expert knowledge of London, and the route from London to Canterbury.[41] Wherever the poem was first composed, in Norfolk or in London, it undoubtedly set out to appeal to an audience which was thoroughly familiar with the Strand, Fleet Street, Saint Paul's, and the road to Dover. As we shall see, some of the alliterative poems display the same kind of knowledge,[42] and remind us that medieval poets and audiences were part of a highly mobile society, and that geographical areas were never sealed against movement and change.

It is possible to make similar observations about the art of the period: East Anglian manuscript painting of the fourteenth century is often popularly described in terms which mark it off from other 'schools' of painting in England, and tend to confine it geographically. And, of course, it is true that some of the best known of the East Anglian manuscripts can be decisively connected with important centres such as Peterborough,[43] with identifiable persons[44] and families.[45] But East Anglian painting had its roots in styles first developed in London centres of the later twelfth and thirteenth centuries,[46] and some of its patrons, and their commissioned works, are clearly associated with areas outside East Anglia. The de Lisle family, for whom the splendid Psalter (British Library MS Arundel 83, part ii) was made, owned lands in East Anglia and Yorkshire. While MS Arundel 83 can probably be localized in East Anglia, other de Lisle manuscripts have distinct Yorkshire references.[47] Moreover, the different styles of painting in the second part of the Arundel Psalter—one strongly influenced by contemporary French work, and another by Italian—warn us against supposing that East Anglia at this time was in any way 'self-centred'.[48]

There are, too, stylistic links between East Anglian book painting and that produced by craftsmen working and travelling in central England, in Nottinghamshire particularly, and therefore well placed for absorbing and transmitting influences from one side of England to the other. The marginal grotesques in an early fourteenth-century manuscript such as the Grey FitzPayn Hours[49] are reminiscent of some later East Anglian borders: this book was illuminated for Sir Robert Grey of Codnor, Derbyshire, to the north-west of Nottingham. The exquisite Tickhill Psalter[50] and the Psalter of Queen Isabella[51] are also products of this central English 'school' of painting. But we cannot remind ourselves too often that such a 'school' was in reality a travelling *atelier*, moving about a large geographical area. Its productions therefore reflect the lives and possessions of a variety of patrons, as well as the varied training of the artists themselves. The Psalter of Queen Isabella, made for the wife of Edward II, perhaps between 1303, when they were betrothed, and 1308, when they were married, spans east and west in its celebration of Saints: while its Calendar refers specifically to Saints of the west midlands, its Litany refers to those of East Anglia and the south-east of England.[52] Such a manuscript should certainly make us hesitate about precise localization, and should call to mind the actual life of the woman for whom it was made: her life as reigning queen, moving between London and the provinces, her arrest, with Mortimer, her lover, at Nottingham Castle in 1330, and the last years of her life, spent at Castle Rising in Norfolk. At her death in 1358, her books included romances—'a white leather book concerning the deeds of Arthur'—missals, a Bible and an Apocalypse in French, and a 'Psalter wrapped in two silken cloths'.[53]

For the varied activities and the widely dispersed estates of the nobility in the fourteenth century created another 'network' which had its own direct influence upon art and literature. The Beauchamps of Warwick, with their core of lands in Warwickshire, Worcestershire, and Herefordshire, were also Earls of Essex, and had lordships in Wales. The Montacutes of Salisbury held lands in the southern counties, but also in Wales; they owned two islands—Lundy and the Isle of Man. At their highest point of power during the fourteenth century, the Mortimers were second only to the Prince of Wales and John of Gaunt as landowners—in Ireland, Wales, and the border country, as well as in Dorset and East Anglia. The estates of the Mowbrays were in Lincolnshire and Yorkshire, but also extended over Leicestershire to Warwickshire. Richard Fitzalan, Earl of Arundel and Surrey, an almost exact contemporary and friend of Edward III, amassed not only a considerable fortune but also a large estate over the fourteenth century. Although a great deal of his land was in the south, he received the old Mortimer Lordship of Chirk, in the Welsh Marches. The Inventories made at his death in 1376 list possessions stored in Arundel, London, and Wales. The Staffords, whose lands in the early fourteenth century were exclusively in the west midlands, rapidly acquired estates, through advantageous marriages, in the south-west and the south-east, from Cornwall to Kent and Surrey.[54] The territorial domain of a great prince such as John of Gaunt stretched over England, with concentrations in the midlands and the north: 'draw a line across England from the mouth of the Severn to the Wash, and there are scarcely a score of strongholds there out of the Duke's hands.'[55] Lesser men than these, bent on enlarging their estates in the next century too, took little account of proximity, if a good land-sale came their way: Sir John Fastolf, whose manors were mainly in the east of England, had possessions in Wiltshire, and—if we credit a letter from his secretary, William of Worcester—was at least open to suggestion about land-negotiations in Dorset.[56]

A description of these estates is an instant reminder of the *Gough Map*: its great roads that traverse England, branching across the midland counties into Wales and up to the north-west, linking not only London with Yorkshire, and London with Derbyshire, but Lincolnshire with London and with the Wirral, must have been life-lines of communication for the nobility and their officials. And in fact contemporary records give an impressive account of journeying about England undertaken by those concerned in all departments of administration. Great lawyers, such as Chief Justice Scrope, travelled as intensively in the king's business between London and Scotland as they did between London and the Continent.[57] The most extreme example of this mobility is provided by the Crown itself: 'the king, going north to fight the Scots, thought nothing of bodily removal, not only of the Wardrobe and Privy Seal, but also of Chancery, Exchequer and Common Law Courts, so that he himself might remain in contact with them.'[58] This highly personal concept of government, which was not in any sense a mere display of power, but a practical way of ensuring efficient administration, kept king, magnates, nobility, gentry, and their households on the move. The Black Prince, in spite of his overseas obligations, 'was well-known in Chester and Cornwall';[59] John of Gaunt closely and personally attended to the affairs of his dispersed lands.[60]

On a day-to-day basis, England must have been thoroughly crossed and re-crossed by those very people who might have had a good deal to do with the patronage and the writing of poetry. It was to John of Gaunt's eldest daughter, Philippa 'living in *Lancaster*'—'en Lancastre le trouvere, ce croy'—that the French court poet, Deschamps, composed and sent his *Ballade* in praise of the Order of the Flower.[61] And to be in Lancastrian employ in the days of John of Gaunt could almost be regarded as a guarantee of some degree of movement about the country. The prominence of the Newton family in the west midlands and in London during the later decades of the fourteenth century could have had a Lancastrian *raison d'être*. We know something of the career of Simon Newton, 'a west-midland man of some importance between 1363 and 1380', who owned lands in Derbyshire and Warwickshire, was King's Esquire, and later Governor of Hammes Castle, near Calais.[62] We can also find that a Thomas Newton was one of those 'chers et bien amez' to whom Gaunt granted, in 1382, 'man-oires, terres et tenementz' in the counties of Staffordshire and Leicestershire.[63] He was 'escheator in Notynghamshire and Derbyshire' in 1390, and in 1392 was confirmed Sheriff of London.[64] Sir John Cheyne, who may have originated in Gloucestershire—he owned considerable property in that county—was clerk in Gaunt's service in the 1370s and 1380s: he was treasurer of the household, and receiver for the honour of Tutbury Castle, Staffordshire, and of Gaunt's lands in Derbyshire. Whether or not Cheyne's subsequent employment on important diplomatic missions meant that he saw less of the roads to the west country in the last years of the fourteenth century, he must, at one period of his life at least, have moved frequently on Gaunt's business between the west midlands and London. Men such as the Newtons and Sir John Cheyne were probably of some education and culture. We know that a copy of *Sir Gawain and the Green Knight* was familiar to a branch of the Newton family in the later fifteenth century: the poems of Humfrey Newton (1466-1536) of Macclesfield, Cheshire, show signs of this in their diction and style.[65] Sir John Cheyne owned and bequeathed a Psalter 'glossed by Richard the Hermit'—Richard Rolle's English translation of the Psalter.[66]

Others with whom Gaunt was connected illustrate this pattern of 'east-west' activity. Sir John Clanvowe, whose dream-poem, the *Book of Cupid*, has already been mentioned as one of the most graceful 'Chaucerian' pieces of the later fourteenth century, was of Herefordshire origin—the Castle of Cusop, near Hay. He is found, not surprisingly, in the retinue of Humphrey Bohun, Earl of Hereford and Essex, and then in Gaunt's retinue, supporting the Duke's party at the Good Parliament of 1376, receiving presents from the Duke, and in 1378 serving him in France in company with other friends of Chaucer's—Sir Richard Sturry and Philip de la Vache. These occupations in London and on the Continent did not necessarily mean that he lost touch with the west country. In the 1380s he was appointed to many commissions dealing with Wales and the border counties, and he was granted money and land in those parts—'steward of the lordship and constable of the castle of Haverfordwest', and 'keeper of the forest of Snowdon'.[67]

Sir Richard Sturry, who was also of Gaunt's party, and who led an active political and military life in the capital and abroad, was the son of a Shropshire landowner; at one time he was keeper of the castle and lordship of Aberystwyth.[68] That he had literary interests we can suppose from his friendship with Froissart,[69] his acquaintance with Chaucer, and his possession of a copy of the *Roman de la Rose* at his death in 1395.[70]

But apart from Gaunt and his following, there were many other families whose lives spanned London and the provinces. John Stanley and his kinsman Thomas Stanley, who were respectively Controller of the Royal Household and Keeper of the Rolls in the 1390s, came of south-west Lancashire stock. Sir John was also hereditary Forester of the Wirral.[71] Over the fourteenth and fifteenth centuries, the Stanleys appear to have had contacts with various kinds of poets and poetry. For one branch of the family, the important collection of Chaucer's minor poems, and of 'Chaucerian' pieces by Sir John Clanvowe, Sir Richard Ros, and John Lydgate—now Bodleian MS Fairfax 16—was made, before 1450.[72] But, like the Newtons, the Stanleys had access also to alliterative poetry and poets. During the fifteenth century, the unique manuscript of the alliterative *Destruction of Troy* was copied and bequeathed by Thomas Chetham, a minor landowner in their service.[73] And *Scottish Ffeilde*, one of the last of the alliterative poems, was written after 1515 to celebrate the exploits of Edward, Lord Stanley, at the Battle of Flodden.[74]

All of these facts compose a picture of a restless, not a static society, in which ambition and political or dynastic allegiance encouraged, even necessitated, movement and actively discouraged the isolation of particular areas and classes of people. It would be surprising if areas and classes of literature could be any more decisively marked off from each other. The geographical patterns traced by patronage, politics, and literary affiliations are complex and abundant. One rather pleasing example comes from the year 1398, and concerns an English poem on the *Legend of Saint Christina*. This was written during the imprisonment of Thomas Beauchamp, Earl of Warwick, on the Isle of Man from 1397 to 1399, by his sole remaining squire, William Parys.[75] The description of the circumstances of composition, and of the relationship between poet and patron, are unusually exact. We know that one of the Beauchamps, earlier in the century, had a strong interest in literary matters: here, now, a squire in the family service is capable of writing a consolatory poem for his master:

> Sire Thomas Beawchamp ane erle was he;
> In Warwik-shire was his powere;
> Now is he of so poure degre,
> He hath no mane save one squiere.
> In prisone site þer lorde alone;
> Of his mene he hath no moo
> But William parys, be seint Johne!
> That with his wille wolle noght hime fro.
> He made this lyfe in ynglishe soo
> As he satte in prisone of stone,
> Ever as he myghte tent þer to,
> Whane he had his lordis service done.[76]

It has been suggested that Parys was a reader of Chaucer, and that his poem confirms the influence of Chaucer upon court literature of his time.[77] Certainly Parys is a skilful versifier, who can manage a rhetorical 'figure' with ease:

> Where are his knyghtis þat with hyme yede
> Whane he was in prosperite?
> Where are the squiers now at nede
> That sumetyme thoughte þei wold not fle?

but his rhythms are distinctively non-Chaucerian; he uses the
old, native four-stress line, not Chaucer's Italian-inspired five-
stress line; the movement of the verse recalls many medieval
Ballades on fortune and evil times:

> Lord, what is thys world wele!
> Rychesse, reule, and ryche Aray,
> Alday to spende and not to spele,
> Wel sone were-it, and wastyth away.[78]

Whatever the extent of Chaucer's direct influence upon
Parys, it is certain that the squire would have known of his
poetry: he probably attended the Earl of Warwick in London
too. In fact, his own family may have been of some importance
in London affairs; Simon de Paris, mercer, and Roger de Paris
held alderman's office in the reign of Edward II, and the
family's affairs prospered throughout the century. Some members were in royal service,[79] others concerned primarily with
trade and City government. But in the 1380s and 1390s, the
name of Parys is not infrequently found in records of the west
midlands. Robert Parys, who was Chamberlain of Edward, the
Black Prince, was also 'chamberlain of Chester'.[80] Nicholas de
Parys owned manors and tenements in North Wales.[81] The
fact that a Thomas Parys is mentioned in 1390 in connection
with the properties of 'John Beauchamp of Holte, knight,
deceased'[82] may mean that there was a particular Warwickshire and Worcestershire link between the Beauchamp and
Parys families. The castle of Holt, in Worcestershire, belonged
to a cadet branch of the house of Warwick; Sir John Beauchamp, later Lord John Beauchamp, Baron of Kidderminster,
was Justice of North Wales, and, in 1387, Steward of the Royal
Household.[83] Some recruiting to the service of the Warwicks
was no doubt done in the west midlands, and the poet-squire,
William Parys, may as easily have been a westerner as a
Londoner by birth. He certainly took care to stress that
Thomas Beauchamp's power lay in 'Warwik-shire'.

So this modest poem, written from the centre of political
disaster, suggests a network of personalities, places, and influences, extending from the far west to the south-east of England.
If it was true of the class structure of the fourteenth century that
'society as a whole was mobile, active ...',[84] it was certainly

true of fourteenth-century life in a more general and practical sense. The *Gough Map* was a much-needed traveller's guide, for those whose business lay at many points between London and York, or between London and Carlisle. In the retinues of the nobility many northerners and westerners were drawn to the capital: no doubt, too, household officials, recruited from City families, became more familiar than we might think with the wilder borderlands of their country.

Another 'poet-squire', of small but distinct talent, reminds us of this: John Halsham, who died in 1415, a landowner of some status in Sussex, Kent, Norfolk, and Wiltshire.[85] Although his main seat was in Sussex, where he held the manor of Bramber from Thomas Mowbray, Earl of Nottingham, he had connections with Yorkshire too—perhaps through relatives, but also perhaps through the Mowbrays, whose Yorkshire possessions were extensive. For in Yorkshire, in 1384, he abducted Philippa Percy, daughter-in-law of the Earl of Northumberland, and daughter of David Strabolgi, Earl of Atholl. They later married, and the rest of his life was spent conventionally enough, as a country squire in Sussex.[86] There, probably, his only surviving English *Balade* was written: two stanzas of rhyme royal, on mutability and fortune, gracefully reminiscent of Chaucer's minor poetry—the *Parliament of Fowls*, for instance:

> The worlde so wide, th'aire so remuable,
> The sely man so litel of stature,
> The grove and grounde and clothinge so mutable ...[87]

And, as it develops, thoughtful and dramatic, reminiscent of some of the courtly poetry of the fifteenth century—of Charles, Duke of Orleans, or of William, Duke of Suffolk:[88]

> The bet y serve the more al out of mynde.
> Is thys fortune, not I, or infortune?
> Though I go lowse, tyed am I with a lune.[89]

The pattern is stable, though traced in miniature: the 'gentleman-poet', here particularly influenced by Chaucer, with noble connections and lands and interests dispersed over a wide area of England. If John Gower's family came south from Yorkshire with the Strabolgis in the earlier fourteenth century,

John Halsham may have gone north from Sussex with the Mowbrays in the 1380s. His *Balade* did not remain in obscurity in Sussex; it occurs in several manuscripts, and was known and used by Lydgate in the 1420s.[90]

It is also worth stressing the importance of one other section of the community—that of the clerks who, coming from all levels of society and equipped with varying degrees of education, moved with great freedom between secular and religious worlds and had entry into all types of secular education.[91] Their social mobility is remarkable, especially from the early fourteenth century onwards. In the development of a machinery of government for the City of London it was the clerks, in company with the lawyers, who disturbed the control long exercised by the 'patrician' families of the thirteenth century, and in whose activities we first discern 'a quickening sense of growth'.[92] And if we may expect to find some of the unnamed authors of medieval literature among the young squires of aristocratic households, we are probably on even better ground when we consider the clerks in this type of service. A household of standing might employ a number of clerks for duties in the chapel, or for general administrative purposes: in 1387 that of the Montacute family had three 'Clercs gents' and four 'Clercs vadletz' of the chapel.[93] John of Trevisa's *Dialogue between a Clerk and a Lord*[94] is a literary version of a real-life situation, in which he served the Lords of Berkeley as chaplain and translator. In the search to put a name to the author of *Sir Gawain and the Green Knight*, we have been advised to 'keep under focus ... the south-Lancashire and west-midland clerks in the household of the duke of Lancaster'.[95]

Outside the special contexts of City or aristocratic service, the clerical classes embraced a wide variety of professions, from country parson to cathedral canon and chantry priest. They constituted, in fact, 'the one national audience', and an audience which had always 'cut across local boundaries'.[96] *Piers Plowman* was written by a cleric in minor orders, who had conformed to what we now recognize as a familiar pattern—moving from the west of England to London to earn a living, and, if early possession of manuscripts is admissible evidence, as successful in reaching knightly readers and owners in Bedfordshire as clerical readers and owners in Yorkshire. The

British Library manuscript of the A-text, Harley 6041, was originally owned by the Bedfordshire family of Hoo: Sir William Hoo was in royal service under Richard II and Henry IV, dying between 1412 and 1415.[97] In 1396 and in 1431, copies of *Piers Plowman* were bequeathed by two Yorkshire clergymen—a canon of York, Walter de Bruge, and a Rector of Arncliffe, John Wyndhill.[98]

There is, indeed, no literary area to which a poem such as *Piers Plowman* can be assigned: composed in London, drawing on a verse tradition commonly—although, as we shall see, not always accurately—associated with the west of England, and accepted, in its three versions, by metropolitan as well as provincial readers, its versatility may have been the result of careful calculation on Langland's part.[99] On the other hand, we can legitimately remark upon the acceptability of a full-scale alliterative poem to a 'national audience', and take this into account when we are locating poetic forms and influences. For if certain texts remain as hard-core evidence for local and easily definable literary areas, other texts confirm what the maps and known lives of medieval people tell us: that boundaries are blurred and flexible, and are easily over-ridden by the demands of business or patronage.[100] Much of the sorting into 'areas' and 'schools' of poetry has been done by scholars and critics and would probably have surprised medieval poets and their audiences. Although jokes of a regional nature were no doubt as popular in the fourteenth century as they have been ever since, the simple historical possibility that a man such as John of Gaunt could have been the patron of Chaucer and of the *Gawain*-poet, of Oton de Graunson and of Richard Maidstone,[101] spanning east and west, Latin, French, and English, must work against the credibility of severely limited areas of poetry and poets in later fourteenth century England. It is historically impossible to believe that, with the amount of movement involved in lives of public or private service, certain types of literature could have remained unknown, and, even more, incomprehensible outside their particular places of composition.

The older, rather rigid divisions of alliterative and non-alliterative localities have already begun to be questioned. The assumption that the writing of alliterative poetry was strongly and almost exclusively limited to west midland and north-west midland areas in England will no longer stand. We might note, as a preliminary, that the tail-rhyme romances, with their free circulation throughout eastern England, contain a good deal of alliterative language: this stanza from *Amis and Amiloun*:

> Her maidens gan answere ogain
> And seyd, 'Madame, we schul þe sain
> þat soþe bi Seyn Savour:
> Of erls, barouns, kniȝt and swain
> þe fairest man and mest of main
> And man of mest honour,
> It is sir Amis, þe kinges boteler;
> In al þis warld nis his per,
> Noiþer in toun no tour;
> He is douhtiest in dede
> And worþliest in everi wede ...[102]

is not an unusual example of tail-rhyme composition. And although it appears true that the more northerly the poem, the more alliterative it will be (*Ipomadon* is an example), the tail-rhyme poets, as indeed the romance poets generally, seem to have accepted a proportion of alliterative language. But this is not the most dramatic evidence. It has been shown that the heroic narrative of Arthur's conquests and last battles, the *Morte Arthure*, can more easily be associated with southern Lincolnshire in the early fifteenth century than with the west midlands.[103] A copy of this richly alliterative poem, full of traditional verbal formulae, was apparently in circulation among members of the wealthier middle classes and the lower gentry at this time, in the neighbourhood of King's Lynn. A poem is only copied and sent about if a demand for it exists. If the *Morte Arthure*, with its highly specialized alliterative vocabulary, was understood and appreciated by men such as 'Syr William Cuke, preste of Byllesbe' and 'John Salus', burgess of Lynn,[104] it seems wrong to overstress regional limitations for any medieval alliterative verse. The acceptability of the *Morte Arthure* in the north-east midlands is an exciting and crucial point to make. It might tempt us to ask whether Langland's rejection of that splendid alliterative diction, for which the *Morte* and *Sir Gawain* are famous, was really on grounds of its difficulty—or whether his decision had more to do with propriety of style. However this may be, the evidence for the knowledge, the copying, and even the writing of various kinds of alliterative verse in the east midlands and London is substantial enough to make *Piers Plowman* an unremarkable production of the capital.

It seems certain that a fair amount of vigorous stanzaic and alliterative verse came to Langland's notice in London, and influenced his style as well as his content. *The Simonie*[105] is often highly reminiscent of *Piers Plowman*, not only in sentiment, but also in its verbal, syntactical, and alliterative usages:

> Pride prikede hem so faste, that nolde theih nevere have pes
> Ar thei hadden in this lond maked swich a res
> That the beste blod of the lond shamliche was brouht to grounde ...
>
> (ll. 433-5)

> And there hii clateren cumpelin whan the candel is oute ...
>
> (l. 120)

It exists in three manuscripts, two of which have indisputable East Anglian and London provenance;[106] the poem clearly belongs to eastern England. Its marked though uneven use of alliterative language, and its acceptability to a London audience (inclusion in the commercially-inspired Auchinleck compilation makes this obvious) are two significant and related facts. Langland probably drew upon a great many shorter satirical poems, and it is interesting that two which seem likely candidates, *The Song of the Husbandman* and *The Simonie*, are both alliterative, but of widely differing provenance. *The Song of the Husbandman* comes from the Herefordshire manuscript, Harley 2253. Langland's reading-matter, as indeed his poem, defies regional compartmentation.

We might also reconsider the facts about some unrhymed alliterative poems of the period after 1350: *Chevalere Assigne,* for instance, which tells the popular story of the Knight of the Swan, and comes to us in an east midland version of the fifteenth century.[107] But its original date of composition was probably safely within the fourteenth century. It is not consistently alliterative, nor is it rich in special alliterative formulae, but it clearly understands, and at times exploits, as Chaucer did, the effectiveness of such language for dignified introductions and for battle-rhetoric:

> Alle-weldynge God . whenne it is his wylle,
> Wele he wereth his werke . with his owne honde;
> For ofte harmes were hente . þat helpe we ne myȝte,
> Nere þe hyȝnes of hym . þat lengeth in hevene ...
>
> (ll. 1-4)

> A bryȝte shelde & a sheene . to shylde þe fro strokes ...
> Take þat launce up in þyn honde . & loke þou hym hytte,
> And whenne þat shafte is schyvered . take scharpelye another.
>
> (ll. 298, 300-1)

Chevalere Assigne, in its present state, raises speculation: we can assume that its uneven alliteration is the result of corrupt transmission—that it was originally a regular alliterative poem, written in the north or north-west of England, and later tampered with by eastern scribes who were only just familiar enough with alliterative poetry to keep the alliteration on vital occasions. This in itself would be an interesting conclusion. But it is also possible that *Chevalere Assigne* represents a looser, more variable type of alliterative verse, written outside the west and north-west midlands. It is not the only poem to open with more decisively alliterative language than it is prepared to sustain—*Piers Plowman*, composed substantially in London, comes to mind. It is one of many works, some not predominantly alliterative at all, and some certainly not written in the west midlands, which testify to the widely recognized power of alliterative language to set a scene, or to evoke a mood. A non-alliterative poem of the south or south midlands begins sonorously, and alliteratively:

> In blossemed buske I bode boote,
> In ryche array, with ryches rank.
> ffaire floures under foote,
> Savour to myn herte sank.
> I sawe two buyrnes on a bank,
> To here talkynge I tok hede ...[108]

In this way, a debate between 'meed and much thank' is inaugurated—a debate which in content is faintly reminiscent of Lady Meed's encounter with Conscience in *Piers Plowman* (B-text, Passus III) and in formal style of presentation faintly reminiscent of the earlier alliterative debate between *Winner and Waster*.

Conversely, we might note that poets writing in the west country, in the fourteenth century, did not necessarily use an alliterative measure: clearly some choice of forms was open to them, as it was to poets in other parts of England—and a choice which could operate within a single work. The *Troy Book*,[109] in Bodleian MS Laud 595, was adapted from the Latin prose of Guido delle Colonne, somewhere in the north-west midlands, about 1400. It is a short-couplet poem, only sporadically alliterative, except in its prologue to the fighting at Troy, when it rises to the martial occasion and 'thickens' into recognizable alliterative style:

> In this talkyng may ȝe here telle
> Off ferly fyght, ffele and felle,
> Of comely kynges corouned and kene,
> That Troye distroyed alle be-dene,
> And brende her houses on a blase ...
>
> (ll. 3247-51)

A good example of the problems raised by trying to assign particular types of poetry to particular areas of medieval England is provided by the short and brilliant alliterative piece called, by its only editor, a *Satire Against the Blacksmiths*.[110] It is found in British Library MS Arundel 292 (fo.71b) which can be dated 1425-50. The poem itself is probably not earlier than the later fourteenth century. Its elaborate verbal display, some of its vocabulary,[111] and certain external facts favour 1400 or later. Its theme—protest against the nightly clangour of blacksmiths at work:

> Swarte smekyd smeþes smateryd wyth smoke
> Dryve me to deth wyth den of here dyntes.
> Swech noys on nyghtes ne herd men never ...
>
> (ll. 1-3)

reminds us not only of Chaucer's testimony, in the *Miller's Tale*, that medieval blacksmiths kept nocturnal business hours.[112] It reminds us also of the *Petition* addressed to the Lord

Mayor of London, in 1394, by the Blacksmiths themselves—
that 'by reason of the great nuisance, noise and alarm experienced in divers ways by the neighbours around their dwelling
... that no one should work by night, but only from daylight
until nine....'[113] This record of an attempt to bring in a 'Smithy
Hours Act' tells us nothing of the poet of our alliterative complaint, but it does tell us of a later fourteenth-century urban
preoccupation, focusing our attention upon London rather
than upon any city of the west or north. There are several other
reasons for connecting the poem with the east of England.
Arundel 292 is a manuscript originally owned by Norwich
Priory, and certain of the texts in it are of particular East
Anglian relevance.[114] As part of the Arundel collection, it came
into the Library of the Royal Society 'ex dono Henr. Howard
Norfolkiensis', to judge from the stamped inscription on fo.3b.
The Arundel collection of manuscripts can be traced back in
part to Lord William Howard, who was active as a book-
collector as early as the later sixteenth century.[115] The description of blacksmiths as 'brenwaterys'—'burnwaters'—in line 22
of the poem seems to be a unique word-formation, except that
it occurs once as a surname, from the Cambridge area, in
1252: 'Roberti Brennewater'.[116]

Facts such as these lead us to query the automatic association
of alliterative verse with the west of England: it remains to be
proved that this powerfully alliterative work has authentic
western affiliations.[117] And indeed, its language and alliterative usages are sufficiently 'mixed' to give grounds for
believing that it might be the work of a poet of the east or south-
east of England, who knew and appreciated many of the set
formulae of alliterative writing, but who also innovated in a
spirited manner.

For certainly it contains some traditional alliterative clusters
of words:

> Dryve me to deth with den of here dyntes[118]
>
> (l. 2)
>
> Stark strokes þei stryken[119]
>
> (l. 14)

But these, it may be significant to note, were common enough
also in rhyming romances of the medieval period. Its com-

pound word formations, 'barmfellys', 'fere-flunderys', 'cloþe-merys', 'brenwaterys', are made to old native patterns, but in most cases are not recorded outside this particular poem. The alliteration is full and expressive, but idiosyncratic: so, 'gnawen and gnacchen' (1.9) is unique, and so, too, is 'spytten and spraulen' (1.8). A heavily alliterative line such as

þe cammede kongons cryen after 'col, col!'

(l. 5)

uses vocabulary familiar in alliterative and non-alliterative works alike—in the *Reeve's Tale, Piers Plowman,* and the *Chester Plays,* as well as in official records of the period.[120]

In short, we have here a poem which aims to appeal and please by a vigorous, and even by an exaggerated use of alli-terative language. Although it is in touch with, it is not tied to traditional alliterative combinations of words, but ranges widely. Its poet was appreciative of alliterative techniques, and exploited the descriptive richness of alliterative vocabulary. We must assume that his public was equally receptive. And if it is not certain, it is at least possible that this public was of East Anglia or of London. Various kinds of alliterative writing, elaborate, modified, and simple, can be associated with the east of England, from the northerly limits of Yorkshire and Lincolnshire to the southerly limits of London. Although Chaucer's audience may have appreciated the joke about 'rum, ram, ruf', they may also have appreciated the special qualities of alliterative verse, particularly when it dealt with appropriate and accredited subject-matter. In this context, it now seems even more reasonable that the alliterative passages in the *Knight's Tale* and the *Legend of Good Women* were meant to evoke a serious and admiring response and that the form of *Piers Plowman* did not at all surprise fourteenth-century London.

Nor, perhaps, did the contemporary poem, *Saint Erkenwald,*[121] which makes fewer concessions than *Piers Plowman* in density of alliterative vocabulary and yet on a number of counts must be very closely connected with London in the 1380s. This verse narrative of a miracle in Saint Paul's worked by the saintly Bishop Erkenwald, makes insistent and expert reference to London:

þe metropol and þe mayster-ton hit evermore has bene

(l. 26)

The setting of the story is convincingly first-hand, in terms of fourteenth-century London life; Saint Erkenwald is recalled from a pastoral visit to view a newly-discovered tomb in Saint Paul's:

> In Esex was Ser Erkenwolde, an abbay to visite ...
>
> (l. 108)

The citizens of London, from apprentices to Mayor, come thronging to the scene:

> Burgeys boghit þer-to, bedels ande othire,
> And mony a mesters-mon of maners dyverse.
> Laddes laften hor werke & lepen þiderwardes,
> Ronnen radly in route with ryngande noyce ...
>
> (ll. 59-62)

And it is interesting that the description of the tomb, with its late-Gothic ornaments

> ... ...   thryvandly hewen,
> With gargeles garnysht a-boute, alle of gray marbre ...
>
> (ll. 47-8)

and its gold lettering (l. 51), calls to mind contemporary accounts of the splendid shrine of Saint Erkenwald in old Saint Paul's.[122] The whole poem is redolent of the City, but especially of the area about Saint Paul's—the shops in Saint Paul's Churchyard (l. 88), and the Bishop's Palace (ll. 113 ff.). It is difficult to resist the conclusion that poet and intended audience were not only interested in, but intimately acquainted with London. Indeed we need not quarrel with the judgement of the poem's first editor: 'its place of origin must have been the city of London.'[123] We know that the unique manuscript of the poem—British Library MS Harley 2250—was in the hands of western owners in the fifteenth and sixteenth centuries, but that one of those families, the Booths of Lancashire and Cheshire, had strong connections with London and St. Paul's: Laurence Booth was Dean of St. Paul's in 1456.[124] This east-west movement need not now disturb us, in the face of such evidence as we have discovered about the constant ebb and flow of people of all stations about the capital. Perhaps the poem was written for westerners living and working in London, by a poet who himself was an immigrant. Perhaps he could count upon some interest among native Londoners for his 'enbelicit' alliterative language. It would, of course, be helpful to know whether he was also the author of *Sir Gawain and the Green Knight* and *Pearl*; the likenesses of vocabulary and metre were very early commented upon.[125] If common authorship were ever proved, it would demonstrate finally what is implicit in these most elaborate of fourteenth-century alliterative poems—that there is nothing purely provincial about either the poet or his art. *Saint Erkenwald* is simpler than the four poems in MS Cotton Nero A. X which are usually grouped together as the work of the 'Gawain-poet'. But it is still a very elegant composition, and might reasonably be seen as a major poet's obeisance to a particular milieu, occasion, or patron. There is nothing unlikely in the idea that *Saint Erkenwald* may have come as naturally from London as *Piers Plowman*. Whatever adjustments to a special situation we may notice in *Piers Plowman* and *Saint Erkenwald*, they are not more significant than the association of two distinctively alliterative poems with Cornhill and Old Saint Paul's in the later fourteenth century.[126]

The verbal reminiscences that can be found in formal Latin pageant verse of London, alliterative poetry of the north-west midlands, and Chaucerian verse have already been suggested elsewhere.[127] Such connections will not surprise us: men such as Richard Maidstone, the *Gawain*-poet and Chaucer are more likely to have known each other's work than not. Their lives, their patrons, and their reading need not have been dissimilar. It is impossible to think of the *Gawain*-poet, with his wide and sophisticated range of techniques, writing alliterative verse for want of familiarity with, or expertise in any other form. The stanza design and the intricate verbal manœuvrings of *Pearl* should put this beyond doubt. Although the dialects in which many—though not all—of the alliterative poems are written are decisively western, and their vocabulary sometimes local and traditional, their themes are by no means parochial or provincial. They are often politically involved in a very national sense, more frequently commenting upon king and country than upon local gentry and local issues. This is as true of *Winner and Waster*, with its analysis of the government of Edward III and its specific London references,[128] as of *Richard the Redeles,* written from Bristol, that 'blessid borugh',[129] but directed towards the king and the nation:

> ... my rede shuld also
> For to conceill, and I couȝhe . my kyng and þe lordis;
> (Prol. ll. 48-9)

When we think, therefore, of 'literary areas', we must do so in the most general terms. And it is worth reflecting upon the evidence offered to us by manuscript collections of the four- teenth and fifteenth centuries. Their principles of selection are not always easy for us to define, but one thing is clear: they show practically no tendency to group or segregate particular kinds of medieval verse on metrical grounds. On the whole, the miscellaneous or encyclopaedic collection is the norm, but even when some unifying purpose can be distinguished, it has more to do with subject than with verse-form: with the provision of sermon or romance materials, texts for meditation or instruc- tion.[130] The fourteenth-century Vernon manuscript is an excellent example: it is a west midland miscellany of verse and prose,[131] but all of sound moral and instructional nature, well described by the manuscript heading 'Sowlehele'.[132] The choice of verse for such a volume cuts right across metrical considerations: the stanzaic and heavily alliterative *Pistill of Susan*[133] has a place beside the moral romance in tail-rhyme, the *King of Tars,* and a great variety of shorter verse types. British Library MS Additional 22283, transcribed only a little later than the Vernon MS, has three tail-rhyme romances and the *Pistill.*

Earlier fourteenth-century collections, of unified or miscel- laneous content, are similarly unconcerned about metre. The Herefordshire manuscript, Harley 2253, mingles vigorous alliterative, stanzaic poems of courtly or satirical nature with others predominantly non-alliterative: the *Song of the Husband- man* or *Annot and Johan* with rougher couplet narratives such as the *Harrowing of Hell* and *King Horn.*[134] From the contents of the London-based Auchinleck manuscript, it is quite clear that readers of the 1330s found romance in couplet or tail-rhyme, poetry with a strong alliterative element or none at all, equally acceptable.

It might be thought that the situation would have changed

after 1350, with the revival of interest in a more decisive and uncompromising alliterative measure—the long, unrhymed alliterative line. But there was, in fact, little change. Poems using this measure, such as *Piers Plowman* and the legend of *Joseph of Arimathie*, were collected into the Vernon manuscript in company with tail-rhyme and couplet poems. The early alliterative work, *William of Palerne*, occurs in one fourteenth-century manuscript only—King's College, Cambridge, MS 13: it is bound with a narrative of the Passion in couplets. In Lincoln's Inn MS 150, a late fourteenth or early fifteenth-century collection, rhymed romances such as *Libeaus Desconus* and *King Alisaunder* are bound with the alliterative *Piers Plowman*.[135]

Most fifteenth-century collections bear this out. Bodleian MS Digby 102 has already been noticed (p. 71, above) as containing a C-text of *Piers Plowman*, and a wide range of religious verse in stanzaic, rhymed forms. Some of the shorter poems in this manuscript deal, in a greatly simplified way, with familiar themes of Langland—'Meed and Much Thank', 'Truth, Rest and Peace', 'Wit and Will',[136] and illustrate, once more, the principle of inclusion on grounds of subject, not on that of metre. British Library MS Harley 2250 sets the alliterative, unrhymed *St. Erkenwald* into a miscellany of non-alliterative religious verse and prose. The celebrated Thornton manuscripts[137] gather their material from alliterative and non-alliterative poetry of all types. In the Additional manuscript the alliterative *Siege of Jerusalem* and the tail-rhyme *Sege of Melayne* are separated from the unrhymed alliterative debate poems, *Winner and Waster* and *The Parliament of the Three Ages*, by romance and religious verse of various kinds and forms. The division would seem to be on account of subject-matter: the first two poems are grouped with religious narratives of a 'heroic' or 'geste' cast—the *Northern Passion* and the *Cursor Mundi*. Another stanzaic alliterative poem, the *Quatrefoil of Love*, is set apart from alliterative verse, among prayers and poems of a more lyrical quality.

In the Lincoln manuscript, the alliterative *Morte Arthure* is placed with non-alliterative romances—the tail-rhyme *Octavian* and *Isumbras*. The important fifteenth-century collection, British Library MS Cotton Caligula A.ii, has the stanzaic alliterative *Pistill of Susan* and the loosely alliterative *Chevalere*

Assigne among a large number of rhymed romances and much religious verse.[138] Admittedly, these are late medieval collections, but they do confirm what many fourteenth-century manuscripts tend to suggest—that neither alliterative nor tail-rhyme verse was singled out for special treatment and attention on grounds of metrical form and poetic vocabulary. The Thornton manuscripts were probably put together in Yorkshire, by a Robert Thornton, landowner in Ryedale.[139] One part of the Cotton Caligula A.ii manuscript belonged to a Cambridgeshire family: the second part, in which *Chevalere Assigne* and the *Pistill of Susan* occur, is thought by one editor to be a southern compilation, possibly from a monastery.[140] They certainly prove the availability of alliterative writing to compilers, copyists, and readers of the more easterly regions of England, and speak against an exclusive west and north-west midland provenance for alliterative poetry.

In fact, manuscripts such as that which must originally have contained only the four alliterative poems *Sir Gawain, Pearl, Patience,* and *Cleanness*[141] appear to have been the exception rather than the rule. The only other alliterative poem which occurs alone in manuscript form is the *Destruction of Troy,* copied by Thomas Chetham in the earlier sixteenth century and passed on as 'an heirloom' by his son, John.[142] On the whole, our evidence goes to show that medieval taste in books was for the compendium or miscellany, rather than for the single work, for diversity rather than unity, either of subject-matter or form. Even the *Gawain* manuscript shows a considerable range of style and theme: all four poems are alliterative, but *Pearl* and *Gawain* employ also some form of stanzaic patterning proving, incidentally, that whatever the mid-fourteenth century 'alliterative revival' was, it was not a simple reversion to an unrhymed, non-stanzaic alliterative line. The manuscripts give little indication that there was, even in the fourteenth century, an exclusively 'alliterative' or 'tail-rhyme' and regionally confined reading public. Reading—and listening—practices, like the practices of compilers of verse manuscripts, seem to have been far more flexible.

At the very limits of the medieval period, in the early sixteenth century, a member of the Chetham family, of south Lancashire, chose to copy out two long poetic works, now MSS

Hunterian V.8 and Chetham Library, A.6.11. They were the long alliterative chronicle-romance, the *Destruction of Troy*, and Gower's *Confessio Amantis*.[143] From what we have seen, such a span of taste does not seem unusual. The Chethams, as well as being landowners in their own right, were in the service of the Stanleys, Earls of Derby, whose literary tastes, during the fifteenth and early sixteenth centuries, were equally varied.[144]

At about the same date, an alliterative poem, showing clear acquaintance with *Piers Plowman* and perhaps also with *The Parliament of the Three Ages*, was copied into a collection of courtly verse strongly associated with Wyatt and other Tudor 'makers'.[145] The poem mentions Kent—'for al Kent I woud not com in his klaws' (l. 47), and its editor sees no reason for connecting it in any way with the west or north of England. It is an alliterative poem of London and the south-east, 'not unappreciated in fashionable circles even as late as the sixteenth century.[146]

But we should not attempt to deny categorically that there were regional concentrations of certain kinds of poetic activity in the medieval period. The traditional placing of alliterative poetry in the west and north-west of England, of tail-rhyme poetry mainly in the east of England cannot be radically questioned—only viewed somewhat differently, in the light of all the evidence. So many of the alliterative poems come to us in some type of western language or with western connections— the discovery of the only text of the alliterative debate *Death and Life*[147] in a house in Shropshire, in 1769, has its own point to make. So many of the poems use vocabulary of special western provenance: some of them are localized in their introductory lines in 'the west':

> Bot I schall tell yow a tale þat me by-tyde ones,
> Als I went in the weste, wandrynge myn one ...[148]

What clearly became, as the century drew on, a purely literary formula, must at one time have referred to a real situation. The fact that Langland, in London, still set his dream on the Malvern hills, and that many anonymous writers prefaced their poems with a wild, western landscape, rendered alliteratively:

> Bi west, under a wylde wode-syde,
> In a launde þer I was lente,
> Wlanke deor on grounde gunne glyde ...[149]

does provide some contemporary evidence for the western orientation of alliterative verse. It is important that this orientation was recognized by poets. Less commonly do we find an alliterative poem, stanzaic or unrhymed, referring to eastern districts of England: a striking example of this, however, is the alliterative lyric from MS Harley 2253 which tells of the beauty of a lady renowned

> Bituene Lyncolne ant Lyndeseye, Norhamptoun ant Lounde ...[150]

Such evidence must not be ignored: it reminds us that the *Morte Arthure* was in circulation in that very area, in the fourteenth century. But we must still say that alliterative poetry seems to have been specially fostered in the west and north-west of England, probably in courtly and religious centres—provided we allow that it was well received in northern areas generally, whether western or eastern, and that it was certainly not an alien or despised form of composition in East Anglia or in London. Chaucer—if we believe what we read in *Sir Thopas* and the *Knight's Tale*—had a lower opinion of non-alliterative rhymed romance verse than he had of alliterative verse.

One fact should be recorded however: alliterative verse never seems to occur in any manuscript collection of Chaucerian poetry. The limitation of these manuscripts to a recognized 'school' of composition—the works of Chaucer, his friends and disciples, Sir John Clanvowe, Hoccleve, Lydgate, Sir Richard Ros—is very marked. It looks as if the public for whom these composite manuscripts were made, probably in commercial scriptoria or bookshops of the fifteenth century, had fairly well-defined tastes in poetry which did not favour alliterative composition. There are, for instance, no alliterative works in the catalogue of books owned by Sir John Paston. His library must have been collected in London and East Anglia: Chaucer, Lydgate, and the minor Chaucerians figure prominently in it.[151] The wealthy landowner, Sir Thomas Cumberworth, whose properties lay mainly in Lincolnshire, at Somersby, but who also had manors in Yorkshire and a house in London, bequeathed devotional prose treatises to priests and a 'boke of the talys of cantyrbury' to his niece, in the mid-fifteenth century.[152] A comprehensive booklist of Latin, French, and English works, which is connected with mid- and later fifteenth century clerical owners in East Anglia and London, mentions 'the talys of Caunterbury' and 'Hocklyf de Regimine': we cannot be certain whether the item 'the Sege of Iherusalem a part' refers to the alliterative or rhymed poem of that name.[153] The appearance of the couplet *Siege*—more usually known as *Titus and Vespasian*—in a newly discovered manuscript volume of Chaucer's minor poems, in company with poems of Hoccleve and Lydgate,[154] makes the alliterative version a less likely candidate. The east midland and London scriptoria which produced many of the finest Chaucer, Lydgate, and Hoccleve manuscripts in the fifteenth century seem to have had little reason to number alliterative works in their repertoire.

But finally we must distinguish not so much between geographical areas in which alliterative verse was known or unknown to poets and their public as between areas in which it attained a particular kind of cultural status and those in which, on the whole, it did not. All evidence points to the fact that knowledge of a variety of alliterative verse styles was almost as widespread in the earlier fourteenth century as knowledge of non-alliterative styles. Poems such as *The Simonie*, from a London manuscript, and the *Song of the Husbandman*, from a Herefordshire manuscript, are indicative. Further, the refinement and sophistication of the rhymed couplet at the hands of Chaucer, and of the unrhymed and rhymed alliterative line at the hands of some anonymous western and northern poets, are parallel phenomena of the age. Both Chaucer and the *Gawain*-poet were consciously enlarging and enriching the English poetic language: they responded to the same sort of stimuli, exerted, we may be sure, by books, patrons, and a growing sense of national achievement and identity. Such a sense operated as an impulse not to reject, but to emulate, absorb, and reshape what other countries and cultures had to offer. The greater potential of the west country as an 'alliterative area' is to some extent a matter of historical fact: behind the fourteenth century lay the accomplished alliterative prose of the 'Katherine Group' of treatises and saints' lives, and the vast alliterative bulk of Laȝamon's *Brut*. Already, by the earlier fourteenth century, the lyrics of the Herefordshire manuscript, Harley 2253, were showing the number of uses, courtly and satirical, to which alliterative language could be put, and the number of metrical patterns to which it could be adapted. It is not surprising that, after 1350, the demand for English verse of similar dignity, verve, and colour to French should have inspired poets living and working predominantly—but not exclusively in—the west and north-west of England to try their hand with a metre both locally familiar and already successfully proved.

Nor is it surprising that Chaucer, living and working predominantly in a courtly society whose literary habits were still as much French as English, should have chosen to experiment with that kind of English verse which could most easily be moulded to continental forms, French and Italian. Alliterative verse, with all its sonority and richness, could never have been a sufficiently flexible medium for the poet who was 'grant translateur, Geoffroi Chaucier'. And he was content to know and respect it rather than to use it, except occasionally.

To the study of medieval literary geography, the age of the Elizabethan antiquaries writes its own postscript. It is now usually accepted that the manuscript containing *Pearl*, *Sir Gawain and the Green Knight*, *Patience*, and *Cleanness* was acquired by Sir Robert Cotton in the later sixteenth or earlier seventeenth century from the library of Henry Savile, scholar, antiquary, authority on heraldry, and known as 'one of the most accomplished men of his time'.[155] His family was of Yorkshire stock, and his estates centred on Banke, or Blaidroyd, near Halifax. His extensive library is catalogued in British Library MS Additional 35213 and Harley 1879.[156] The Harley catalogue (fo. 8b) lists, as item 274, an 'owld booke in English verse beginninge Perle pleasant to Princes pay', a description which fits, except in one point,[157] the manuscript now bound up in MS Cotton Nero A.X. Sir Robert Cotton is known to have obtained a good many of Henry Savile's books, and the *Gawain* manuscript is very likely to have been one of them.[158]

We know nothing of the history of the manuscript between the late fourteenth and the late sixteenth century. Many of Savile's books came originally from religious houses in Yorkshire—from Byland, Rievaulx, Fountains, and Mount Grace: the dispersal of the great monastic libraries, after the Dissolution, opened a vast store-house to the antiquary and the private book-collector. One of Savile's intermediary sources may have been the library of John Nettleton, who is mentioned, about

1565, as one of a group of collectors of manuscripts from the monastic libraries.[159] A number of his volumes bear the name 'Nettleton' in shorthand inscription, as well as that of 'Savile'. This takes us back at least one generation in the process of tracing manuscripts back to their medieval origins. The Nettletons of Hutton Cranswick, in the East Riding of Yorkshire, were moderately wealthy landowners, and may have been one of a number of recusant families in Yorkshire, possibly including the Saviles:[160] such families would have had an added interest in collecting books from the old monastic libraries. The John Nettleton whom we know as a book-collector is likely to have been the son of John and Jane Nettleton, whose wills, proved in 1553 and 1565 respectively, provide for the University education of their children.[161] Outside the Savile collection, John Nettleton's name occurs several times in the British Library Thornton manuscript (Additional 31042: fos. 49a and 139b), as well as in other medieval liturgical and theological books.[162]

Many 'old books in English verse' no doubt remained in the hands of northern families during the fifteenth and earlier sixteenth centuries, and were ultimately passed, from collector to collector, into the large 'professional' libraries of men such as Savile and Cotton. It would be pleasing to be able to complete the history of the *Gawain* manuscript, taking it back beyond Savile's ownership to an earlier local owner, of similar type to Nettleton, or to a religious house in Yorkshire. Working from the other end of the scale, we can trace a manuscript such as Additional 31042 from a Yorkshire copyist of the fifteenth century, Robert Thornton, Lord of East Newton, in Ryedale, to John Nettleton, of sixteenth-century Hutton Cranswick. The transition is comparatively easy. And it is just as easy to imagine that Henry Savile of Banke obtained the *Gawain* manuscript from some source not far from its original home. Banke was fairly near the Yorkshire border, and the language of the poems in the Cotton manuscript has been defined as that of south-east Cheshire, or north-east Staffordshire.[163]

But it is worth pointing out that Nettleton and Savile were not confined to the north of England for their book collecting. Henry Savile spent a good deal of his life in London, making his home in the parish of Saint Martin-in-the-Fields, and died there, in 1617.[164] If he wrote to Camden about antiquities near Otley,[165] he was also engaged in gathering books from Lincoln-shire, Northamptonshire, and Kent. His volumes of Lydgate, Skelton, Hoccleve, and Chaucer were probably bought from London and East Anglian bookshops. He had significant con-nections with the London antiquaries, Camden and Cotton, and with Oxford scholars.[166] Even his links with John Nettle-ton are not unambiguously northern: Nettleton died in 1597, 'prisoner in the King's Bench in Southwark': his will was proved in the Archdeaconry of Surrey.[167] Whatever story lies behind it, the death of a Yorkshire book-collector, in Elizabe-than London, reminds us of a familiar pattern: Yorkshire estates and London parishes, Hutton Cranswick and Banke, Southwark and Saint Martin's-in-the-Fields are points in an old-established network of communications, political, social, and literary, between London and the provinces. We have no means of knowing precisely how, and where, Henry Savile obtained the *Gawain* manuscript. But it is, no doubt, to the powerful influence exerted by the London-based antiquarians and scholars of the later sixteenth century that we owe the final gathering-up of many important medieval works into more permanent collections.

4 Alliterative Verse and *Piers Plowman*

The easy acceptance of a clear regional localization for the alliterative verse of the fourteenth century is often accompanied by another kind of acceptance—that of certain idiosyncratic and long-established features of style and approach which mark it out from other varieties of medieval English verse. We are asked to believe in 'shared assumptions' about the art of alliterative poetry: verbal, metrical, and philosophical links are held to justify a theory of an 'alliterative poetics', even, perhaps, an alliterative ethos of 'moral insight and historical truth:'[1] it is also widely assumed that the alliterative poets of the fourteenth and fifteenth centuries inherited in some real, but mysterious, way a tradition of these things from earlier, pre-Conquest centuries of alliterative composition.[2] The fact that the potential of this inheritance was rather suddenly realized at about 1350, after a longish period of uncertain fortune, has been recognized by the term 'revival': it still satisfies most literary historians as a description of the re-appearance of full-scale alliterative verse-writing from 1350 onwards.

Nothing in this account is quite at odds with the truth, but it is, perhaps, a rather simplified tale. As we have suggested, there are some signs that medieval readers were less decisive, less interested than present-day critics in taking note of the distinctions between alliterative and non-alliterative writing.[3] Only Chaucer's 'publishers' seem to have been at pains to exclude alliterative verse when compiling their lists of contents. And while the idea of the continuity of an alliterative tradition must still be retained, it should now be possible to make a more judicious statement about what we mean by 'continuity' and 'tradition'.

We can try, in the first place, to avoid drawing the alliterative poets together, as a school, on grounds other than those which they patently provide us with: their use of similar metres need not predispose us to find in them a community of aims and attitudes which will, for instance, set them off against Chaucer or other non-alliterative writers. And we can, further, be prepared to find that certain poets, alliterative and non-alliterative, distinguishing themselves by their special excellence from their fellow artists, will encourage us to propose a very diverse set of groups: there are some valid reasons for associating all medieval English poets, with the exception of Chaucer, just as there are other reasons, almost equally valid, for singling out Langland, and associating all others. We are still bound, however, to find proper reasons for our quite natural inclination then to set Chaucer and Langland together, against the rest: there may be few connections, save those of defining, even isolating, genius, and no way, ultimately, of seeing the poetry of this age as a 'whole'.[4]

The relationship of alliterative to non-alliterative poetry is certainly not summed up by Chaucer's famous dismissal in the *Parson's Prologue*.[5] When the anonymous translator of the *Historia Destructionis Troiae* into alliterative verse reaches the sad episode of Troilus and Criseyde, he excuses his brevity—and that of his Latin source—by recommending:

> Whoso Wilnes to wit of þaire wo fir
> Turne hym to Troilus, and talke þere ynoghe ...[6]

It is unlikely that his 'Troilus' is Guido delle Colonne's own source—the *Roman de Troie* of Benoît de Sainte Maure; a far more likely identification is Chaucer's own *Troilus and Criseyde*.[7] The alliterative poet seems to be referring us to the authoritative treatment of this poignant subject, and several things are implied by his words. They suggest, for instance, that there was no lack of communication between writers working in such different media, and that they may have regarded their compositions as alternative, rather than opposed, reading matter. The translation of Guido's Latin poem was undertaken for a knightly patron, based, it seems probable, in the provinces.[8] Chaucer's version of Boccaccio's *Filostrato*, undertaken in a known London context, and dedicated to established figures in court and city circles—'the moral Gower and the philosophical

Strode'—was nevertheless accessible to the alliterative poet, and, in fact, seems to have affected his handling at several points. Thus in spite of his refusal to dwell upon the 'wo' of their parting, he adds two lines to his Latin source which effectively call to mind Chaucer's painful description of Troilus watching uselessly for the return of Criseyde:

> Tristly may Troiell tote over the walle,
> And loke upon lenght, er his love come!
>
> (*Destruction of Troy*, ll. 8178-9)

Similarly, it may be from his reading of Chaucer's equally painful description of Troilus handing Criseyde over to Diomede that he takes some significant detail and some emotive comments. In both the *Destruction of Troy* and in *Troilus*, but not in the Latin of Guido, Diomede grasps the reins of Criseyde's horse as he leads her away:

> He rode to þat riall, and the reyne toke ...
>
> (*Destruction of Troy*, l. 8078)

> ... and by the reyne hire hente ...
>
> (*Troilus and Criseyde*, v. 90)

and although the anonymous poet has nothing to compare with Chaucer's 'sodeyn Diomede', he neatly expresses that same mixture of passion and calculation by referring to the 'wild and cold heart' of the Greek prince (*Destruction of Troy*, ll. 8077, 8080).

It is certainly true, however, that he makes a distinction between his particular kind of interest in the Troilus story, and Chaucer's, marking off Chaucer's version as one of sentiment—'þaire wo'. *The Destruction of Troy*, with its immense scope, its moral and historical preoccupations, easily adopts the position of its Latin prose original, seeing the parting of the lovers and the betrayal of Troilus as an *exemplum* of the instability of women:

> There is no hope so unhappy, þat hastes to noght,
> Ne so unsikur at asay, as to set uppon wemen ...
>
> (*Destruction of Troy*, ll. 8062-3)

But in its chosen material and attitude it can hardly be said to be especially 'English alliterative': the poet's willingness to have the events of history yield general moral lessons, and his satisfaction in restating, from a particular case, grave disquiet about trusting in the female sex, are both familiar features of medieval literature, whether Latin or vernacular. Indeed it is true of Chaucer's *Troilus* alone that it hesitates before it draws the traditional conclusions about the folly of its hero's love for a fickle woman. Even Chaucer's Italian model, Boccaccio, comes nearer to a plain opinion on such matters than Chaucer: his advice is courtly, secular, and flippant, but it is based soundly on the general homiletic scepticism about woman as an intrinsically inferior creation:

If you take [my verses] to heart as you read, you will not lightly place your trust in any woman. A young woman is both inconstant and eager for many lovers, and prizes her beauty more than her mirror warrants. She is full of vanity about her youthfulness, and the more attractive and desirable it is the more she prides herself upon it. She has no sense of merit or judgment and is forever fickle like a leaf in the wind.[9]

Henryson, when he wrote his bitter sequel to Chaucer's *Troilus*, making sure, as Chaucer had refused to do, that Criseyde is brought to justice for her sins, was righting the medieval balance of the story, which had been uncertainly adjusted by Chaucer:

> Ne me ne list this sely womman chyde
> Forther than the storye wol devyse.
> Hire name, allas! is punysshed so wide,
> That for hire gilt it oughte ynough suffise.
> And if I myghte excuse hire any wise,
> For she so sory was for hire untrouthe,
> Iwis, I wolde excuse hire yet for routhe.
>
> (*Troilus*, v. 1093-9)

It is important, therefore, to expect the comparison of alliterative and non-alliterative poetry to yield only a limited amount of data to help in the establishing of an alliterative 'continuum'.[10] One more example may be taken from Chaucer and the poet of the *Destruction of Troy*. The Prologue to the *Destruction* has already been claimed as a witness to the rather self-conscious truth-telling vocation of the alliterative poets:

> The alliterative poet protests that he is to be counted, above all else, a truth-teller. The prologue of the *Gest Hystoriale* [of the *Destruction of Troy*] treats the theme at length.[11]

But in fact, like the supposedly precise reference to the long-established tradition of alliterative verse composition in that Prologue,

> By lokyng of letturs þat lefte were of old ...
>
> (*Destruction of Troy*, l. 26)

most of the basic material can be found in the Latin Prologue by Guido; the alliterative translation is only really distinctive for its special phrasing and style. We might point, however, to the interesting fact that the rhymed-verse translation of the *Historia*, the so-called *Laud Troy Book*, does not elect to deal with Guido's Latin Prologue in such detail: its version is compressed and unspecific:

> Many speken of men that romaunces rede
> That were sumtyme doughti in dede,
> The while that god hem lyff lente,
> That now ben dede and hennes wente.[12]

But if we were then tempted to move from contrasting the alliterative and non-alliterative renderings and propose that the first could still, in spite of its lack of originality, be considered an authentic piece of 'alliterative theory', we ought also to take into account Chaucer's similar word in the Proem to *Anelida and Arcite*:

> For hit ful depe is sonken in my mynde,
> With pitous hert in Englyssh to endyte
> This olde storie, in Latyn which I fynde,
> Of quene Anelida and fals Arcite,
> That elde, which that al can frete and bite,
> As hit hath freten mony a noble storie,
> Hath nygh devoured out of oure memorie ...
>
> (*Anelida and Arcite*, ll. 8-14)

What we find, in Guido's Prologue, in that of the anonymous *Destruction of Troy*, and in Chaucer's *Anelida*, is a common enough medieval sentiment about the importance of stories of

the past to the present age. It is present in the twelfth-century
Prologue to the romance of *Cligés*, in which Chrétien de Troyes
reviews the descent of chivalry and learning from Classical
times to medieval France, and emphasizes the part played by
old books in that transmission:

> De la fu li contes estrez ...
> Li livres est mout anciiens
> Qui tesmoingne l'estoire a voire;
> Por ce fet ele miauz a croire.
> Par les livres que nos avons
> Les fez des anciiens savons
> Et del siecle qui fu jadis ...[13]

From there the story was drawn ... The book is very old, from which
the story is taken, and this makes it easier to believe in. From such
books, which we still have, we learn the deeds of men of old, and the
times now long-past ...

And it is present in Prologues to works as various as the thirteenth-century Anglo-Norman romance, *Gui de Warewic*:

> D'els deit l'om ben sovenir
> E lor bons faiz dire e oir;
> Ki mult ot e co retient
> Sovent mult sage devient.[14]

A man ought to keep them in mind [sayings of the past] and repeat
and listen to the good deeds [recounted]. He who listens well and
remembers often will become considerably wiser ...

and the *Life of the Black Prince,* written by Sir John Chandos,
probably about 1385:

> Si ne se doit homme pas tener
> De beaux ditz faire et retenir
> Cils qe sen sceuent entremettre
> Eins les doient en liure mettre
> Pourquoy apres ce qils sont mort
> Et si ount fait lui iuste recort
> Car cest almoigne e charitee
> De bien dire e de veritee
> Car bien ne fust unques perduz
> Qen ascun temps ne feust renduz ...[15]

Yet ought men not to refrain from making and remembering fair
poems—all such as have skill thereto; rather they should enter them

in a book, that after their death true records may be kept; for to relate the good is verily alms and charity, for good was never lost without return at some time ...

Alliterative and non-alliterative poets, English, French, or Latin, may turn to such material. It is found again as part of John Gower's Prologue to his *Confessio Amantis*:

> For hier on erthe amonges ous,
> If noman write hou that it stode,
> The pris of hem that weren goode
> Scholde, as who seith, a gret partie
> Be lost ...[16]

And when we find that Guido's words about the practical and moral function of poetry in the transmission of the past provide the fifteenth-century monk-versifier, John Lydgate, with a Prologue to Book IV of his *The Fall of Princes*, it is clear that no value can be attached to them as a piece of special alliterative doctrine:

> Lawe hadde perisshed, nadde be writyng;
> Our feith appalled, ner vertu of scripture;
> For al religioun and ordre of good lyuyng
> Takth ther exaumple be doctryn of lettrure.
> For writyng causeth, with helpe of portraiture,
> That thynges dirked, of old that wer begonne,
> To be remembred with this celestial sonne.[17]

The same situation arises when we consider the Prologue to the early alliterative debate poem, *Winner and Waster*. It has been suggested[18] that here we have good evidence for a distinctive 'alliterative' concept of the high function of poetry and of the falling-away of poetic standards in the present age:

> Whylome were lordes in londe þat loued in thaire hertis
> To here makers of myrthes, þat matirs couthe fynde,
> Wyse wordes with-inn, þat writen were neuer
> Ne redde in no romance þat euer renke herde.
> Bot now a childe appon chere, with-outten chyn-wedys,
> þat neuer wroghte thurgh witt three wordes to-gedire,
> Fro he can jangle as a jaye, and japes can telle,
> He schall be leuede and louede ...[19]

But the voicing, here, of discontent with contemporary poets, and sober respect for those of the past, draws upon a common stock of medieval tradition: Chrétien de Troyes complains, in *Erec*, about the doubtful quality of minstrel verse:

> D'Erec, le fil Lac, est li contes,
> Que devant rois et devant contes
> Depecier et corronpre suelent
> Cil qui de conter vivre vuelent.[20]

... a story which those who earn a living by telling stories are accustomed to mutilate and spoil in the presence of kings and counts ...

And fourteenth-century chroniclers almost uniformly repudiate the 'bourdes et menteries' of the jongleur *chansons de geste*. Froissart, presenting the first part of his *Chroniques* to Queen Philippa of England, before 1360, wrote as scornfully as the poet of *Winner and Waster* about the irresponsibility of 'jongliours et enchantours', who corrupted 'par les chançons et rimes controuvées la juste et vraie histoire ...'.[21] Perhaps the closest analogue to the alliterative Prologue comes from Chandos Herald's *Life of the Black Prince*, which laments the passing of seriously intentioned poets and the vogue for 'chatterers and buffoons':

> Ore veu homme du temps iadys
> Qe ceux qui faisoient beaux ditys
> Estoient tenu pur aucteur
> Ou pur ascune amenceueur
> De moustrer les bons conissance
> Pur prendre en lour coers remembrance
> De bien e de honure receuioir ...

In olden times it was clear that those who composed fine poems were indeed looked up to as authors, or in some sense as recorders—to demonstrate sound knowledge, drawing upon remembrance of good things, and receiving honour ...

> Car combien qe homme nen face compte
> Et qe homme tiendroit plus grant acompte
> D'un Jangelour ou d'un fauxe menteur
> D'un Jogelour ou d'un Bourdeour
> Qui voudroit faire une grimache

> Ou contreferoit le lymache
> Dount homme purroit feare un risee
> Qe home ne ferroit sanz demoeree
> D'un autre qui saueroit bien dire ...[22]

For although men hold them [true poets] in little esteem, and take more account of a chatterer, a liar, a juggler, or a jester, who tries to raise a laugh by pulling faces or doing contortions, and more readily attend to such than to one who knows how to write poetry properly ...

If we have ever been inclined to try to characterize English alliterative verse in a simple 'nationalistic' way, as more truly representative of native modes and themes than European-based, non-alliterative verse, then affiliations such as these, with a long tradition of French and Anglo-Norman poetry, might ask us to be cautious.

It may be doubted whether, in fact, alliterative poets 'shared' any assumptions about poetry other than those which they also shared with a vast number of non-alliterative writers. If they 'take themselves rather seriously',[23] so, too, did many English poets: their choice of 'grave themes' and their belief in the power of language link them as much with that elder contemporary of Chaucer's, 'moral Gower', as with each other. They, like him, expound the doctrine of the Trinity:

One essence dwells in these three, one god [is] three. He can be nothing more nor less ... Fire, heat, and motion are three things, and they appear as such. Just as a glowing fire always contains these three things, so ... [24]

They, like him, often invoke 'God alone', not the Muses, before embarking upon their poems: again, it is Chaucer who stands away from both alliterative and non-alliterative practice. The *House of Fame*, with its appeals to 'the god of slep' (l. 69), 'Cipris' (l. 518), and 'Appollo' (l. 1092), is equally remote from Gower's *Vox Clamantis*—

I do not invoke the muses for my undertaking, however, nor do I make offering to the gods. But I shall sacrifice to God alone. Merciful God of the Spirit, fire the innermost depths of Thy servant's breast ... [25]

—and from the *Destruction of Troy* and the *Morte Arthure*.[26]

And if, further, we seek a wider context for those works which subscribe to the notion of the poet in an advisory, even critical capacity with regard to king and realm, then Gower, with his Latin verses on King Richard II, *O Deus Immense*, his *Vox Clamantis* and *Tripartite Chronicle*, tracing political and moral patterns which run through the reign of Richard and culminate triumphantly in the accession of Henry IV, must come to mind. These are the poems which are nearest, by general intention and theme, to the alliterative *Mum and the Sothsegger*: composed over the last year of Richard's life and the early part of Henry IV's period of rule, the anonymous poem from the 'blessid borugh þat Bristow is named' begins by offering stern but compassionate advice to Richard—

> Now, Richard þe redeles, reweth on ȝou-self,
> þat lawelesse leddyn ȝoure lyf, and ȝoure peple boþe,[27]

and develops into a treatise on government for Henry, ending with a congratulatory description of his reformed household and personal virtues:

> Now is Henry-is hous holsumly y-made,
> And a meritable meyny of þe moste greet ...
> But he hymsilf is souurayn, and so mote he longe,
> And þe graciousist guyer goyng uppon erthe ...[28]

Gower had been more actively involved in poems of practical advice to Richard while there was still the possibility of reform:

> Rex qui plus aurum populi quam corda thesaurum
> Computat, a mente populi cadit ipse repente.[29]

The king who values his people's money more than their hearts falls quickly from their favour.

The alliterative poet can only address him retrospectively, analysing the causes of his fall, and counselling fortitude; he had always *meant* to write Richard a work of criticism—

> This made me to muse many tyme and ofte,
> For to written hym a writte to wissen him better,
> And to meuve him of mysserewle ...
> *(Mum and the Sothsegger, Prol., ll. 30-2)*

But now all that is left is the sad reckoning of mistakes, and the hope that the deposed king will not 'gruchen a grott aȝeine

Godis sonde ...' (Prol., l. 35). Both poets agree, however, on
Henry's glorious restoration of peace, order, and justice:

> R. regnum vastat vindex et in omnibus astat;
> Mulset terrorem pius H., que reducit amorem.
> O Deus, Henrico, quem diligo, quem benedico,
> De regnum tutum nulla gravitate volutum.[30]

The vindictive R[ichard] laid waste his kingdom and stood over
everyone: H[enry] mitigated fear and brought back brotherly love.
O God, grant to Henry, whom I cherish and bless, a safe kingdom
overturned by no kind of violence ...

And both poets provide, basically, a 'mirror for princes',
building upon a tradition of verse commentary and exhortation
which spans the thirteenth and fourteenth centuries with works
in Latin and the two vernaculars. So Henry III, in 1265, had
been castigated in Latin for his foreign favouritism—

> Hinc alienigenas discant advocare
> Angli, si per advenas volunt exulare ...
> Eschaetis et gardiis suos honorare
> Debet rex, qui variis modis se juvare
> Possunt ...[31]

Hence let the English learn to call in strangers, if they wish to be
exiled by strangers ... The king ought to honour with escheats and
wards his own people, who can help him in various ways ...

and Edward III, in 1347, had been seriously advised to resume
warfare against France, and to discontinue the ignoble truce
between the two countries:

> Bellans, victor eris; treugas cape, decipieris ...[32]

By fighting you will be the victor; accept a truce and you will be
deceived.

Recognition of this larger context for alliterative verse is important in that it gives us a fuller perspective in which to consider
those 'shared assumptions' which have been said to characterize the alliterative poets. It will be seen that these 'shared
assumptions' are assumptions that are shared by the great
body of writers of the thirteenth and fourteenth centuries,

in Latin, Anglo-Norman, and English, who write out of a preoccupation with moral, social, and political issues. These assumptions, these preoccupations, are not in any clearly defined way exclusive to or exclusively characteristic of the alliterative poetry of the period.

At the same time, those who are persuaded by the weight of such arguments may still have reservations concerning one particular set of 'shared assumptions', those, that is, that have to do with choice of metrical form. The extent to which an adherence to the long unrhymed alliterative line makes a common bond among writers of alliterative poetry is a matter of debate, but it would be well to recognize here too that a variety of affiliations may be adduced for alliterative verse, and for individual writers of alliterative verse. There are kinds of alliterative writing in English, not readily identifiable as either 'prose' or 'verse', which may well have been extremely influential in providing the structures for both continuity and change[33] in alliterative verse, and which have the added advantage for argument of having actually survived. Furthermore, there is a wide variety of alliterative writing in Latin and Anglo-Norman which provides another rich array of parallels and precedents. There are, for instance, Latin prose romances, such as the *Historia Meriadoci* and the *De Ortu Walwanii*, written, perhaps, on the Welsh border, in the late thirteenth century, which use alliteration and seek an elevated style in which synonymy and richness of diction are prominent.[34] Both in floridity of practice and in historical interest, the *Historia Meriadoci* has a kinship with the alliterative *Morte Arthure*. In fact, it might even be suggested that the account given in the *Historia Meriadoci* of Arthur hunting out Griffin in the mountains of Snowdonia reflects the historical reality of Edward I's wars against Llewelyn in much the same way that the events of the *Morte Arthure* have been said to reflect the historical reality of Edward III's campaigns abroad.[35] There is also a kind of Latin alliterative verse with very marked alliteration which may have specific association with English alliterative poetry. It has been argued, for instance, that the poem *Patience* owes a particular debt to the *Naufragium Jonae Prophetae* of the twelfth-century Latin poet Marbod of Rennes:[36] the intricate prosody and diction of the *Naufragium* are temptingly reminiscent of the more elevated kinds of alliterative poetry. The poet of *Patience* may have learnt something of prosody from Marbod, and it is worth recalling here that another work by Marbod, the *Oratio ad Sanctam Mariam*, is an acknowledged source for the *Lofsong of Ure Lefdi*, one of the lyrical 'prose' pieces associated with the South-West Midland 'Katherine group' of the early thirteenth century.[37] This group of devotional pieces and saints' lives, some of them in a heightened rhythmical and alliterative prose of distinctive character, have often been claimed as predecessors of some kind for the alliterative poetry of the fourteenth century. There are further Latinate associations, for if we look in the *De Ornamentis Verborum* of Marbod,[38] we shall find that several of Marbod's examples of ornamental style read like Latin 'versions' of the rhetorical prose of the early thirteenth-century West Midlands School. If we seek additional models and influences which would help to explain why established rhymed and stanzaic usages were supplanted, in the hands of some poets, by unrhymed alliterative verse, then Latin alliterative prose and poetry might provide a practical answer. Such forms of writing might have been, if not necessarily a direct influence, then a persuasion towards change.

Even closer to English alliterative writing is the Latin rhymed alliterative verse of Richard Rolle, especially his *Canticum Amoris*.[39] The connection here is demonstrable in that Rolle is himself the author of rhymed alliterative verse and rhythmical alliterative 'prose' in English which is part of the body of alliterative writing traditionally associated with the poetry of the 'revival'. The models which supplied inspiration for this early fourteenth-century contemplative writer, in earlier English prose, such as that of the Katherine group, in Latin alliterative prose and verse, provide some of the materials for an alternative hypothesis concerning the 'origins of the alliterative revival', one that is both more complex and better evidenced, historically, than the simple myth of continuity and revival.

Finally, it should not be forgotten that Anglo-Norman poetry in *laisses* may have provided an important model for English alliterative poets. The long unrhymed alliterative line may have seemed to them an excellent substitute for the long lines with assonance of the *laisses*, and one particularly suitable for full-breathed narrative poems of the *geste* type. The *Chronique de la Guerre entre les Anglais et les Ecossais* of Jordan Fantosme, written for Henry II in 1175,[40] may be taken to exemplify such poetry. Its themes are historical, with moral commentary, and, with its circulation among provincial noble households of the east and north-east midlands, it provides a suggestive precedent for later English alliterative poetry.

If we come now to consider the greatest of the alliterative poems of the fourteenth century, *Piers Plowman*, the case for an exclusive community of intellectual and poetic assumptions among alliterative poets seems more questionable still. The presentation of Langland's poem in a conventional alliterative context may have some importance in terms of the writing of certain kinds of literary history; but it has little importance in terms of our understanding of the special quality of Langland's thought and art. Even his handling of the alliterative verse form itself, which might be thought to contain evidence of some general agreement about what constituted alliterative form, is boldly individual, suggesting that he shaped his practice from rougher materials, semi-alliterative, hybrid in nature, which may have existed upon the very borderlands of prose and verse.[41]

   The fact is that when we try to associate *Piers Plowman* closely with other alliterative works, the real value of the association is always doubtful. Comparisons usually serve to isolate *Piers Plowman* rather than to connect it. So, although there is some interest in speculating upon the part played by the satirical debate, *Winner and Waster*, in Langland's basic alliterative reading,[42] and some interest, too, in defining the derivative relationship of later dream-allegories and complaints such as *Mum and the Sothsegger, Death and Life,* and *Pierce the Ploughman's Creed* to his poem, the rewards of such comparative study are limited. The earlier work is a fragile statement of what was to become one of Langland's richer themes. The later works pay their debt to a small area of *Piers Plowman*; their interpretation is narrow, often partial. Certain materials, artistic forms, verbal effects are borrowed, but there is nothing substantial to suggest that the later authors were capable of benefiting from, even if they admired, Langland's innovatory power, his subtle and comprehensive understanding, his high and felicitous spirituality. The political effect of the poem—if we are to take the letter of John Ball to the commons of Essex seriously—was strong and immediate. *Piers Plowman* was without doubt one of the best-read texts of the fifteenth and early sixteenth centuries. But it did not inspire alliterative compositions of similar scope and quality.

We may observe how Langland's stern and tormented compassion for the poor is vulgarized into a form of sensationalism by the portrait of the ploughman in *Pierce the Ploughman's Creed*:

> His ton toteden out as he the londe treddede,
> His hosen overhongen his hokschynes on everiche a side,
> Al beslombred in fen as he the plowe folwede ... [43]

And we may observe how the author of *Mum and the Sothsegger*, confused and angered by similar worldly disorders, adopting Langland's *persona* of the wandering poet in order to dream himself into some kind of order, yet demonstrates sympathies quite alien to those of Langland. In his attitudes to the lower classes, for instance, he is often nearer to Gower than to Langland: his sentiments are reactionary, his pity is held in check by a rigid hierarchical sense of order. It would, in fact, as we have seen (p. 95 above), be as relevant to consider *Mum and the Sothsegger* in juxtaposition with the *Vox Clamantis* as with *Piers Plowman*: both the former combine traditional class satire with sharp political commentary; both are conservative, critical, and mandatory.

Not surprisingly, we do hardly better when we turn to non-alliterative poetry for those associations which elude us. There is, quite clearly, a massive amount of subject-matter held in common by Langland and Gower in the *Vox Clamantis*, the *Mirour de l'Omme*, and *Piers Plowman*; their pessimistic and thorough account of all levels of medieval society makes a common basic use of materials provided by moralists of an earlier age as well as by their own sombre gaze upon the contemporary scene. But Gower's unshakeable orthodoxy, his purposeful lack of understanding of the subterranean movements of unrest in the late fourteenth century, refer him to one element only in Langland's complicated and stressful analysis. And if we look outside poetry altogether, to a long prose treatise such as *Dives and Pauper*, which, in the early fifteenth century, debates subjects of immense interest to Langland, and is, indeed, comprehensive, the situation remains the same. Many of the materials of the treatise are Langland's too, but the handling of them is often significantly different. The salvation of man, for example, could be considered Langland's 'O Sentence', and *Dives and Pauper* is concerned with this, urgently. Its urgency, however, is put to the service of its anticipated class of readers: the secular upper classes—and it is consistently anxious to reassure the rich that their salvation need not be in doubt. Dives is comforted for his fears 'that God had not loved rich men ...' by the statement that 'the holye patriarkys weryn wol ryche and þow God lovedde hem wol wel ...'.[44] At the very centre of *Dives and Pauper* is the doctrine of the orthodox medieval pulpit—'paupertas est odibile bonum', 'poverty is a hateful good', and the necessity of the poor for the salvation of the rich is a theme it shares with many a forceful sermon:

> the rich man has been created for the benefit of the poor, and the poor man for the benefit of the rich ... in order that God may test the love of the rich ... [and] to increase the merit of the poor ...[45]

Langland was familiar with these stable sentiments, but his use of them is extremely complex, even, we might say, characteristically unstable! He sees, with Biblical support, that it is easier to win heaven through poverty than through wealth—

> The heighe wey to heveneward ofte Richesse letteth;
> *Ite inpossibile diviti, etc.*
> Ther the poore preesseth bifore with a pak at his rugge
> > (*Piers Plowman*, B. XIV. 212-13)

and that the Deadly Sins have little chance of success in their assault upon the poor—

> If Wrathe wrastle with the poore he hath the worse ende ...
>
> And if Glotonie greve poverte he gadereth the lasse.
> > (B. XIV. 225, 230)

But the context in which all this is set out is that of a keen realization of the texture of poverty—of the experience of *being poor*. It is the 'cold beddyng', the 'straw' for sheets, and the 'weeping for cold' that Langland ensures we remember (B. XIV. 231-6), not the good fortune of the poor to be such poor material for the active operation of sin.

The better-known literature of the fourteenth and fifteenth

centuries, alliterative or non-alliterative, prose or verse, gives us some content, some preoccupations to remind us of *Piers Plowman*: it can do little to give us an introduction to or a confirmation of Langland's most striking and idiosyncratic methods of procedure—both conceptual and artistic. It is as if the reading of *Piers Plowman* proved too rich for more than part of its substance to be absorbed into fresh literary forms.

And if we were to ask, then, what is the unique nature of this richness, if we had to identify the central quality of Langland as writer and artist, the quality which distinguishes him and his work from so much contemporary and later writing, it would surely be the quality of disturbance. He is a disturbed and disturbing poet, who works often in a highly original way, through techniques of disorientation and alienation, through reversals of accepted forms and processes—whether in the literary fields of allegory and satire or in the spiritual fields of visionary insight. Langland's singularity in the fourteenth-century English literary landscape is a remarkable phenomenon. But what may cause us almost as much wonder, from a historical point of view, is that more of the literature and art of his day is not as 'singular', as 'disturbed'. There is no need to prove at any length that the later fourteenth century in England, as in northern Europe generally, was a pattern of tensions: a period when dissent, whether social, political, or religious, showed some need to develop into revolution—impossible though it may have been, at that particular moment. It was a period when, for the first time, the Church's traditional and flexible methods of containing dissent, its methods of accommodating the inevitable collisions of intelligence and authority, began to fail. Gordon Leff points out that it was the increasing rigidity of the medieval church in the later fourteenth century which both encouraged the growth of unorthodoxy, and ensured that there was no way of dealing with it, save persecution: 'the Church froze in its own positions. ...' It became 'an institution which of its nature could not both abide by the present order and assimilate the future'.[46] In these decades, accelerated change and experiment, dissatisfaction with accepted institutions, critical scrutiny of accepted structures are all-pervasive.

We may note the difference of temper between the attitudes

to warfare in the reign of Edward III and in that of Richard II; the peace-movement which centred upon King Richard and his party in the later years of his reign reflected not only political realism but also perhaps a more general sense of disillusionment with traditional medieval theories about the glorious and beneficial nature of the exercise of martial skills. The disillusionment with war is both political and ideological, and Chaucer's *Knight's Tale*, with its bitter version of the 'redoutynge of Mars and of his glorie' —

> A thousand slayn, and nat of qualm ystorve;
> The tiraunt, with the pray by force yraft,
> The toun destroyed, ther was no thyng laft ...
> *(Canterbury Tales*, I. 2014-16)

may be a better guide to the spirit of the times than the official biography of the Black Prince, produced about 1386, which celebrates a life of campaigning in heroic terms already, possibly, a shade old-fashioned.[47] More dramatic still is the evidence from the lower registers of English medieval society of the breaking of old bonds, once thought divinely sanctioned. The Peasants' Rising of 1381, though defeated, was heavily symptomatic of change; its most celebrated historian sees it at the heart of 'a period of considerable self-confidence, even assertiveness among tenants and labourers alike ... In this period the grip of traditional forms of lordly power over tenants was faltering. ...' A new political awareness shows significantly, 'a loss of respect for the traditional élites ...'.[48] And if it is true that already 'the historic process of dissolution ...' of medieval society had begun, some 'dissolution' can also be observed in the sphere of religious thought. Not only must we take into account the radical denials of basic Church doctrine by John Wiclif: the vigour with which the established Church countered such denials might persuade us that all was still well. But there are signs of innovation and speculative boldness everywhere, not least the subtle unorthodoxies of Uthred of Boldon, monk of Durham and Oxford historian, whose unusual doctrines of salvation, prompted by a wide, charitable sense of God's justice ('All flesh shall see the Salvation of God') Langland himself may have known.[49] A whole range of new demands were being made upon the Church, by classes freshly literate, by classes barely literate; challenging the official educational propaganda came an increasing strength of 'unorthodox opinions [arising] spontaneously from the cogitations of men and women searching for explanations that accorded with the realities of the life in which they were enmeshed ...'.[50] It is not surprising that Bruce McFarlane could find strong words to describe a turbulent period:

the contemporary spirit in religion was puritan, biblical, evangelical, anarchic, anti-sacerdotal, hostile to the established order ...

and could see its characteristic rhythm as that of rebellion:

... a moral revolt by the laity against the visible Church, a rejection of sacerdotalism in favour of the personal, immediate contact between the believer and his Creator ...[51]

Naturally we need to remind ourselves that such rebellions as often met with defeat as with victory; the history of the fifteenth century is in many respects a history of retrenchment— even of repression. And we need to recognize that sentiments of protest, dissent, revolt were often held in uneasy balance with those of acquiescence and conformity. What is clear, however, is that in the later fourteenth century, orthodoxy was frequently confronted by searching questions and was even forced to stand upon alien ground in order to make its defence. The dialogues which recorded such encounters were dangerously disposed to become conflicts and we might expect to find that certain artists would, while attempting to work within the orderly debate, draw their most forceful writing out of the conflict between a desire to reaffirm older loyalties and beliefs, and an equally strong desire to assert new convictions or at least explore their significance. The potential of 'danger' can be gauged even in that well-controlled English debate poem *Pearl*: we can sense the constant possibility that the author will be tempted to disturb the finely balanced theme of the debate—the necessity of embracing pain in a context of faith—by allowing disproportionate and sympathetic emphasis to the spectacle of human wilfulness dashing itself against the pure, unalterable justice of God's will. The excitement of reading *Pearl* is partly dependent upon our live suspicion that the power of the poetry will eventually work against the exigencies of the doctrine. In this case,

that does not really happen: debate is not 'disturbed' into conflict: the growing-points of dissent are refused growth. The last
words of *Pearl* are made acceptable, not in a state of exhaustion
but in one of reconciliation. A sense of danger is part of our
experience of reading Chaucer, too; there are ways in which
the dilemmas of the age emerge in his poetry—most crucially
when he is dealing with old-established source-materials. Here
we may, for instance, discover him facing austere medieval sets
of values in a mood of alternating complacency and restlessness: obedience may unpredictably give way to impatience. So,
when we compare the *Clerk's Tale* and its sources, there is a
world of difference between Petrarch's vision of the terrifying
beauty of the story—its meaning only to be precipitated from
'a cloud of loves and martyrdoms'[52]—and Chaucer's view,
scaled-down to take in a whole range of variable human responses, irritable, angry, affectionate, admiring by turn.

But it is not in the poetry of the *Pearl* author, and not in that
of Chaucer, that the major perturbations of the later fourteenth
century are given most powerful and original expression. For
that we have to go to Langland, who is quintessentially a product of his disturbed age. In fact, he makes his poem out of
disturbance, refusing to leave it—or his readers—in any state
of final solution and turning from the *andante cantabile* of faith to
the *appassionato* of inquiry. For comparable works, and comparable developments within the span of an artist's work, it is
perhaps more rewarding to go to the painters and sculptors
than to the writers of the later Middle Ages. Not, however, to
those of England in Langland's lifetime. Charles Muscatine
commented relevantly upon the conservative nature of English
art in the reign of Richard II: 'it does not much suggest a
milieu of turbulence or crisis. Similarly, English architecture,
now in its great "early Perpendicular" period, suggests solidity
and dignity rather than tension or decay.'[53] Nothing in the
pleasant litanies of English miniature painting during those
years—in the Bohun manuscripts, for instance—compels us to
think of what may lie beyond the sweetness of devotion solicited
and bestowed. The relevant comparisons must come from
Europe, and from the fifteenth century: from the art of the
extraordinary Rohan Master, whose decorated books, commissioned by the House of Anjou in the violent years of the

earlier fifteenth century, reveal an increasingly violent and disruptive talent;[54] from that of Hieronymus Bosch, whose paintings constantly border upon crisis, and unnerve us with their savage (conceptual) but cool (painterly) juxtapositions. And there is one particularly moving (though late) analogy for that quality of 'disturbance' in Langland which is not only a manifestation of basic conflict in the mind of the poet, in the temper of his age, but is also a driving force, insisting to Langland that *Piers Plowman* should always be re-made, re-written, and that creation should be fresh and continuous, to the very end of his last version of the poem. The analogy is with the progress of Michelangelo, through the last sequence of *Pietà* sculptures, from the Palestrina to the Rondanini group, exploring the meaning of that moment of despair in the Christian narrative in forms of art increasingly harsh, more original as they became more grotesque: 'In the humility of his last years, Michelangelo has pared away everything which could suggest the pride of the body, till he has reached the huddled roots of a Gothic wood carving.'[55] Although the artists, the subjects, the media, even the centuries are different, there is something similar here: life-work ending not with a benediction, but with a principle of continuous change and growth. In one view, not necessarily perverse, the *Pietàs* of Michelangelo and the three texts of Langland's poem are stages in an unfinished process, tributes to the political value of 'disturbance' as creative energy no less than as creative humility:

You must return to that unsophisticated spot where the angel discovered you when he brought you the first blinding message ... If the angel deigns to come, it will be because you have convinced him not with tears, but with your humble resolve to be always beginning, to be a beginner ...[56]

We might, in fact, examine the singularity of Langland as a fourteenth-century English poet by taking as our focus of attention the theme of 'disturbance' in his work, and proposing that our identification of this theme should not be simply a matter for critical regret, but one of the more compelling reasons for recommending *Piers Plowman*, in all its successive forms, as the greatest vernacular poem of the later Middle Ages. In this it is necessary both to associate ourselves with and to separate ourselves from opinions such as those expressed by Charles Muscatine, who not only sees Langland's 'poetry of crisis' reflecting the 'instability of the epoch in its very structure and style as well as in its argument', but also judges poem and poet 'victims' of that crisis, that instability.[57] Muscatine's account analyses a kind of defeat which the poem, despairing though it often is, does not consistently admit to. It neglects one crucial element in *Piers Plowman*, which speaks of, and demonstrates, triumph. For *Piers Plowman* is essentially a record of confrontations; it may sometimes, in its ruthlessly honest and almost impossibly ambitious attempt to come to terms with the social, political, and intellectual forces which were powerfully changing the medieval world, be led into contradictions, wrestle and fall into exhaustion. But it is, in the first place, an incomparable record of a historical and personal struggle. It is, secondly, incomparable as a record of rewards which did not come to Langland in the high simplicities of apocalyptic narrative, nor in those of liturgical ceremony. They came in fleeting moments of insight, when the disordered parts of his inner and outer world were subjected to a unifying process of change and regeneration. And this is still the great wonder of the poem, that, in spite of the desperate grounds for pessimism discovered by dreamer and reader as the exploration pushes deeper into that inner and outer 'wildernesse', it reveals also, with some optimism, a universe blessed by metamorphoses. If Langland turns impatiently, contemptuously, upon the restless flux of ordinary human existence—'how bisie thei ben about the maze ...' (B. I. 6)—he celebrates another restlessness within man's experience. In this divine version of earthly flux, disturbance is translated, becoming a more purposeful, though hardly less mysterious dynamic, working between God and his creation. The dreamer's changing comprehension of what he sees: the changing figure of Piers Plowman; the changing face of the everyday familiar world; all bear witness to the way in which 'disturbance' can be reinterpreted in a context of spiritual energy. There is nothing ultimately 'disturbing' about the sudden recognition of Christ in ten thousand places 'lovely in limbs and lovely in eyes not his ...',[58] although normal vision has been 'disturbed' to achieve it:

> For our Ioye and our Iuel, Iesu crist of heuene,
> In a pouere mannes apparaille pursueth us evere,
> And loketh on us in hir liknesse ...
>
> (B. XI. 185-7)

Put at its most basic, the quality of disturbance in *Piers Plowman* can be detected in a series of conflicts between the poet's allegiance to the orthodox and divinely sanctioned structures of medieval institutions and beliefs, and his irritable consciousness of the facts of medieval existence which made the preservation of such structures both unlikely and unjust.

Commentators upon *Piers Plowman* have found difficulty in assessing the degree of responsibility felt by Langland towards these matters; Langland criticism has found it possible to move between opposed, and not unreasonable conclusions—that he is at heart a reactionary, at heart a revolutionary. But scrutiny of his poem for evidence to support one or other of these views brings us rather exactly to the question of disturbance: so often in *Piers Plowman* we are involved in disturbing sequences, as the dreamer listens to debates which both present the established case and undermine it. The poetry itself need do no more than emphasize the dilemma. In Passus XIV of the B-Text, for instance, Haukyn's forceful defence of his 'sinful garment of human nature':

> 'I have but oon hool hater', quod Haukyn, 'I am the lasse to blame
> Though it be soiled and selde clene; I slepe therinne o nyhtes:
> And also I have an houswif, hewen and children ...'
>
> (B. XIV. 1-3)

which has often been 'lathered' with sickness and adversity, is followed by the orthodox and conservative advice of Patience that, after repentance, Haukyn, 'the active man', should throw himself upon God's mercy, and 'care not for the morrow':

> 'And I shal purveie thee paast', quod Pacience 'though no plough erye,
> And flour to fede folk with as best be for the soule ...'
>
> (B. XIV. 29-30)

Activa Vita's scepticism about the good sense of this counsel— 'thanne laughed Haukyn a litel ...' is silenced by the almost rapturous passage of poetry in which Patience celebrates the

meaning and the sufficiency of the spiritual food—'fiat voluntas tua'—he proposes for Haukyn. The doctrine of 'pacientes
vincunt' is reiterated, and, in positive terms, the external
advantages of the poor over the rich are stressed:

> Thanne may beggeris, as beestes, after boote waiten,
> That al hir lif han lyved in langour and defaute.
> But God sente hem som tyme som manere joye
> Outher here or elliswhere, kynde wolde it nevere ...
>
> (B. XIV. 117-20)

But what succeeds to this seems to be a gradually increasing
anxiety as to the certainty of such heavenly rewards for reliance
upon 'fiat voluntas tua' here on earth; the confident statements
of the lines quoted above become the adjurations of a later
passage:

> Now, lord, sende hem somer and som maner ioye,
> Hevene, after hir hennes goyng that here han swich defaute ...
> Ac poore peple, thi prisoners, lord, in the put of meschief,
> Conforte tho creatures that muche care suffren ...
> Conforte thi carefulle, Crist, in thi riche ...
>
> (B. XIV. 164-5, 174-5, 179)

Again, however, this somewhat tentative material is followed
by a firm and entirely orthodox analysis of poverty and its
efficacy:

> So pouerte propreliche penaunce is to the body,
> And Ioye to pacient pouere, pure spiritual helthe ...
>
> (B.XIV. 284-5)

We might, after such an unrelenting sermon, expect the col-
lapse of the spirited Haukyn—but his weeping and his penitent
words are curiously moving, with their implication that to live
is to sin: it is hard to do otherwise:

> 'So hard it is', quod Haukyn, 'to lyve and to do synne.
> Synne seweth us evere ...'
>
> (B. XIV. 325-6)

Our reading of all of this will depend upon many different
factors—one of which, perhaps, is whether we are literary historians or literary critics. The critic may be disposed to judge
such unexplained transitions, such fluctuating pressures, as

artistic failure—the poet failing to integrate his diverse materials and reconcile his faith, intelligence, and compassion in
a way which will allow the poem to register unity. The historian
may be disposed to see here and commend to us the documen-
tation of a moment in the fourteenth century when the currents
of reform and reaction were significantly locked.

'Disturbance as conflict' can also be observed in Langland's
handling of his allegory—in, for instance, his management of
the relationship of the allegorical to the literal mode. Disturbance of traditional allegorical norms is often what we encounter,
but this may not be a phenomenon which we can afford to pass
over as ineptitude, nor need it be, in the words of another critic,
'an attack on the habit of thought encouraged by allegory'.[59] It
may have something to do with Langland's strong apprehension of the condition of living in the painfully real medieval
world, or at least, his willingness to let that apprehension have
freedom of entry into his poetry; whatever the reasons, the fact
is that Langland's allegorical usages are very different from
those of the *Pearl*-poet, or those of the author of the *Roman de la
Rose*. Traditionally, the relationship between literal and allegorical characters is that of learner and instructor (in the case of
the personified vice, that of learner and tempter). *Pearl*, with its
fallible dreamer and magisterial Pearl-maiden, or an early
Passus of *Piers Plowman* such as that which discusses the meeting of the dreamer and Holy Church, illustrates the normal
situation perfectly. Despite the vigour of the literal characters,
they must be shown to have limited access to the truth; if they
argue persuasively, appeal movingly, their term of authority
must be brief; traditionally they must not be left uncorrected.
Yet in *Piers Plowman* there often seems to be uncertainty about
the acceptance of the ultimate truth and authority of the allegorical characters; there are juxtapositions, collisions of literal
and allegorical characters from which no entirely satisfactory
conclusion comes. The literal contribution to a debate may be
lastingly, not temporarily impressive; the life of an allegorical
character can be precariously sustained, and there is more than
one moment in the poem when some sturdy literal character
may invite the reader to conclude, with relief and a little amusement, that those allegorical creatures who appeared to lecture

him so convincingly are really nothing but chapter-headings in
a medieval text-book of faculty psychology.

Such a moment comes, for instance, when the literal, historical character, Trajan, breaks into Scripture's assurance to
the dreamer that salvation is to be achieved through the due
processes of baptism, repentance, confession, contrition, and
suffering—all enclosed in the mercy of God 'as oure bokes
telleth' (B. XI. 138). Trajan's irruption into the allegory is
startling and impressive—

> 'Ye? baw for bokes!' quod oon was broken out of helle ...
> (B. XI. 140)

His testimony is fresh and irrefutable: as a 'trewe knyght',
though a pagan emperor, he was saved 'by love and by lernyng
of my lyvynge in truthe ...' (l. 152). It may come again when in
Passus XIII of the B-Text, after a confident but generalizing
passage by Patience on love and patience as ideal rulers of the
world and bringers of total peace, the worthy Doctor of Divinity
who had, not four days earlier, 'bifore the deen of Poules /
Preached of penaunces that Poul the Apostle suffrede' (B. XIII.
65-6), sets cogent and impatient arguments of a contemporary
political nature against the orthodox religious view:

> 'It is but a *dido*', quod this doctour 'a disours tale:
> Al the wit of this world and wight mennes strengthe
> Kan noght parfournen a pees bitwene the pope and hise enemys,
> Ne bitwene two cristene kynges ...'
> ... And putte the table fro hym ...
> (B. XIII. 172-6)

But however we decide to interpret the individual episodes,
they contribute to an over-all rhythm or set of rhythms in *Piers
Plowman* which poignantly expresses a familiar area of man's
'disturbed experience' about himself and his world—the distance between theory and practice, between theological justice
and Christo-centric compassion, even between visionary ela-
tion and waking melancholy. For so often the dreamer himself
experiences not only that disillusionment with allegorical authority which, as we have seen, is such a perplexing and original
feature of the 'poem', but also the sad fading of such allegory
into thin literalism, the wrenching passage back from the

dream, 'weary and wet-shod', after treading in spiritual pastures. Should we, then, finding 'disturbance' so often at the heart of the matter in *Piers Plowman*, take an ultimately pessimistic view of Langland's thought and art? And is there any hope that the poem can reach us except as a critical chart of human difficulties, as a seismograph of universal pain?

I have suggested that we could rest our defence of *Piers Plowman* on its unique position as a medieval work which is just such a precise chart, such an accurate seismograph. There is, of course, much more that it does. The greater proportion of the poem is concerned with documenting conflict, dissent, anger, and humiliation as they obstruct the poet-dreamer's desire for absolute faith. But if Langland is characterized by his fierce destructive energies, his restless dissatisfactions, and his deep sense of alienations, he is also characterized by the strength of his inner vision. Much of his aggression and his bitterness must be seen in the context of that vision, as, on a later but comparable occasion, Rilke saw:

then you set about that unexampled act of violence, your work, which more and more impatiently, more and more despairingly, sought among visible things equivalents for the vision within ... [60]

We should not neglect the fact that the poem documents a personal revelation of truth—a revelation which may only illuminate the dark places of the poem at certain key moments, but which is a clear, unambiguous witness to some sense of miracle, transcending rather than denying the chaotic and problematic 'character of the times', the 'crisis' in the poet and his world.

Here we still need to associate Langland with the upper reaches of medieval spirituality—whether recorded in the Latin writings of the internationally famous, or in the humbler vernacular treatises of the men and women of northern Europe and Scandinavia who were Langland's contemporaries. In many important ways they were subject to similar pressures, and sought—at higher levels, admittedly, than Langland— similar solutions. There is, for instance, more in Walter Hilton's work, whether original or translated,[61] more in that of Julian of Norwich, than there is in any alliterative or non-alliterative poem to explain how Langland came to make his great transpositions from the human mode of turbulence and disturbance to the divine mode of active regeneration, in which his most splendid creative work was done. Here we must point to the development of the concept of a figure such as Piers the Plowman, the concept of his nature and function in the poem. And we should also point to other kinds of special creative development—the use of deliberately disconcerting, alienating techniques[62] of presentation not simply as an urgent message about inner and outer confusion, that progress from personal to cosmic turmoil,[63] but as a message about the interpenetration of the ordinary, habitual world with the materials and processes of vision.

On both counts, of course, Langland was probably as much indebted to his knowledge of the Scriptures as to his knowledge of the spiritual writings of his century. Familiar with the historical world of the New Testament, he knew that ordinary men could see water turned into wine, could see with new eyes—'their eyes they have closed, but *at any time* they should see with their eyes, hear with their ears, understand with their hearts ...' (Matthew 13:15). The existence of the miraculous was 'as old as loaves and fishes': its intervention assured by the concluding miracle of the Resurrection:

Whereby are given to us exceeding great and precious promises, that by these ye might be partakers of the divine nature, having escaped the corruption that is in the world.

(2 Peter 1:4)

Moreover, a reading of the New Testament alone could have suggested to Langland the mystery of appearances—a mystery which he turns to such startling dramatic advantage in the B-Text of his poem, as the dreamer watches Piers the Plowman assume a more complex relationship to Christ, to Saint Peter, to the Good Samaritan, and questions keenly what is in front of his very eyes:

Is Piers in this place?

(B. XVIII. 21)

For the New Testament, like Langland's poem, is concerned to challenge accepted ways of seeing, to alert man to the sense of strangeness which must precede understanding; its narrative often presents the disciples in full perplexity about Christ:

some say thou art John the Baptist, some Elias and others Jeremaias
or one of the prophets ...

(Matthew 16:14)

Nothing could better prepare us for the mysterious comings
and goings of Piers in the later passus than the account of
Christ's appearances after the Resurrection:

and their eyes were opened, and they knew him, and he vanished out
of their sight ...

(Luke 24:31)

And nothing could better illustrate the ability of Langland to
seize upon the mysterious potential of the statements of Christ
about 'appearance' than his use of the concise question and
answer in Matthew 25:44-5,

Lord, when saw we thee anhungered or athirst or a stranger or
naked?
    In as much as ye did it not to one of the least of these, ye did it not
to me.

as the basis for those great moments of illumination where
Christ *is* recognized in poor men travelling:

... for pilgrymes are we alle,
And in the apparaille of a pouere man and pilgrymes liknesse
Many tyme god hath ben met among nedy peple ...

(B. XI. 242-4)

All of such indebtedness is undeniable. But there are ways in
which some of Langland's spiritual contemporaries seem to
bear with particular relevance upon his artistic and conceptual
procedures. Charles Muscatine has called attention to what he
perceives as the 'paradoxical space' of the poem—its 'insecurity
of structure', its 'shifting spatial relations';[64] if we accept his
analysis, we must take a predominantly negative view of the
reasons for Langland's invention of this 'strange, surrealistic
structure' within which to express his 'passionate criticisms, his
earnest exhortations'. But there are contemporary theories
which may explain why the loosing of the bonds of ordinary
spatial logic, of sublunary geography, could have appealed to
Langland in a positive rather than negative way. Although
Langland need certainly not have known the English contem-

plative text the *Cloud of Unknowing*, he need not have been unfamiliar with the reasoning which lies behind the author's reply
to his disciple's anxious position:

'Where then shall I be? Nowhere, according to your story'.

'Now, as a matter of fact, you're on the right track: for there I want
you to be. Nowhere in the body is everywhere in the spirit. Be very
careful that your spiritual activities are nowhere as far as the body is
concerned ... Who is the man who calls this "nowhere"? It must be
our outer, not our inner man: our inner man calls it "everywhere".'[65]

It is indeed in these English spiritual writers that we sometimes come closest to the situations described in *Piers Plowman*:
there is as much in Walter Hilton's *Letter to a Hermit*[66] as there
is in any English or French dream-poem to help us understand
the dilemma of Langland's dreamer—the rhythm of his waking
and dreaming life, the complex warring of intention and capacity, the struggle to find a guide to lead him to salvation. The
breadth of concept witnessed to in a work such as Walter
Hilton's *Goad of Love*, translated from the pseudo-Bonaventuran
Stimulus Amoris, is Langland's breadth too: an ethic of service
which has visionary implications:

Right so doth such a man that travaileth, and serveth an holy man or
a sick or doth any other work to worship of God, and only beholdeth
our Lord Jesus Christ in him. He feedeth his brother and is fed of
God, he stretcheth out his hands and his limbs to help his brother,
and his heart delighteth in God. For why? he serveth his brother not
as a man, but as to our Lord Jesus in a man, aye thinking thus that
our Lord said: 'As oft as ye do to the least of mine ye do it to me'.[67]

And as for the creation of Piers the Plowman—that demonstration of the miraculous way in which the ragged but vital movements of life in ordinary man can be transposed into the
regular movements of a life regenerated by the will of God—we
need surely to associate such a creation with these writings
which are inspired by a belief in the possibility of a miracle of
growth at all levels of good lives, no less than by a belief in the
conviction that the best life of dedication to love must also be a
dedication to service. It would be difficult to get closer to Langland's concept of the changing Piers than in Richard of St Victor's *Four Degrees of Rapturous Love*, one of the great founding
texts of later English contemplative prose:

In tertio sitit in Deum. In quarto sitit secundum Deum ... totum
Domino committit ... In tertio gradu animus elevatus ad Deum totus
transit in ipsum ... in quarto egreditur ex compassione ... In tertio
itaque gradu quodammodo mortificatur in Deum; in quarto quasi
resuscitatur in Christum ... Qui ad hunc caritatis gradum ascendit,
absque dubio in hoc gradu amoris est qui veraciter dicere potest :
Omnibus omnia factus sum et omnes facerem salvos.

In the third degree of love, the soul thirsts to have its being in God; in
the fourth, it thirsts for God's sake ... committing all its being to God
... In the third, the soul is raised to God and passes wholly into him ...
In the fourth, it goes forth driven by compassion ... In the third
degree, one is put to death in God; in the fourth, one is raised in
Christ ... He who ascends to the fourth degree of love is truly in the
state of love that can truly say: 'I am made all things to all men so that
I may save all'.[68]

For Langland, then, with his many narratives spanning all
ages of Christian history 'past, present and to come, till time
shall be no more', the acceptance of earthly instability is part of
painful and then triumphant recognition of the nature of the
spiritual world. Instability and disturbance can be offered,
therefore, not entirely negatively, as failure, but more positively as a comprehensible stage in the progress towards triumph. It is a kind of reassurance and reconciliation and finality
that is rare in *Piers Plowman*, but it is there, most notably in the
passus recounting the events of the Crucifixion and the Harrowing of Hell (B. XVIII). It is, however, a finality that is
quite inaccessible to Chaucer, whose endings and reconciliations are often made in a spirit of stoicism or weariness, with
rarely the sense that they are the ineluctable consequence of
what has gone before, and often coming with surprising sud-
denness, as in *The Knight's Tale, Troilus and Criseyde*, or even the
little 'balade de bon conseyl', *Truth*.

5 Chaucer and Medieval English tradition

The placing of Chaucer's poetry in 'Medieval English tradition' is something to be undertaken with caution, for, as we have seen, there is no simple way of accounting for what that tradition was. He can, indeed, be presented as a sensitive recorder of many of the varied educated and literary interests alive in the London of his day: if we should not describe him as a 'court-poet' in the narrowest, most exclusive sense, it is partly because we have learnt to describe the 'court of Richard the Second' more widely, and have allowed for the intersection of many different lines of medieval metropolitan society at that court. There are, it is true, some contemporary literary activities of which his poetry—though not, perhaps, his prose— seems to fail to take account. At one time, we might have asserted that he shows little knowledge of, or taste for, the long alliterative poem in which Langland, at so little distance from him, was examining the state of man's soul and of Christendom. But it could not be quickly assumed that the Plowman and Parson of his *General Prologue* to the *Canterbury Tales* do not owe something to a reading of a version of Langland's poem, nor that his handling of the pilgrimage form, with its late and tentative move from secular preoccupations to celestial, its surprisingly monumental homiletic conclusion, was not in some way provoked or stirred by what he read of pilgrimage in *Piers Plowman*.[1] The speculations raised by this idea are very wide. It might be tempting to conclude that he had seen only an A-version of *Piers Plowman*, since he gives a fairly simple interpretation to the *motif* of pilgrimage: Langland's labyrinthine winding of interior and exterior journeying in the later parts of the poem had no apparent effect upon Chaucer, if in fact he had read more extensively into the work. The A-text, which circulated as an entity, in its own right, could have suggested sufficient for Chaucer's social panorama in the

Canterbury Tales: although it is only a drafting-out of the issues
which Langland later studied in depth, Chaucer could have
taken from it what was useful to his rather different purposes.
If he *did* read even the A-text, however, we would like to know
what he made of the clear instructions given to Langland's
eager pilgrim, Piers, to stay at home, and win his pardon, pay
his dues, on life's pilgrimage, and not on any prescribed route
to the shrine of Saint or Saviour.[2] Whatever he found useful in
Langland's poem, it was certainly not Langland's constant and
explicit moral commitment to particular courses of action,
physical and spiritual, nor was it Langland's sense of the interesting complexity of faith. Two kinds of pilgrimage Chaucer
may have recognized: his friend, Sir John Clanvowe, wrote a
treatise on *The Two Ways*.[3] But the vision of a series of over-
lapping pilgrimages, past, present, and to come, is not part of
his world-view, however we may try to find it so.

One important possibility must be recognized or, rather,
restated, for it is by no means new: that Chaucer and Langland
drew upon many of the same materials for their comment upon
society, rather than upon each other. The vast body of satiric
and homiletic literature, in Latin and in the current vernaculars of England and Europe, which analysed, arraigned, and
proposed solutions for the *malaises* of all sections of society—a
literature set at almost every level of literacy, and public—
clearly fed a great deal of both Langland's and Chaucer's
socio-religious observations upon the world of men about
them. Both of them drew upon serious and satirical 'estates'
literature, both of them are sensitively aware of particular controversies of the fourteenth century, controversies, for instance,
centred about the place and function of the Friars in medieval
society which were debated and acted out most dramatically in
the London of their lifetime.[4]

There is, indeed, a very real sense in which later fourteenth
century writers such as Langland, Gower, and Chaucer can be
seen as perfectly explicable products of the moral and intellectual climate of later fourteenth-century London. So, too, as we
have seen, can the anonymous author of *St. Erkenwald*, the
author of the vigorous alliterative polemical piece known as
Friar Daw's Reply, and the prolific Carmelite Friar, Richard
Maidstone, who, from his court connections with men such as

John of Gaunt, must have been known to Chaucer and Gower, and produced on demand Latin polemical tracts, English verse translations of the *Psalms*, and Latin panegyric poems for royal occasions.[5]

But to do Chaucer and, of course, all of these writers full justice, such interesting evidence of a common cultural background of materials and assumptions must not be elevated into a theory of common literary characteristics which might then be awarded a definitive term, designating a 'school' of writing. Recent attempts to do this have invited us to look hopefully for similar methods and characteristics in poets as diverse as Chaucer, Langland, and the *Gawain*-poet,[6] instead of demonstrating that the major characteristic of literary activity in England from 1350 to 1400 is its capacity to accommodate, in a wide but unified cultural setting, so many different 'norms' of subject-matter, method, and form. Such a capacity it must have inherited, to some degree, from the period immediately preceding it, when English authors expressed themselves in Latin and two vernaculars, and in a variety of literary ways, drawn from many European and more strictly native traditions.[7] It may, indeed, be true that this 'capacity' is the only real 'medieval English tradition' we should propose, and that it was the fifteenth century, with its passion for orthodoxy, formalization, and selection, which first introduced us to the idea of literary norms and schools of writing. It was certainly the fifteenth century which first identified and endorsed a 'Chaucer tradition', making what Chaucer had newly created into established English poetic practice.[8] Meanwhile, we have two lines of evidence from the fourteenth century to argue that certain ways of writing poetry were not wholly respected or liked by certain other poets: but no contemporary comment makes it clear to us that Langland was considered sectarian or old-fashioned for choosing an alliterative metre, nor that Gower's choice of working in three languages was considered unusual. In such circumstances, it seems wiser not to attempt to tie poets together except with those very bonds of mutual tolerance which they themselves seem to have accepted, and which seem to have been accepted by their own 'publishers' and readers.

Given the facts of some shared materials and interests, and of a situation of extreme fluidity in the matter of literary standards and idioms, Chaucer is both allied with and disengaged from his English contemporaries—which is exactly what a reading of *Piers Plowman, Sir Gawain and the Green Knight*, or *Pearl* might lead us to expect. The characteristic of all major fourteenth-century writers (whether of prose or of poetry) is a readiness to experiment with and depart from received forms—*The Cloud of Unknowing, Troilus and Criseyde, Piers Plowman*, and *Patience* are all, in their own ways, unusual and independent works. And this can be their only enduring and appropriate claim to be related to each other, and to that splendidly individualistic period which encompassed, after all, the Bohun manuscripts, the Percy Tomb at Beverley, and the west front of York Minster, with their distinctive versions of that other elusive norm—'late Gothic'.

Even then, we have not properly settled the question of how to relate Chaucer to his 'age'. The examples of Gothic art quoted above were all taken from English tradition, and although to some degree English Gothic is agreed to be 'international' in make-up and calibre, we should be wrong if in trying to approach a definition of Chaucer's particular fourteenth-century role we chose our artistic analogues from an English range alone.

For what, of course, marks Chaucer out from his English contemporaries, in degree and intensity rather than in actual substance, is his far wider knowledge of and far more significant attachment to the literature of Europe—and in particular, to that of Italy. Here we could return, briefly, to the Bohun miniature painting style, and point to the important Italianate elements in its dramatic facial expressiveness, its feeling for strong movement, its experiments with perspective:[9] all of these are, it is true, characteristic of Chaucer's poetry. We could also, however, find them characteristic of Langland's *Piers Plowman*. A Bohun initial detailing Christ on the road to Calvary can be a moving commentary on Langland's Christ—

> 'Pitousliche and pale—as a prisoun that deieth ...'
> (B. XVIII. 58)

as, indeed, it can be of an earlier description of that moment— the lyric of the school of Richard Rolle, 'My dere-worthly derlyng, sa dolefully dyght ...'[10]

But more suggestive analogies, more complex affiliations with the art and literature of fourteenth-century Europe, can be discussed in the case of Chaucer. Granted that a reading acquaintance with Dante as well as with many French romance-writers and dream-allegorists must be assumed for the anonymous poet who is probably responsible for the four works in MS Cotton Nero A.X.,[11] it is still to Chaucer that we must turn if we wish to see the strongest impact of European literature upon a receptive English artist of the later fourteenth century. Though this may seem to be a truism, its full significance has not always been appreciated by Chaucer's admirers and critics. For that 'strong impact' is no guarantee of simplicity of effect; a 'richly receptive artist' is not necessarily an easy artist to account for, or elucidate. Nor, by his nature, is he predominantly and consistently interested in simplicity and coherence of effect. His attempts to come to terms with the multifarious and sometimes contradictory nature of his source-materials may only temporarily lead him to a resolved pattern. But of course, that pattern, when it is arrived at, may be the more strictly designed and adhered to because of the artist's consciousness of the pressure upon him to order the wealth he has at his disposal, and in which he delights.

It is a fairly constant feature of major writing on Chaucer, from Dryden onwards, that it has been reluctant to admit an inability to find answers to all the special problems presented by Chaucer's poetry. And, indeed, it has been expert in minimizing, even disguising those problems. Chaucer criticism still deals in the skilful administering of *placebos* to readers whose own sensibilities must register that Chaucer is characterized among medieval English poets for the extent to which he will allow his ranging materials to pose questions, dictate problematic situations, suggest richly ambiguous characters and scenarios—not all of which can or will be dealt with in the logical formal structure of the total work. We should not, of course, call Chaucer quite 'unique' in these respects, for there is something to be said about 'problems of accommodation' in a medieval poem so frequently and publicly admired for its perfect organization as *Sir Gawain and the Green Knight*. There, the very various kinds of material—original Arthurian legend, sexual temptation-story, inner allegory of faith and purity, rhetorical and descriptive set-pieces—are put together with skill and confidence. But it is interesting that most critics are concerned to explain why there should be no real difficulty for the reader in interpreting the part played by the Green Knight throughout the poem, in reconciling the Green Knight's account of the whole perilous game in which Gawain becomes involved with the hero's own assessment of his deeply and unendingly compromised position as the 'game' closes down.[12] We are mistaken to search always for answers which will absolve medieval poets from the occasional difficulties brought upon them by their creative enthusiasm for coalescing and re-shaping older themes and stories. We have no absolute assurance that the *Gawain*-poet knew what to do with the archetypal Morgan-le-Fay in his newly furbished version of the old narrative, nor can we ever be sure that his action in allowing Sir Gawain to forget, apparently, the presence and efficacy of the magic green girdle as he approaches the terrifying Green Chapel[13] is a deliberate and sophisticated part of the poem's theme or whether it is a plain failure to integrate different parts of the theme—a lack of attention which can be explained by the special nature of medieval literary conditions and literary values.

But the *Gawain*-poet does not present us with dilemmas of the same magnitude as those we find in Chaucer. If he is, in fact, the author of the dream-elegy, *Pearl*, he gives us there a faultless example of control of materials: our sympathies for the desperate, bereaved dreamer, confronted by the dazzling but unapproachable figure of his lost 'litel quene', are never allowed to reach breaking-point. Our tracing of his wilful indulgence of grief and his reformation of will is never made unbearably painful, and the narrator, who is poet, protagonist, and interpreter, keeps us in reasonable approbation of that divine plan illustrated by the human 'fable', even before vision confirms what reason has accepted.[14]

We have already examined some of the motives which impelled a large number of writers, working in many diverse areas, to promote the claims of English over those of French as the prime vernacular of the mid- and later fourteenth century.[15] It will be appropriate, therefore, to remind ourselves that Chaucer's choice of English for his literary language is unlikely to have been a crude nationalistic gesture, a warm-hearted feeling for a strengthening 'native' movement in poetry. It is much more likely to have been inspired by a desire to emulate those famous traditions of France, Burgundy, and Italy, where royal and ducal patronage was already encouraging both translation of Latin works into the vernacular, and the collection of libraries strongly vernacular in emphasis.[16] All of this was, of course, dependent upon a theory of the innate dignity of vernacular language, when used by writers of taste and learning. Some such theory, some such situation, we might point out, must have been responsible for the more elegant English lyric verse of earlier fourteenth-century 'miscellanies'—Harley MS 2253, for instance. But Chaucer's very deliberate act of beginning his poetic career by training his skills as a translator of French shows a freshly awakened preoccupation with English as a fit vehicle for the major works of European literature. It is impossible that Chaucer should not have been familiar with the theory, and the practice, of fourteenth-century Italians, such as Dante and Petrarch, on this question of the use of the vernacular.

A sense of the inadequacies of English for the whole range of high literary purpose, and a determination to amend matters were not, of course, his alone. We have seen, in the preceding chapter, that as early as the 1350s certain alliterative authors were taking very conscious steps to 'augment' and 'enrich' the repertoire of English poetic language—not only by calling upon old, native resources of vocabulary, but by initiating styles and idioms from French and Latin tradition.[17] A little later, the author of *Sir Gawain and the Green Knight* moved in the same direction. But Chaucer's endeavours seem to have been marked by a greater self-consciousness, a greater willingness to comment upon the situation in which he finds himself. His feeling for the importance of poetic composition, for its high lineage, for the responsibility of poet and scribe to ensure correct transmission, is given expression, and in a way which forces us to consider what he knew, in particular, of Italian precedent.

The amusing, but somewhat rueful juxtapositions, for instance, in *The House of Fame*, argue a poet who is humorously, but also properly conscious of the strain to which he would like to subject English verse form and style. The *Proems* to the various Books move from jocular 'minstrel'-type appeals

> 'Now herkeneth, every maner man
> That Englissh understonde kan ...'
>
> (ll. 509-10)

to elevated dedications—

> 'And ye, me to endite and ryme
> Helpeth, that on Parnaso duelle,
> Be Elicon, the clere welle ...'
>
> (ll. 520-2)

The *Proem* to the third, unfinished Book is both apologetic and aspirant: its Dantesque echoes are strong—it looks to Apollo, while it disclaims that very skill it still seeks to achieve:

> 'Nat that I wilne, for maistrye,
> Here art poetical be shewed:
> But for the rym ys lyght and lewed,
> Yit make hyt sumwhat agreable ...'
>
> (ll. 1094-7)

The House of Fame is only a half-serious work, in which stylistic experiments are conducted, sometimes in consonance with the nature of the subject-matter—

> Thoo atte last aspyed y
> That pursevantes and heraudes,
> That crien ryche folkes laudes,
> Hyt weren alle; and every man
> Of hem, as y yow tellen can,
> Had on him throwen a vesture
> Which that men clepe a cote-armure,
> Enbrowded wonderliche ryche
>
> (ll. 1320-7)

and sometimes at variance—

> Telle me this now feythfully,
> Have y not preved thus symply,
> Withoute any subtilite
> Of speche, or gret prolixite
> Of termes of philosophie,
> Of figures of poetrie,
> Or colours of rethorike?
>
> (ll. 853-9)

It has been asserted that in certain respects the poem is reminiscent of the livelier conversational moments of those earlier English romance narratives which Chaucer could easily have read, but which he certainly—in his *Ryme of Sir Thopas*, for instance—held in scant 'official' respect.[18] This may indeed be so, but the over-all character of the work argues a basic instability of attitude—an uneasy desire to capitalize upon what is old and familiar, and, at the same time, to embark upon trials of strength in pursuit of what is new and alien, without any very clear sense of where such ambitious behaviour will lead. In this sense, the *House of Fame* is a sacrifice, although not a painful one, to the principle of free experiment in composition which engrossed Chaucer from the very start of his career and which accounts for all of the most interesting, if not the neatest, of his works.

His hope for some kind of prestigious acclaim, not only on behalf of his alliance with a 'heroic' and 'tragic' tradition of subject-matter, but also on behalf of his attempt to place an *English* poem in that tradition, is clearly expressed in two stanzas of *Troilus and Criseyde*: here now, in entirely sober juxtaposition, come the aspiring thought and the despairingly modest disclaimer. The poem is, on European but especially Italian precedent,[19] associated, however tremblingly, with the great verse-writings of the past; the anxiety of the poet is to excuse his modest vernacular imitation, and yet, simultaneously, to present it as an act of faith in the eventual status to be won by that vernacular—a status of which stability and dignity are twin properties:

> But litel book, no makyng thow n'envie,
> But subgit be to alle poesye;
> And kis the steppes, where as thow seest pace
> Virgile, Ovide, Omer, Lucan, and Stace.
>
> And for ther is so gret diversite
> In Englissh and in writyng of oure tonge,
> So prey I God that non myswrite the,
> Ne the mysmetre for defaute of tonge.
>
> (V. 1789-96)

Even that curious insistence of Chaucer upon a fictitious
Latin source for his *Troilus and Criseyde*—

> The whiche cote, as telleth Lollius,
> Deiphebe it hadde rent fro Diomede ...
>
> (V. 1653-4)

may not so much prove an ambivalent, even shamefaced regard
for the vernacular nature of the Italian sources he was, in fact,
using, as a desire, perhaps, to equate the importance of his
activity with that of Boccaccio, who, though he personally in-
vented the whole of the first half of the Troilus and Criseyde
story, did build upon a series of earlier authors, some of them
Latin.[20] It is as if the situation of the English poet had to be
seen to be broadly comparable with that of the greatest European vernacular writers: a relationship between a chosen language and the Latin of tradition—which was enhancing rather
than exact in its implications. No doubt Chaucer remembered
words such as those with which Boccaccio bade farewell to his
Teseida:

> ma tu, o libro, primo a lor cantare
> di Marte fai gli affanni sostenuti,
> nel volgar lazio più mai non veduti.
>
> E perciò che tu primo col tuo legno
> seghi queste onde, non solcate mai
> davanti a te da nessuno altro ingegno,
> ben che infimo sii, pure starai
> forse tra gli altri d'alcuno onor degno; ...
>
> le vaghe nostre vele qui caliamo,
> e le ghirlande e i don meritati,
> con l'ancore fermati, qui spettiamo ...
>
> (XII, st. 84-6)[21]

But you, oh my book, are the first to make the Muses sing the lofty
struggles of Mars in the common tongue. And since you are the first
to plough these waves, perhaps you will stand worthy of honour ...
Here we lower our wandering sails, and having dropped anchor here
await the garlands and gifts that are due.

The final dedication of his poem to Strode and Gower, two
competent Latinists, and the translation of the last stanza from
the most highly-esteemed vernacular poet of the whole Middle

Ages, Dante,[22] are double 'status' assurances, both equally important. And for all this, in the poem as a whole nothing impeded Chaucer's independent handling of his material, just as nothing impeded Boccaccio in his free inventive range over the whole Troilus story.

The fact that Chaucer's alignments are with a variety of European modes of art and thought should prepare us to find in his work a wealthy complexity of form, content, and attitude. Such discoveries are not always easily assimilable into orthodox critical theory, but they do, nevertheless, help to define the way in which Chaucer stands out from his English contemporaries, and, ultimately, the way in which he creates English tradition, rather than conforms to any existing native pattern.

This is already quite unmistakeable in his early dream-poem, the *Parlement of Foules*, which draws upon a number of well-known medieval texts, Latin, Italian, and French, for its materials, making out of them not a single-toned, unified composition, but one which admits some dissonance to its loose-knit harmonies. His presentation, for instance, of the court and palace of Venus, within the 'park, walled with grene ston' to which he is led in his dream, is both rich and, in the context of the whole poem, ambiguous. It is worthwhile to inquire why this is so. Most writers on the *Parlement* are sure that Chaucer held particular orthodox medieval views on the significance of the goddess Venus, and that his account is based firmly upon the belief that she 'represents the misdirection and corruption of a desire originally natural and good'. He is describing what he 'deplored', but 'beautiful evil is still beautiful':[23]

> And in a prive corner in disport
> Fond I Venus and hire porter Richesse,
> That was ful noble and hautayn of hyre port.
> Derk was that place, but afterward lightnesse
> I saw a lyte, unnethe it myghte be lesse,
> And on a bed of gold she lay to reste,
> Til that the hote sonne gan to west.
>
> Hyre gilte heres with a golden thred
> Ibounden were, untressed as she lay,
> And naked from the brest unto the hed
> Men myghte hire sen; and, sothly for to say,

> The remenaunt was wel kevered to my pay,
> Ryght with a subtyl coverchef of Valence—
> Ther nas no thikkere cloth of no defense.
>
> (*Parlement*, ll. 260-73)

But the necessity for convincing ourselves that Chaucer is here describing 'what he deplores' is based not so much upon the actual words he uses as upon a hypothesis about the logic and consistency of the poem's argument.

If, indeed, in his brief account of the book he was reading before he fell asleep, 'Tullyus of the Drem of Scipioun',[24] Chaucer intended to give strong direction for the theme of his own dream-vision, we should have very good grounds for thinking that this amorous corner of the walled garden simply illustrates certain statements which Chaucer found in the old Latin text, and strengthened by his recollection of Dante's treatment of the lustful in the second circle of Hell.[25] In Chaucer's version, Scipio asks his grandfather, the elder Scipio, for advice on 'the weye to come into that hevene blisse' (line 72), and receives clear moral precept:

> And he seyde, 'Know thyself first immortal,
> And loke ay besyly thow werche and wysse
> To commune profit, and thow shalt not mysse
> To comen swiftly to that place deere
> That ful of blysse is and of soules cleere.
>
> But brekers of the lawe, soth to seyne,
> And likerous folk, after that they ben dede,
> Shul whirle about th'erthe alwey in peyne,
> Tyl many a world be passed, out of drede ...'
>
> (ll. 73-81)

What follows, in the English poet's dream, might then be said to exemplify, generally, those two categories of human existence, with Nature, 'vicaire of the almyghty Lord' (l. 379), and Venus as presiding deities. It is, however, one thing to predict a possible moral theme for a poem by Chaucer, and another to find it consistently carried through, in terms not only of content, but also of tone. This is precisely illustrated by the very opening events of the dream, as the elder Scipio, now for a second time the dream-guide, leads the poet to the gate of the park; for a poem which may be about to deal with virtuous law-abiders and lecherous law-breakers, the inscription over the gate is curiously out of key. It reminds us not so much of a world of clear moral contrasts, as of the delicious and terrifying world of *fin'amor* where pain and pleasure are paradoxically joined, and where the lover risks himself to experience, not necessarily to happiness:

> 'Thorgh me men gon into that blysful place
> Of hertes hele and dedly woundes cure;
> Thorgh me men gon unto the welle of grace,
> There grene and lusty May shal evere endure ...'

> 'Thorgh me men gon', than spak that other side,
> 'Unto the mortal strokes of the spere
> Of which Disdayn and Daunger is the gyde ...'
>
> (ll. 127-30, 134-6)

At this point, it is Chaucer's distance from the moral seriousness of Dante, describing a similar situation, which must impress us: if he borrows the motif of the poet led by an august guide to an awesomely inscribed gate from the *Inferno* (III. 1-9), he borrows nothing of its original significance. This is a different medieval context, and one, in fact, in which we might more reasonably expect to be confronted by Venus and her court of paradoxical joys than by figures representing the 'two ways' of man's life on earth, according to Christian doctrine. What we notice is a shift of attention and emphasis: the episode at the gate does not develop logically out of introductory proposals, but has a tangential quality. It preserves the *idea* of contrast, already promoted, but it changes its nature and its meaning. We might well, from the general flavour of the passage, as well as from specific statements—

> 'For this writyng nys nothyng ment bi the,
> Ne by non, but he Loves servaunt be ...'
>
> (ll. 158-9)

suspect that when the park does yield up its goddess of love, it will not do so in any strict moral context of good and evil, punishment and reward, and certainly not in a setting designed to clarify the corrupt finalities associated with this 'misdirected desire'. What has replaced that earlier unequivocal attitude to human behaviour and human destiny is an attitude of greater

objectivity; the dreamer senses, as lover and poet, and not
without some shivering anticipation, the richness rather than
the simplicity of the garden's promises. He is invited to approach experience, with all its exciting contraries—

> 'For with that oon encresede ay my fere,
> And with that other gan myn herte bolde;
> That oon me hette, that other dide me colde'—
>
> (ll. 143-5)

and also to use the materials of his observation in the service of
salvation, and 'hevene blisse':

> 'And if thow haddest connyng for t'endite,
> I shal the shewe mater of to wryte.'
>
> (ll. 167-8)

For his description of Venus, in a paradisal landscape,
Chaucer turned to Boccaccio's *Teseida*, augmenting it from
Boccaccio's own primary source, the *Roman de la Rose*, and, in
two cases, from lines of Dante.[26] The nature of the Italian original is important here, for Chaucer transferred to his English
version not only a great deal of Boccaccio's material but also
something of his approach to that material: he is indebted, in
current medieval terminology, for *sens* as well as *matiere*. In the
Teseida the Venus episode forms part of the narrative dealing
with the sacrifices and prayers of the three lovers, Palamon,
Arcita, and Emilia, to their respective deities. Palamon's
prayer seeks out his goddess, Venus, in a garden set among
pine-trees, on Mount Cithaeron: escorted by Desire, the
prayer moves through a familiar earthly paradise, which fills
her with eager admiration—'rimirando ... dell'alto loco e del
bello ornamento' (VII, st. 53), 'wondering at the noble place
and its fine lay-out'. There is, in fact, no reason inherent in the
narrative why Boccaccio's goddess, in her high garden, should
be regarded with anything but 'admiration'. The poem
presents three aspirant human beings, three sponsoring deities,
and the problem of which will prevail. The interest of that
problem would be diminished by comment in the poetry upon
good, evil, justice, or tyranny as represented by the gods.[27] All
that is needed is an impressive account of their various powers;
this Boccaccio gives in some detail, but in the neutral manner

of one who is not called upon to judge or interpret, but rather to describe and celebrate.

So, whatever his opinion of Venus outside the particular limits of this section of the poem, he records her appearance, qualities, and behaviour in an elaborate tableau, and in an elaborate garden setting, with the very slightest hints of moral directive to the reader. As in Chaucer's English version, the garden is of unblemished, ideal beauty:

> Con la quale oltre andando, vide quello
> ad ogni vista soave e ameno,
> in guisa d'un giardin fronzuto e bello
> e di piante verdissime ripieno,
> d'erbette fresche e d'ogni fior novello,
> e fonti vide chiare vi surgeno,
> e intra l'altre piante onde abondava,
> mortine più che altro le sembiava.
>
> (VII, st. 51)

Going further with her, the Prayer saw sights that were sweet and pleasant in the shape of a beautiful, leafy garden, full of the greenest plants, and fresh new grass, and of every kind of spring flower: among the plentiful plants, amongst which myrtle seemed to abound more than anything else, clear fountains had their springs ...

All kinds of birds and gentle animals inhabit the garden: birdsong and instrumental music fill the air. Then the approaches to the temple of Venus begin to reveal those tableaux which present, in allegorical form, the life of devotion to Venus: the presence of figures such as 'Voluttà' (Pleasure), 'Ozio' (Idleness), 'Van Diletto' (Imaginary Delight), and 'Lusinghe' (Flattery) (st. 54-6), among groups which also include Cupid, Memory, Elegance, Affability, Courtesy, Refinement ('Gentilezza'), Beauty, and Youth, should not surprise anyone familiar with the ingredients of the courtly love-philosophies of the high Middle Ages. Boccaccio, indeed, goes so far as to include more sinister personifications—with Flattery walk 'il folle Ardire ... e Ruffiania ...' (Foolhardiness and Procurement) (st. 56). But we should not conclude that this is a simple condemnation of Venus and her 'doctrine', any more than we should take the five black arrows of the God of Love, in the *Roman de la Rose*—Pride, Churlishness, Shame, Despair, Unfaithfulness[28]—to be the inbuilt ineradicable flaws in his code of amorous behaviour. Rather, they point to the possible dangers, the sins against the laws of love which Youth, hand-in-hand with Beauty and Pleasure, will do well to avoid: Boccaccio sees the two groups in the same garden, but he sees them separately, just as Guillaume de Lorris distinguishes Love's golden arrows of Beauty, Honesty, Generosity, Companionship, and Fair-Countenance from his five arrows of darker import:[29]

> Poi presso a sé vide passar Bellezza
> sanza ornamento alcun, sé riguardando;
> e gir con lei vide Piacevolezza,
> e l'una e l'altra seco commendando;
> poi con lor vide starsi Giovanezza,
> destra e adorna, molto festeggiando;
> e d'altra parte vide il folle Ardire,
> Lusinghe e Ruffiania insieme gire.

> (VII, st. 56)

Then nearby she saw Beauty pass, without any ornament, looking at herself: with her went Pleasure, each paying compliments to the other. Upright, well-dressed Youth accompanied them, making merry. And on the other side she saw Foolhardiness, Flattery, and Procurement, walking together.

It is important to register the tone of the passage. Boccaccio observes, but he does not—at least, in his poetry—comment: he takes an essentially cool view, if warmth of moral indignation is what we are expecting. Warmth is certainly there, but it relates mainly to the poet's enthusiasm for the decorative elegance of the scene. In fact, he gives some indication of this when he tells us of Palemone's prayer 'wondering at the noble place and its beautiful adornments', 'rimirando, in sé sospesa alquanto,/ dell'alto loco e del bello ornamento' (st. 53).

The description of the temple of Venus is similarly angled towards the gratifying of wonder rather than moral curiosity. The nature of the passion celebrated is never disguised, but the poetry deals in exposition and not in criticism. Thus it is no surprise to find Priapus, representing crude sexual appetite, presiding in the flower-garlanded, sigh-filled hall of altars, while Venus, sexual appetite refined and beautified by legend, history, and art, lies in a perfumed inner oratory, her body glimmering in the half-light:

il luogo vide oscur nel primo gire;
ma poca luce poscia per lo stare
vi prese, e vide lei nuda giacere
sopr'un gran letto assai bello a vedere.

Ella avea d'oro i crini e rilegati
intorno al capo sanza treccia alcuna;
il suo viso era tal, che' più lodati
hanno e rispetto bellezza nessuna;
le braccia e 'l petto e' pomi rilevati
si vedean tutti, e l'altra parte d'una
veste tanto sottil si ricopria,
che quasi nulla appena nascondia.

(VII, st. 64-5)

the place seemed dark as she first went in, but, after a while she could
make out a little light, and saw Venus lying naked on a large, most
beautiful bed. She had golden hair, bound softly about her head; her
face was such that, in comparison, those lauded for beauty have no
beauty at all. Her arms and breast and rounded apples were bare to
the gaze, and the rest of her was covered with a garment so thin that
practically nothing was hidden.

Alien as it may seem to later standards of taste, the existence of
Priapus and Venus under one roof offends more for what may
seem its bland association of the ludicrous and the serious than
for its destructive gloss on the character of 'love'. As Boccaccio
presents his microcosmic lover's universe, calamity is figured
in various aspects, some more grotesque than others. Frus-
trated and fulfilled desire is the double theme of the life dedicated to Venus, as is also the powerful force of passion, whether
manifested in beauty or ugliness. Boccaccio elaborates this with
significant imagery, but he is certainly not preparing his
readers to look upon Venus and see only Priapic lust. It is indicative of the tone of the episode that Palemone's prayer moves
eagerly through the temple observing everything, and goes in
to Venus 'sanz'altro rispetto, / in abito quale era mansueta'
(st. 63), 'without further hesitation, in a humble manner'.
What she sees is a goddess far removed from the Venus of some
northern European writers—of Guillaume de Deguilleville,
who portrays in his *Pélérinage* a woman defouled with dung and
clay, riding on a fierce boar;[30] of the anonymous *Echecs*

Amoureux, translated by the English monk, John Lydgate, as *Reson and Sensualite*:

> Venus was fresh and yonge of age
> And passyng fair of hir visage ...
> For, finaly, to hir servise
> She drough al tho by violence
> Swich as kam in hir presence,
> Benigne of port, wyth chere smyling,
> Hyr eyen glade ay laughyng,
> Lyght of corage, of wil chaungable,
> Selde or never founde stable ...
> Queynte of array, who lyst take hede,
> A cote y-lacyd al of rede,
> Rycher than outher silke or golde ...
> But wel I wot, men myghte se
> Hir shappe throgh-out, so was it maked,
> Lych as she had in soth be naked ...
> And hild also in hir ryght honde,
> Rede as a kole, a firy bronde ... [31]

There is no fear that Lydgate's reader might be seduced, except under conditions of duress, by this laughing, restless, brand-threatening woman: the poet makes sure that his moral position is firm and inviolable. Not so Boccaccio, whose poetry here rests upon moral neutrality to create a vision of delicacy and ripeness, that ideal of sensuous grace which Botticelli would later present as his lightly veiled deities of love and spring, Venus and Flora. The rest of the description confirms this: Venus is attended by figures symbolizing sensuous fruition—Bacchus and Ceres, 'con li suoi savori', 'with their sweet gifts' (st. 66). She extends with one hand a welcome to the arts of sexual invitation, 'e essa seco per la man tenea / Lascivia', 'she herself held wantonness by one hand', and with the other hand she reminds us of her triumph in the Valley of Ida, when she was preferred to her sisters for her great beauty:

> ... e 'l pomo il quale, alle sorori
> prelata, vinse nella valle idea.

> (st. 66)

The air is heavy with 'mille odori', 'a thousand scents', but certainly not with 'disapproval'. The literal and symbolic detail, the mythological references convey richness and excitement in a sexual context. There is no gloss in the poetry itself.[32]

And if it is true that only later, in Botticelli's lifetime, did the moment come when 'the image gained ascendancy over the text, Venus conquered her commentators',[33] at least in the *Teseida* we can sense the possibility of such a moment. Boccaccio's attitude to Venus as revealed in his notes to the *Teseida* may be morally impeccable: it was not, however, given total control of the imagination in his poetry.

We should, I think, underestimate the quality of Chaucer's taste and perception if we assumed that he was not attracted by any of these things when he made use of Boccaccio's stanzas on Venus for the *Parlement of Foules*. Many medieval texts (*Les Echecs Amoureux*, for instance) could have provided him with a portrait of the goddess of love, inspired by some feeling for the dazzle as well as the evil of her nature. But Boccaccio's version was incomparable for that clarity of atmosphere, which allowed decorative beauty to be seen in sharp, distinct form. Momentarily, perhaps, but significantly, the artist showed his interest in the shape of beauty, rather than in its meaning. And there is very little evidence that Chaucer felt the necessity to remould the Italian in any very important way. The changes he makes sometimes heighten Boccaccio's effects: his garden is more explicitly paradisal, in its unchanging temperate climate, its constant daylight, its gifts of eternal youth and vigour:

> Th'air of that place so attempre was
> That nevere was ther grevaunce of hot ne cold;
> There wex ek every holsom spice and gras;
> No man may there waxe sek ne old;
> Yit was there joye more a thousandfold
> Than man can telle; ne nevere wolde it nyghte,
> But ay cler day to any manes syghte.
>
> (ll. 204-10)

But nothing in the English poem hints at the unsuitability of Cupid, Venus, and their court for such a setting. The dreamer discovers, as naturally as did Palemone's prayer, Cupid 'under a tre, besyde a welle' (l. 211), forging his arrows. Moreover, he is 'Cupide, oure lord': the dreamer's mood is of reverent acceptance,[34] in harmony with that of the Italian. At times he even seems to be anxious to remove what might be hastily interpreted as moral comment in Boccaccio's text: 'Van Diletto', 'Imaginary Delight' appears simply as 'Delyt, that stod with Gentilesse' (l. 224): he shies from the Italian 'Ruffiania', 'Procurement', translating it into milder component parts—'Desyr, / Messagerye, and Meede' (ll. 227-8), as if he hesitates to draw the reader's attention to it. Priapus still holds his place of eminence 'in swich aray as whan the asse hym shente ...' (l. 255), but now wreathed with 'freshe floures newe ...' (l. 259) from those gardens over which, in other contexts,[35] he presides. Boccaccio's juxtaposition of Venus with wantonness, or sexual invitation—'e essa seco per la man tenea / Lascivia ...' ('She held wantonness by the hand ...')— he appears to ignore completely. And while he accepts the presence of Bacchus and Ceres at her side, it is the role of Ceres as healer of hunger, symbol of fruition rather than of excessive appetite,[36] which he stresses:

> 'And Ceres next, that doth of hunger boote...'
>
> (l. 276)

His rendering of Boccaccio's painterly description of Venus, as the eye first makes her out in the dusky room, is a magnificent tribute to the qualities of the Italian. No breath of criticism disturbs the still scene; the sensuous atmosphere is perfectly indicated by the gold of the bed, the gold thread in the goddess's hair, and the golden heat outside the temple:

> Derk was that place, but afterward lightnesse,
> I saw a lyte, unnethe it myghte be lesse,
> And on a bed of gold she lay to reste,
> Til that the hote sonne gan to weste.
>
> Hyre gilte heres with a golden thred
> Ibounden were, untressed as she lay,
> And naked from the brest unto the hed
> Men myghte hire sen; ...   (ll. 263-70)

The imitation, by Chaucer, of Boccaccio's attitude to his material is very well illustrated by one short addition to the account of the trophies hung on the walls of the temple: the broken bows of chastity belonging to the followers of Diana, 'maydenes swiche as gonne here tymes waste / In hyre servyse

...' (ll. 283-4). Whatever Chaucer privately thought of the respective virtues of Diana and Venus, in these lines of poetry he writes from the centre of the episode, as suggested by Boccaccio, and presents us with the concept of the wastefulness of chastity. Indeed, it is easy to see how his comment would have arisen. Boccaccio's three examples (st. 61) of women whose bows were broken and hung in the temple—Calisto and the two Atalantas—are given not in any spirit of sad resignation to the misery of their fate. It is, rather, the triumph of love as it is reflected in their stories which seems to preoccupy him—the one immortalized as a constellation, the second ultimately vanquished by the golden apples of Aphrodite, the third destined to become the mother of 'the fair Parthenopaeus, grandson of Oenus of Calidon'.[37] The long list of famous lovers who figure in the temple paintings, enlarged out of Boccaccio by reference to many possible medieval lists, including perhaps that of Dante in the *Inferno* (V. 58-9), reads less as if it is presented as a fuller illustration of Dante's 'hell of the lustful' than as an illustration, impressive both pictorially and poetically, of the wide-ranging power of love. The equivalent stanza in the *Teseida* makes explicit reference to the artistic excellence of the wall-paintings:

> Videvi istorie per tutto dipinte,
> intra le quai, con piu alto lavoro, ...
>
> (st. 62)

She saw stories everywhere depicted ... with the finest workmanship.

And it is only the final words of Chaucer's stanza—'and in what plyte they dyde ...' (l. 294)—which dubiously allow critics to re-interpret his description in the light of the *Divina Commedia* rather than in the light of his Italian source.

A later poet, whose knowledge of Chaucer's minor works was extensive, returned to the old theme of the temple of Delight, with its inhabitants, Beauty, Sadness, Pleasure, Death:[38]

> She dwells with Beauty—Beauty that must die;
> And Joy, whose hand is ever at his lips,
> Bidding adieu; and aching Pleasure nigh,
> Turning to poison while the bee-mouth sips.

> Ay, in the very temple of Delight
> Veiled Melancholy has her sovrain shrine,
> Though seen of none save him whose strenuous tongue
> Can burst Joy's grape against his palate fine;
> His soul shall taste the sadness of her might,
> And be among her cloudy trophies hung.

The emphases in this last stanza of Keats's *Ode to Melancholy* are different from those of either Boccaccio or Chaucer: his conclusions are distanced from theirs by the advanced nature of his aesthetic. But more than a little of the spirit of the two fourteenth-century passages has gone to the making of the *Ode*. If the two medieval poets, Chaucer and Boccaccio, could not have said so directly, they did celebrate the sadness and the beauty of love with reference to its power and privilege and not, as was more usual at their time, to its place in a divinely ordained scheme of reward and punishment. Such a scheme had, of course, formed part of the prefatory announcements of Chaucer's poem, but it is impossible to regard the Venus episode in the dream-garden as no more than an expressive treatment of 'lykerous folk', 'lecherous creatures' and their ways.[39] By going to the *Teseida* for his inspiration Chaucer turned aside from simple moral material, and by choosing not to modify the Italian greatly he put the thematic consistency of his own poem at magnificent risk—no doubt for the sake of the great descriptive and imaginative opportunities which the *Teseida* offered him.

Something similar could also have been offered to him by the secular art of Italy at this time. We shall never know what he saw of Italian wall-painting on his visits to Florence, Milan, and Genoa in the seventies and eighties of the fourteenth century. But it is worth recording that the theme of pain and beauty not only compounded but reconciled in human love was already being treated by Italian artists in ways more sophisticated than northern Europe could demonstrate. Chamber-paintings such as those from the northern castle of Avio present figures from courtly life kneeling and standing, perfectly calm, yet pierced, literally, with the arrows of desire.[40] The allegorical element in the design is still quite strong—as it is also in the poetry of Boccaccio and Chaucer—but the absence of warning commentary, the stress upon the happy acceptance of the wound of love, the evident pleasure taken in depicting the finely clothed, gracefully posed 'servants of love' all combine to celebrate a theme which feeds the imagination more than it satisfies the reason.

It is entirely in keeping with what we later come to recognize as a characteristic procedure of his that Chaucer moves his dreamer without comment or pause from the temple and its surroundings to the outdoor 'council chamber' of the goddess Nature. And it never becomes clear—so summary is the location of this leafy palace—whether the paradisal garden, so lovingly detailed as the dreamer moves towards the temple of Venus, has any very significant and functional relationship with Dame Nature and her comprehensive feathered parliament.[41] As we know, the garden initially belonged to the Venus episode, and was imported wholesale into the English poem. It seems amusingly typical of Chaucer that by the time he reaches the real 'open-air' section of his work, he has lost interest in it and only briefly refers to it as 'the place / That I of spak, that was so sote and grene' (ll. 295-6). For the rest of the poem, he will be concerned with love-debate of a particularly varied and lively kind, innovating brilliantly upon a familiar French literary genre. The garden, with its properties of enclosure, exclusiveness, and concentration,[42] is hardly necessary to the occasion, or to the argument. In fact, it is interesting to observe, looking back over the poem, that Chaucer's heightening of Boccaccio's garden of Venus into an explicitly paradisal area, immune from all kinds of change, was obviously prompted by an excited association of the Italian garden with other famous medieval love-paradises,[43] and not by a careful strategy, anticipating the appearance of Nature, God's deputy. He has begun to neglect the immutable loveliness of the garden even so early as his description of the languid Venus, waiting for the hot sun to sink to the west (l. 266)—a felicitous, though, in the context, illogical mark of her sensual ease. Nature's lightly sketched garden is even more urgently subject to the diurnal movement of the planets; this is no earthly paradise, but the real world, where business is pressing, and nightfall puts an end to open-air discussion:

> And from the morwe gan this speche laste,
> Tyl dounward drow the sonne wonder faste.

> The noyse of foules for to ben delyvered
> So loude rong, 'Have don, and lat us wende!'...
>
> (ll. 489-92)

The encircling wall of 'grene ston', with its forbidding and enticing gate, has disappeared, and Nature's creatures fly without hindrance to their occupations.

We need not labour the point that the *Parlement of Foules* is a mosaic of source-materials, influences, and creative interests were it not that its unity of theme and execution is so often insisted upon.[44] By attributing to it an unnatural and quite un-Chaucerian neatness, we deprive the poet of recognition for those more exhilarating qualities which should mark his particular eminence in a period distinguished by fine English writing. For it is, above all, adventurousness, prompted by an appetite for what many of the great European traditions had to offer, which characterizes Chaucer at his best. Here, in the *Parlement of Foules*, the poet is still an emergent artist, but something characteristic of his future can be glimpsed.

6 Chaucer and Boccaccio: *The Knight's Tale*

And that future was to allow for at least one full-scale attempt to recast the *Teseida*—as the *Knight's Tale* in the Canterbury collection. It is instructive to watch Chaucer at work upon the *Teseida* again, utilizing the whole poem in very different ways, for very different purposes, but encouraged, even when diverging from or rejecting his source, by those special qualities of energy, passionate feeling, curiosity, and restlessness which made Boccaccio's poetry so influential upon European writers of his own and following centuries. For not only did Chaucer receive from Boccaccio important principles about the composition of poetry in the vernacular; he could not have avoided learning something from him, also, about independence of procedure, and the operation of individual judgement, even about the projection of the author's individuality, whether partly fictitious or not, into his verse. There is nothing contradictory in the idea that poems such as the *Teseida* and the *Filostrato*, acting in an exemplary role, taught Chaucer how to develop his own characteristic methods and approaches at the same time as they provided him with material to imitate exactly. Their rich mixture of poetic genres and styles, of subject-matters, their wide range of viewpoint, from that of the professional artist to that of the personally involved lover, their intimation of many legitimately held attitudes towards the life of man at war, man in love, man faced by the working of Fate and the Gods—all helped to foster in Chaucer not simply the desire to translate, but to create afresh, on the basis of their authority. If the English poems which resulted are sometimes more remarkable for their aspiration than for their steadiness of purpose and consistency of execution, it is not, on balance, very surprising. Chaucer, like his Knight, had 'a large feeld to ere' (*K.T.*, l. 886), and although he does not need the modest disclaimer of competence which he allowed to his pilgrim-character, 'and wayke been the oxen in my plough' (l. 887), he does need recognition for his ambitious understanding of the nature of his task.

No other English medieval poet had such a complex pattern of indebtedness and independence in his relationship with major sources. In the *Parlement of Foules*, Chaucer turned to the *Teseida* for a descriptive set-piece on Venus and her 'court'— not so much integrating it with the thematic content of the poem as incorporating it as an episode, sensuous and self-sufficient, in the leisurely narrative of the dream-vision. Some of the problems which emerged in this process have to do with the gods and their dealings with human affairs. In this particular context Boccaccio treats the power of Venus as a matter for wonder and admiration; Chaucer, in his turn, conveys much more than a little of the atmosphere of the Italian to his English version—at some risk to other doctrines about life and love, expressed elsewhere in the *Parlement*. It is, therefore, an encapsulated section of the *Teseida*, brought over almost too intact, which complicates the argument of the *Parlement*. But when Chaucer began to rework the whole of the *Teseida*, critically and appreciatively, it became possible for him to combine many different courses of action.

Every study of the *Knight's Tale* tells us that Chaucer reduced the immense length of the *Teseida* to roughly a quarter of its size, and that out of a romantic epic with pseudo-classical machinery he produced a medieval romance. Taking into account the possibility that an earlier translation was pressed into service as the Knight's 'Canterbury Tale',[1] part of what he did to the Italian may have been suggested by the framework for which the English was intended. The Canterbury-pilgrimage setting, and the semi-dramatic link-up with a chivalric narrator would have made a good deal of the *Teseida* unusable. There are, however, reasons for thinking that the allocation of the story of Palemone and Arcita to the Knight of the *Canterbury Tales* could never have been more than an initial and, after that, intermittent motive force in Chaucer's treatment of the *Teseida*. One of the most significant areas in which change is worked is that which concerns the subject of Gods and men. As a broad generalization, it would be true to say that what is mainly a narrative element in Boccaccio's poem becomes a thematic element in Chaucer's *Knight's Tale*. Chaucer grows interested in the *idea* of man and his subjection to the dictates of the Gods, whereas Boccaccio is content to enrich the story of that subjection with rhetorical and descriptive colour. Where Boccaccio deals in the lament, Chaucer sometimes deals in the protest; where Boccaccio proposes little more than an outlet to sorrow in renewed action, Chaucer attempts a philosophical justification of man's suffering. Predictably, the *Knight's Tale* gains in pathetic, dramatic, and imaginative appeal, but this in itself frequently amounts to a painful commentary upon Boccaccio's narrative and makes heavy demands of Chaucer when he comes finally to the point of resolution and reconciliation.

It is easy to see, on the one hand, how the *Teseida* provided Chaucer with materials and motifs for development, and, on the other, how he altered their significance—sometimes setting them in new contexts and groupings, sometimes angling and supporting them quite differently. The motifs of the instability of Fortune and the enmity of the Gods are already present in the Italian—the first running throughout the poem, referred to often by the principal characters and by the poet himself, and the second accepted as a premiss, a main-spring of part, at least, of the action. Thus Juno's hatred of Thebes—an illogical consequence of Jove's infidelities in that city—is seen to be instrumental in its destruction, and in the wretched afflictions of the two Theban captives, Palemone and Arcita; the third book opens with

> Poi che alquanto il furor de Iunone
> fu per Tebe distrutta temperato ...

The anger of Juno was somewhat lessened after the destruction of Thebes ...

> (*Teseida*, III, st. 1)

And Arcita, banished from Athens, takes a pessimistic view of Juno's continual intervention in his life and that of Palemone:

> E oltre a ciò l'iddii ne sono avversi :
> come tu sai, antica nimistate
> serva Giunon ver noi, e diè perversi
> mali a color che passar questa etate;

e noi ancor perseguendo ha somersi,
come tu vedi, in infelicitate
estrema; e Ercul né Bacco n'aiuta,
per che io tengo mia vita perduta.

(*Teseida*, III, st. 66)

Besides, the gods are unfriendly: As you know, Juno nurses an ancient grudge against us, and has inflicted spiteful injuries on those who went before us. She persecutes us still, and has overwhelmed us with utmost misfortune. Hercules, Bacchus help her—and for this reason, I consider my life lost.

The relationship between the persecutions of the Gods and the unpredictable acts of the 'alta ministra', Fortune (VI, st. 1), is not very clearly articulated; Arcita and Palemone feel themselves to be tormented by both kinds of power, and it could be assumed, if rather loosely from the poetry, that Fortune is envisaged as the instrument of divine pleasure and displeasure. Palemone and Arcita curse 'la malizia / dello' nfortunio loro', 'the spite of their misfortune' (III, st. 3); Arcita, when he is freed but banished from Athens by Teseo, sees his life driven forward by 'l'adirata fortuna', 'angry fortune' (III, st. 76); and Boccaccio himself, in one memorable sequence, meditates on the dramatic vicissitudes in the history of his two heroes, all brought about by Fortune:

L'alta ministra del mondo Fortuna,
con volubile moto permutando
di questo in quel più volte ciascheduna
cosa togliendo e tal volta donando,
or mostrandosi chiara e ora bruna
secondo le pareva e come e quando,
avea co' suoi effetti a' due Tebani
mostrato ciò che può ne' ben mondani.

(*Teseida*, VI, st. 1)

Fortune, that lofty governess of the world, who changes one thing into another over and over, with her inconstant movements, giving and taking away, now showing bright and now dark, as and how and when it suits her, had showed what power she had over worldly things through her treatment of the two Thebans.

His conclusions, after reviewing their capture, imprisonment, falling in love, their deprivations, the one banished, the other a captive, their illegal duel, their condemnation by Teseo and their eventual pardon, are full of amazement and uncertainty: what can be said in the face of such power?

> Deh, chi fia qui che dica che'mondani
> provvedimenti a' moti di costei
> possan mai porger argomenti sani?
> Se non fosse mal detto, io dicerei
> certo che fosser tutti quanti vani,
> questo mirando e ciò ch'ancor di lei
> si legge e ode e vede ognora aperto,
> ben che ne sia come ciò fa coverto.
>
> (*Teseida*, VI, st. 5)

Now who would say here that worldly prudence can explain her movements with sound arguments? I would say, if it were proper to speak so, that all such attempts were entirely worthless, considering this case and others that we read and hear of and see continually, even though the way she works is hidden.

It is interesting to notice, however, that Boccaccio handles these materials with a measure of detachment: they are not allowed to assume more than a limited importance in the poem as a whole. They serve to draw out our sympathy for the miserable Arcita and Palemone, they stimulate our awareness of the predicament of man's life, set between the Gods and Fate. But there is always a sense that Boccaccio resists their power to involve him, his characters, and his readers in deep concern. They do not ever move us strongly, or absorb our interest totally. So, for instance, the poet can cover, in one single-toned stanza (III, st. 1), the pleasure taken by Juno in the fall of Thebes, the subsequent retreat of Mars to his Thracian stronghold, and his own intention to celebrate, now, the battles of Cupid. And as, in the account of the temples of Mars and Venus, the authority of the Gods, expressed in images of great descriptive richness, commands the attention without invoking the passions, so, through the poem, the authority of Fate asks for sad recognition without invoking despair.

Chaucer's reaction to what he found in the Italian may, in the initial stages, appear tentative: in the light of the completed work, however, even the smallest change is full of significance. So when Arcite attempts to reconcile Palamon to their unhappy

imprisonment, and associates, for the first time, the influence
of the malign planet Saturn with that of Fortune as twin causes
of 'adversitee' (l. 1086), we have a clear instance of Chaucer's
desire to benefit from his original, but also to widen and deepen
its implications. The choice of Saturn is not, in itself, startling:
the orbit of Saturn was the most extensive of any planet known
to the fourteenth century, its 'aspect', or position, most hostile:

> So stood the hevene whan that we were born ...
>
> (l. 1090)

But the introduction of planetary influences, absent in the
Teseida at this point, argues not only that Chaucer, with his
scientific interests, was eager to give his readers a more varied
range of reference:

A 'fortunat ascendent' clepen they whan that no wicked planete, as
Saturne or Mars ... is in the hous of the ascendent, ne that no wicked
planete have noon aspect of enemyte upon the ascendent ...[2]

Nor does it only argue that he wished to increase the immediate
pathos of the human situation—two young men assailed by all
kinds of invincible forces. It must also mean that he was preparing to strengthen the motif, already briefly announced by
the Italian references to Juno and her 'furor' directed against
Thebes (III, st. 1), of absolute power wielded by the Gods.
While Saturn is called up first as a 'wicke aspect of disposicioun
...' (l. 1087), it must have been in Chaucer's mind that, as
father of Jove, he stood in close relationship to Juno, wife of
Jove—and, further, to Venus, daughter of Jove. Astrological
patterns, always vividly present to Chaucer, suggested a way of
enlarging and vitalizing that which, in the *Teseida*, is an effective but subordinate narrative device. Once Saturn, in whatever guise, has entered the poem, the serious, even sinister
potential of the narrative can begin to be realized. Palamon's
response to the words of Arcite hints at this: nothing in the
Teseida prompts his prayer to Venus, with its allusions to
'destiny', 'everlasting decree', and 'tyranny':

> And if so be my destynee be shapen
> By eterne word to dyen in prisoun,
> Of oure lynage have som compassioun,
> That is so lowe ybroght by tirannye ...
>
> (ll. 1108-11)

It might be possible to forecast, from those lines, something of Palamon's next address to the Gods, with its contempt for their 'word eterne' (l. 1304). At least they indicate a growing preoccupation with the frailty of human life, faced not only by the evidence of man-made disaster but also by the thought of unalterable and incomprehensible destiny.

And if this subject of men and Gods is beginning to hold promise of a stronger dramatic tension than it ever developed in the *Teseida*, the related, but not identical, subject of men and Fortune is being given a new weight of philosophical reference. This makes itself clear in Arcite's reaction to his release from prison by Theseus. The irony of his situation—free, but banished from all he loves—calls for some comment, and on the whole the theme of Boccaccio's comment is 'Fortune is changeable' (IV, st. 11), an observation which may be used to raise hope as well as to console for the loss of hope. Chaucer also allows Arcite that sentiment initially:

> Wel hath Fortune yturned thee the dys ...
> For possible is ...
> That by som cas, syn Fortune is chaungeable,
> Thow maist to thy desir somtyme atteyne ...
>
> (ll. 1238-43)

But only here is it given a recognizably Boethian development. Chaucer's own translation of the *Consolatio Philosophiae* conveniently 'places' the content of Arcite's speech, which uses Boethian ideas in a limited way, with purely local point, but not in a totally improper or untruthful way. Following the line taken by Boccaccio's characters, Arcite still sets store by the thought that Fortune may eventually reward the unbanished Palamon. If, of course, he were well advanced along the path of Boethian consolation he would not only accept that 'alle fortune (is) good, the whiche fortune is certeyn that it be either ryghtful or elles profitable ...',[3] but he would also have a different concept of what constitutes ultimate happiness, seeing that

the unstablenesse of fortune may nat atayne to resceyven verray blisfulnesse ...

> (*Boece*, Bk. II, pr. 4, ll. 148-9)

He is, however, a character involved in a romance of love and war, and such insights could hardly be expected at that stage of the narrative. His lament over the wilful discontent of man, and his ill-judged efforts to change the appointed course of events are Boethian in expression:

> Allas! why pleynen folk so in commune
> On purveiaunce of God, or of Fortune,
> That yeveth hem ful ofte in many a gyse
> Wel bettre than they kan hemself devyse?
>
> (*K. T.*, ll. 1251-4)

Men weren wont to maken questiouns of the symplicite of the pur-veaunce of God, and of the ordre of destyne, and of sodeyn hap ... Yif we wisten the causes why that swiche thinges bytyden, certes thei sholde cesen to seme wondres ...

   (*Boece*, Bk. IV, pr. 6, ll. 25-7; IV, met. 5, ll. 32-6)

It is true that his applications are sometimes narrow; he is very much concerned with the recent loss and the possible resti-tution of creaturely happiness, and his definition of 'felicitee' remains obstinately centred upon human fulfilment. Where the lady Philosophy describes the stumbling path of the 'drun-kard', man, towards 'the soverayn good' (III, pr. 2, ll. 79, 86), Arcite uses the same metaphor for man reaching out towards all kinds of lesser joys.

But the model is Boethian: Arcite's speech touches lightly and reminiscently upon a whole problematic area of thought, relating to man's pursuit of false happiness, his resilience to adversity, and his difficult acceptance of divine purpose. If it does not press for exact Boethian equivalences or for identical resolutions, it associates itself unmistakeably with rich philo-sophic argument, and illustrates a seriousness of intent which Arcita lacks in the *Teseida*:

> Infinite harmes been in this mateere.
> We witen nat what thing we preyen heere:
> We faren as he that dronke is as a mous.
> A dronke man woot wel he hath an hous,
> But he noot which the righte wey is thider,
> And to a dronke man the wey is slider.

And certes in this world so faren we;
We seken faste after felicitee,
But we goon wrong ful often, trewely.
(*K. T.*, ll. 1259-67)

In strict Boethian terms, Arcite is only partially in command of
the truth: in terms of the character which Chaucer received
from Boccaccio, he is impressively and newly aware of signifi-
cances, echoing the Lady Philosophy in some of her best statements:

God, whan he hath byholden from the hye tour of his purveaunce ...
dooth swich thing, of which thing unknowynge folk ben astonyd ...
(*Boece*, Bk. IV, pr. 6, ll. 217-24)

Such an enlargement of the original subject of 'Fortune' was
no doubt suggested to Chaucer by his imaginative sense of
Arcite's pressing need for more help than that subject could
give him in his predicament. But this introduction of the concept of divine providence may have a relevance beyond that of
the local and dramatic. Chaucer was to use the *Consolatio* increasingly as the *Knight's Tale* proceeded towards its complex
denouement, and here, perhaps, we have the first intimation of
one special and important reason for that use. The *Consolatio*
offered a wealth of materials and methods for coping with those
human dilemmas of pain and belief which were beginning,
even so early in Chaucer's dealings with the *Teseida*, to claim
his attention. A stronger interest in the quality and causes of
human suffering seems to have led him, characteristically, in
two directions, neither of which, characteristically, had been
fully explored by Boccaccio: towards the dramatic presentation
of bewilderment and anger in those who suffer, and towards
the provision of good reason for the ending of that drama in
reconciliation. What we might expect is some correlation between the lively conduct of the first, and the grave conduct of
the second: as the picture of perplexed human beings and enig-
matic Gods is laid in with darker, more vivid strokes, so the
recourse to philosophic comment and explanation must become
more urgent. Chaucer would not have had such need to augment Boccaccio's scattered and somewhat formal references to
the power and operation of Fortune if he had not already com-
mitted himself to heightening Boccaccio's description of the

wretched and persecuted life of man on earth. And as far as the whole poem is concerned, 'correlation' will be of over-riding importance: the power of the human drama should be adjusted to the power of the philosophical solution, and just as the first should not raise unanswerable questions so the second should not uncomfortably suggest answers that undermine the very nature of the narrative.

It is easy to see that a poet of Chaucer's particular talent might well be tempted to exploit the dramatic at the expense of other elements less responsive to imaginative treatment. What is also important to recognize is that there could be dangers in an enthusiastic plundering of the *Consolatio*, a treatise ultimately designed to aid in the rejection of worldly preoccupations and values, for a story which was so focused upon success and failure of a worldly kind. Nothing could, in terms of the medieval contract between poet and source-narrative, prevent the final rededication of the *Knight's Tale* to mundane happiness: it must end in a wedding, not in a death. Chaucer's introduction of Boethian materials of consolation into his version of Boccaccio's poem took, therefore, certain risks: it risked their being found inadequate to deal with newly dominant themes, and unsuitable to comment upon the basic and unalterable narrative.

There are also, however, the Boethian materials of complaint to consider: the *Consolatio* offered a model for the expression of human scepticism and anger as well as for the expression of magisterial wisdom and penitent acceptance. Chaucer availed himself of both, using the Boethian complaint as a means of reinforcing and extending that which he received from Boccaccio as a narrative motif, and had already begun to shape anew: the exercise of absolute authority by the gods, and the pattern of justice and injustice meted out to men. If Arcite was given some of Lady Philosophy's words to re-express, Palamon was given in his turn those of Boethius himself, culpable, and impassioned:

O thou governour, governynge alle thynges by certein ende, whi refusestow oonly to governe the werkes of men by duwe manere? Why suffrestow that slydynge Fortune turneth so grete enterchaungynges of thynges; so that anoyous peyne, that scholde duweliche punysche felons, punysscheth innocentz? ...

O thou, what so evere thou be that knyttest all boondes of thynges, loke on thise wrecchide erthes.

(Boece, Bk. I, metre 5, ll. 31-7, 49-52)

But while it is true that Palamon's outburst— '... O crueel goddes that governe / This world with byndying of youre word eterne ...' (ll. 1303-4)—is loosely based upon this passage from the *Consolatio,* it is altered very considerably, both in direction and in content. Whereas the *Consolatio,* by its very debate-structure, is able to control the effect of such a complaint, and reveal it clearly and immediately as an error of human understanding,

Whan I hadde, with a contynuel sorwe, sobbyd or borken out thise thynges, sche, with her cheere pesible, and nothyng amoeved with my compleyntes, seide thus ...

(Boece, Bk. I, pr. 5, ll. 1-4)

the English poem, already diversely inclined to attitudes both sympathetic and bracing, has no similar power. Palamon's speech, with some of its materials Boethian, takes some colouring from the straightforward statements of the Italian about the 'ancient enmity' of the gods. The tone of Boethius in his appeal is sad, regretful: the tone of Palamon in his is angry, resentful—a heightening of emotions intimated, at least, in the *Teseida's* phrases, 'la malizia / dello 'nfortunio', 'antica nimistate / serva Giunon ver noi', 'il furor di Iunone' (III, st. 3, 66, 1). The new note is struck in 'O crueel goddes', as compared with 'O thou governour', and sustained in the far more emphatic and concrete line 'that governe / This world with byndyng of youre worde eterne'. The vocabulary is bitter and pungent—'table of atthamaunt', 'rouketh', 'slayn', 'prisoun', 'siknesse'—where that of the treatise is melancholy—'slydynge Fortune', 'anoyous peyne', 'fraude', 'fals colour', 'dreden'. The questions asked are direct and desperate with their new application of the Boethian concept of man as a 'divyne beest' to the sickening image of man as not more than butcher's victim—but a victim called upon perversely to suffer more than once.

> What is mankynde moore unto you holde
> Than is the sheep that rouketh in the folde?
> For slayn is man right as another beest,

> And dwelleth eek in prison and arreest ...
> And whan a beest is deed, he hath no peyne;
> But man after his deeth moot wepe and pleyne ...'
>
> (ll. 1307-20)

No doubt Chaucer was remembering the lament of Boethius, 'we men, that ben noght a foul partie, but a faire partie of so greet a werk, we ben turmented in this see of fortune' (Bk. I, metre 5, ll. 52-4). His telling compression of the original ideas, however, and his weighted, emphatic language make Palamon's challenge much more difficult to dispose of in a context which is, in any case, morally ambiguous:

> What governance is in this prescience,
> That giltelees tormenteth innocence?
>
> (ll. 1313-14)

Just how potent such 'ambiguity' is in our judgement of the nature of the speech may be illustrated simply by those lines which refer to the divine powers. Chaucer's substitution of 'crueel goddes' for 'governour' has always been noticed as an adaptation of the *Consolatio* to the 'classical setting of the tale.'[4] The 'cruel gods', addressed generally in the opening words, are then specified at the close of the speech as Saturn, Juno, and Venus:

> But I moot been in prisoun thurgh Saturne
> And eek thurgh Juno, jalous and eek wood ...
> And Venus sleeth me on that other syde
> For jalousie and fere of hym Arcite.
>
> (ll. 1328-33)

Boethius has been merged with Boccaccio, to provide an attack upon the pagan deities, with their wanton malice—an attitude which also inspires Chaucer's dismissive stanza at the end of another poem, based upon Boccaccio's work—*Troilus and Criseyde*:

> Lo here, of payens corsed olde rites,
> Lo here, what alle hire goddes may availle ...
>
> (v. 1849-50)

But in the very centre of the speech, Chaucer allows Palamon to mention 'God' in terms that would be generally acceptable as Boethian or Christian:

> And yet encresseth this al my penaunce,
> That man is bounden to his observaunce,
> *For Goddes sake,* to letten of his wille
> Ther as a beest may al his lust fulfille ...
>
> (ll. 1315-18)

In other words, man, in obedience to God, is bound to observe moral laws, and restrain the promptings of his will. Are we, then to accept Palamon's protests as legitimate in their literary-historical setting but illegitimate in the sense that their Boethian model is designed to be self-evidently fallible? The inconsistency of reference to the 'deities' or the 'Deity' makes, on the one hand, for uncertainty about this; on the other, it makes for an interesting 'open-ended' situation, in which we may begin to think that the poet is motivated less by moral considerations than by the desire to give a favoured theme full, dramatic, and imaginative scope. Palamon's protest reaches for the most effective weapons of vocabulary and argument, without precisely imitating them in their original context, and without hesitating to barb them further. Thus Boccaccio's description of Juno's 'long-harboured enmity', 'antica nimistate', of her 'perverse wrongs', 'perversi mali' done to Thebes (III, st. 66), is given a new seriousness as an accusation against a formidable triad, Saturn, Juno, and Venus. The cruelty of the gods, frequently stated but not lengthily dwelt upon in the Italian, is expounded with the help of persuasive rhetoric and concepts drawn powerfully, if rather ruthlessly, from a distinguished philosophical treatise.

And at the same time the incomplete transposition of materials into a 'classical' format guarantees that the problems are not sealed off as parts of a historically distanced narrative. Subtler ingredients, of a medieval Christian flavour, are suggested in the lines which speak of man impelled 'for Goddes sake' to the control of his basic instincts. It is not only the play of fear and anger which we notice in this passage, as Palamon confronts the effective actions of Juno and Saturn: it is also the working, though from an orthodox Christian viewpoint the imperfect working, of the reason and the conscience. This juxtaposition of widely differing motives and emotions within one loosely-structured whole makes Palamon's 'arguments' so difficult to judge, but so easy to admire. He cannot be condemned out of hand on 'Boethian', or medieval Christian grounds, for his wilful misunderstanding of divine purpose: the firmness of his ground for complaint against the gods is only too well substantiated by the narrative, and by Chaucer's own decisive highlighting of that narrative. On the other hand, Palamon cannot be set aside, as one quite limited by his historical circumstances to nothing but stoic acceptance of the irrational and often cruel interventions of deities such as Juno, Venus, and Saturn in the lives of men. The speech is as forthcoming in dramatic appeal as it is resistant to logical analysis.

And although Chaucer, in the guise of his pilgrim-narrator, agrees to 'stynte of Palamon a lite' (l. 1334), drawing back somewhat from this painful contact with his indignation and misery, even to the extent of inviting the listener or reader to pronounce judiciously upon 'who hath the worse, Arcite or Palamoun?' (l. 1348), the poem never really manages to shrug off the consequences of its full involvement in the theme of 'prescience / that giltelees tormenteth innocence'. Nor are there many signs that Chaucer struggled hard to do so: indeed, he continued to increase the part played by the gods in the story—introducing 'the wynged god Mercurie' to direct Arcite back to Athens and ultimately to his death:

> ... To Atthenes shaltou wende,
> Ther is thee shapen of thy wo an ende ...
>
> (*K. T.*, ll. 1391-2)

Arcite's response is humanly courageous, and, in spite of its brave rhetoric, humanly unsuspecting of the deeper ironies of the god's words:

> ... to Atthenes right now wol I fare,
> Ne for the drede of deeth shal I nat spare
> To se my lady, that I love and serve.
> In hire presence I recche nat to sterve ...
>
> (*K. T.*, ll. 1395-8)

Similarly, the soliloquy of Arcite which Palamon, escaped from prison, overhears is shaped afresh, with special emphasis, not present in the equivalent Italian,[5] upon the malicious role of the gods in the fortunes of the two knights:

> How longe, Juno, thurgh thy crueltee,
> Woltow werreyen Thebes the citee? ...
> And yet dooth Juno me wel moore shame,
> For I dar noght biknowe myn owene name ...
> Allas, thou felle Mars! allas Juno!
> Thus hath youre ire oure lynage al fordo ...
> (*K. T.*, ll. 1543-4; 1555-6; 1559-60)

It is in this general direction that Chaucer's presentation of the temples of the gods, in which the lovers make their separate prayers, differs so crucially from that of Boccaccio. With regard to the temple of Venus, we have already seen how, in the earlier *Parlement of Foules,* Chaucer is capable, even anxious, to preserve as much as possible of the Italian *matiere* and *sens.*[6] Here, the situation is quite different. The temple of love is briskly, almost mechanically described; the nature of the passion inspired by Venus is conveyed solely in terms of formal art—gone is the scented garden, except as a brief reference in a painted landscape, gone are the moving tableaux of beauty, danger, and delight which engaged the poet of the *Parlement*:

> And by hymself, under an ok, I gesse,
> Saw I Delyt, that stod with Gentilesse.
> I saw Beute, withouten any atyr,
> And Youthe, ful of game and jolyte,
> Foolhardynesse, Flaterye and Desyr ...
> (*P. F.*, ll. 223-7)

The zestful poetry of the dream-vision, with its flickering half-lights of pleasure and fear, is replaced by poetic cataloguing which brings out, in the most unambiguous manner, the stark pain of the reign of Venus:

> First in the temple of Venus maystow se
> Wroght on the wal, ful pitous to biholde,
> The broken slepes, and the sikes colde,
> The sacred teeris, and the waymentynge,
> The firy strokes of the desirynge
> That loves servantz in this lyf enduren;
> The othes that hir covenantz assuren;
> Plesaunce and Hope, Desir, Foolhardynesse,

> Beautee and Youthe, Bauderie, Richesse,
> Charmes and Force, Lesynges, Flaterye,
> Despense, Bisynesse, and Jalousye
> (*K. T.*, ll. 1918-28)

The summary words in which the garden of love is designated as a landscape-background—

> ... al the mount of Citheroun ...
> Was shewed on the wal in portreyynge,
> With al the gardyn and the lustynesse.
> Nat was foryeten the porter, Ydelnesse ...
> (*K. T.*, ll. 1936, 1938-40)

measure the distance between this poem and the *Parlement*. The stress is entirely different: Venus has become a goddess of power only—her forces are drawn up against beauty and riches, she is implacable and inescapable:

> Thus may ye seen that wysdom ne richesse,
> Beautee ne sleighte, strengthe ne hardynesse,
> Ne may with Venus holde champartie ...
> (*K. T.*, ll.1947-9)

In the *Parlement of Foules* Venus and Richesse are at one, 'in disport', while Beauty walks outside, in the garden (ll. 260, 225).

And symptomatic of the changed nature of Chaucer's interests in the *Knight's Tale* is the appearance of the Goddess herself as a statue, not as Boccaccio's half-naked woman:

> ... e vide lei nuda giacere
> Sopr'un gran letto assai bello a vedere
> (*Teseida*, VII, st. 64)

She saw her reclining naked on a huge bed that was very beautiful to see

The Venus of the *Knight's Tale* is impeccable, from the point of view of medieval iconography: half-risen from the sea, garlanded with the roses of love, attended by doves, and by her blind son, Cupid. She only departs from accepted tradition by carrying a cittern instead of a shell.[7] But nothing disturbs the hard image of glittering dominion:

> The statue of Venus, glorious for to se,
> Was naked fletynge in the large see,

> And fro the navele doun al covered was
> With wawes grene, and brighte as any glas ...
>
> (ll. 1955-8)

For all her 'glory', Venus here is not unrecognizable as the 'deere doghter' of the vengeful god, Saturn; aggression, not seduction, is the key-note of the passage, which closes with 'arwes brighte and kene', not with the languid fruits of love.

> Biforn hire stood hir sone Cupido;
> Upon his schuldres wynges hadde he two,
> And blynd he was, as it is often seene;
> A bowe he bar and arwes brighte and kene.
>
> (ll. 1963-6)

As might be expected, the temple of Mars is treated with explosive violence. Boccaccio's account, although of a 'cruel place', 'il luogo rio' (VII, st. 32), is dominated to a great extent by the poet's admiration, expressed through the medium of Arcita's Prayer, for the forcefulness of his subject, rather than by his revulsion from its evil implications. The 'lofty struggles of Mars' are as much the theme here as the 'infortune of Marte' (*K. T.*, l. 2021) is the equivalent theme of Chaucer's adaptation. As in the temple of Venus, the expert quality of the painting—'da sottil mano', 'with cunning hand' (VII, st. 36) —recommends itself: more startlingly here, since the pictures are of humanity wasted by war—

> ... e qualunque sforzato
> fu, era quivi in abito musorno ...
>
> (*Teseida*, VII, st. 36)

Whatever was won by force appeared there in sombre form

The whole temple had been built by 'skilful Mulciber, with (all) his art ...', 'Mulcifero sottil, con la sua arte' (VII, st. 38). Moreover, it is worth noticing that most of the qualities and characteristics of the 'religion' of Mars are expressed as allegorical temple-figures, in gestured tableaux:

> E con gli occulti ferri i Tradimenti
> vide, e le 'nsidie con giusta apparenza;
> lì Discordia sedea e sanguinenti
> ferri avea in mano, e ogni Differenza;
>
> (*Teseida*, VII, st. 34)

And she saw there Betrayals with their hidden weapons, and Plots
with honest faces; Discord sat with bloodstained swords in hand, and
every kind of Strife.

The epithet 'l'allegro', for 'Furore', 'lively, vivacious Fury'
(st. 35), illustrates the easy way in which horror can be temporarily accepted as visually interesting; the altars, burning
with the fires of war, are 'luminoso', 'shining, bright' (st. 35),
and become even brighter, 'più chiaro' (st. 40), with the arrival
of the god himself. The earth gives off wonderful scents, 'e diè
la terra mirabile odore', and the armour of the statue of Mars
moved 'with a sweet sound', 'le cui armi risonaro / tutte in sé
mosse con dolce romore ...' (st. 40). The attitudes of Boccaccio
to his materials are, in this whole sequence, from a moral viewpoint, extremely fluid. Pity and revulsion are contributory
elements; dominant always, however, is an appreciative sense
of the power of the God and of his activities which may not be
identified precisely as admiration, but which comes very close
to that emotion.

Chaucer's handling of the Italian here seems to be characterized partly by a greater reserve, and partly by a greater determination. On the one hand, he seems reluctant to imitate
Boccaccio in his relish for the landscape and the temple of
Mars: on the other hand, he seems anxious to channel and
direct the description in the service of one particular theme.
This becomes very clear in his adaptation of the Martian landscape of Thrace—a landscape real in the *Teseida*, painted in
the *Knight's Tale*. It is not only the difference between art and
reality which matters here; in any case, for reasons much
debated by Chaucerian commentators, Chaucer appears to
hover between the two in the detail of his description. The
narrator appears to *visit* the painted forest, *hear* the ominous
storm tossing the trees and the angry clangour in the temple
itself:

> First on the wal was peynted a forest,
> In which ther dwelleth neither man ne best,
> With knotty, knarry, bareyne trees olde,
> Of stubbes sharpe and hidouse to biholde,
> In which ther ran a rumbel in a swough,
> As though a storm sholde bresten every bough.
> And dounward from an hille, under a bente,
> Ther stood the temple of Mars armypotente,

Wroght al of burned steel, of which the entree
Was long and streit, and gastly for to see.
And therout came a rage and swich a veze
That it made al the gate for to rese.
The northren lyght in at the dores shoon,
For wyndowe on the wal ne was ther noon,
Thurgh which men myghten any light discerne.
The dore was al of adamant eterne,
Yclenched overthwart and endelong
With iren tough; and for to make it strong,
Every pyler, the temple to sustene,
Was tonne-greet, of iren bright and shene.   (ll. 1975-94)

Boccaccio's text is very systematic here, making precise distinctions between the real landscape outside, the 'insane and violent creatures', 'l'Impeti dementi', Sin, Anger, Treachery, and Deception (st. 33), who inhabit the temple, and the paintings of conquered peoples upon its walls. It would not be wise to conclude too hastily, as some have done,[8] that Chaucer was turning back to the ultimate source of Boccaccio's account in the *Thebaid* of Statius, where there is a more dramatic movement between the phenomena of real-life and art:

terrarum exuviae circum, et fastigia templi
captae insignibant gentes, caelataque ferro
fragmina portarum bellatricesque carinae,
et vacui currus protritaque curribus ora,
paene etiam gemitus : adeo vis omnis et omne
vulnus. ubique ipsum, sed non usquam ore remisso
cernere erat : talem divina Mulciber arte
ediderat[9]

All around were spoils of every land, and captured peoples adorned the temple's high front, and fragments of iron-wrought gates and ships of war and empty chariots and faces ground by chariot-wheels, ay, almost even their groans! truly every form of violence and wounds. Himself was everywhere to behold, but nowhere with softened looks; in such wise had Mulciber with divine skill portrayed him.

His reading of Latin, which was never expert, may not have included the *Thebaid*, and it is far more likely that his presentation is an inconsistent reshaping of Boccaccio's Italian: the decision to transform a real landscape and location into a painting on a temple wall is only intermittently observed.

It remains true, however, that Chaucer's rejection of Boccaccio's winter scene in Thrace, which has a severe beauty of
its own—

> ne' campi trazii, sotto i cieli iberni,
> da tempesta continua agitati,
> dove schiere di nimbi sempiterni
> da' venti or qua e or là trasmutati
> in varii luoghi ne' guazzosi verni,
> e d'acqua globi per freddo agroppati
> gittati sono, e neve tuttavia
> che 'n ghiaccio a mano a man s'indura e cria...
>
> (VII, st. 30)

... on the Thracian plains, under wintry skies, torn by continual
tempests, where ranks of perpetual cloud are blown here and there in
stormy winters, and water-drops freeze as they fall, and snow too,
that gradually hardens and turns to ice.

and his concentration, instead, upon the 'selva steril di robusti
/ cerri', 'forest of barren and massive oaks' (st. 31), which
shrouds the temple of Mars, betrays much more than a rather
formal taste in landscape-description. There is a terrible grandeur in Boccaccio's snow-swept Thracian plains, just as there is
grandeur, too, in his whole concept of Mars and his domain—
elements which Chaucer might understandably have found less
appropriate to his changed purposes. For it is a narrow, more
single-toned interpretation which he offers of all the gods, but
in particular, of Mars: not his 'lofty struggles', but his ugly
omnipotence, to be focused in the temple statue—

> The statue of Mars upon a carte stood
> Armed, and looked grym as he were wood ...
> A wolf ther stood biforn hym at his feet
> With eyen rede, and of a man he eet.
>
> (*K.T.*, ll. 2041-2, 2047-8)

Predictably, then, the extensive winter-scene is reduced to the
'colde frosty regioun' (l. 1973) and Boccaccio's gnarled forest,
cut off significantly from pastoral life, 'né v'era bestia alcuna
né pastore ...' (st. 31), becomes Chaucer's sole exemplar. His
alterations are slight, but significant, in that they establish a
claustrophobic and threatening sense of evil which is never,
afterwards, relieved: Boccaccio's furies, weaving among the

trees 'with loud clamour', 'grandissimo romore' (st. 31) are replaced by an undefined, tempestuous thunder—'As though a storm sholde bresten every bough ...' (l. 1980). Boccaccio's temple of clear-burnished steel, reflecting the sun, though indirectly,

> tutta d'acciaio splendido e pulio,
> dal quale era dal sol riverberata
> la luce ...
>
> (st. 32)

shines more darkly in Chaucer's version; the single epithet in 'Wroght al of burned steel' (l. 1983) does not produce the same effect as the Italian 'splendido e pulio'. Only the iron supporting pillars are 'bright and shene' (l. 1994); only cold 'northern light' (l. 1987) penetrates, through a tunnel-like entrance. Even the expansion of Boccaccio's 'la stretta entrata', 'the narrow entrance' (st. 32), to 'the entree / Was long and streit' (ll. 1983-4) helps to enforce this impression of a dark cave, or tomb, reached through a cramped passage, down which the fierce winds of violence desolately blow:

> And therout came a rage and swich a veze
> That it made al the gate for to rese
>
> (ll. 1985-6)

The extent of Chaucer's involvement with what Mars signifies, in every part of human life, may perhaps be judged from the vivid and direct use of the formula 'I saugh' (ll. 1995, 2011, etc.) for the account of the inside of the temple. Suggested, probably, by the 'videvi' (st. 35, 37, etc.) of the Italian which introduces the spectacle confronting the personified Prayer of Arcite as she reaches the goal of her journey, it is likely to be an indication that, in his excited enlargement of the theme of human disaster, Chaucer loses touch with the fiction of Knight-narrator (a fiction never particularly strong for him) and writes more personally. The catalogue, whether of images or of paintings, is relentlessly thorough, and, where Boccaccio's description had been vivid, even melodramatic, this is chilling both in its exactness and in its resonance. The detail, which Chaucer only occasionally remembers as detail in a *painted* temple, refers in a precise and agile fashion to the conceptual basis of violence—

> Ther saugh I first the derke ymaginyng
> Of Felonye, and al the compassyng ...
>
> (ll. 1995-6)

to its everyday manifestations in the life of man—

> The careyne in the busk, with throte ycorve;
> A thousand slayn, and nat of qualm ystorve ...
>
> (ll. 2013-14)

to the traditional figures of allegory, which define its component parts—

> The crueel Ire, reed as any gleede ...
> Contek, with blody knyf and sharp manace ...
> Yet saugh I Woodnesse, laughynge in his rage,
> Armed Compleint, Outhees, and fiers Outrage ...
>
> (ll. 1997, 2003, 2011-12)

and some of its most famous victims in history—

> ... the slaughtre of Julius,
> Of grete Nero, and of Antonius
>
> (ll. 2031-2)

This variousness of reference is the key to the nature of the passage: whatever literary, astrological, and iconographical sources Chaucer had for his expansion of the Italian,[10] the final impression is, in one word, disturbing. The impact of the decor of Boccaccio's temple is strong, but distanced slightly by the fact that the aggressive pageant is displayed either in terms of formal allegory—

> Videvi ancora l'allegro Furore,
> e oltre a ciò con volto sanguinoso
> la Morte armata vide e lo Stupore
>
> (VII, st. 35)

She saw quick Fury also, as well as armed Death with bloody face, and Stupefaction.

or, when the actors are human, in terms of group-activity—

> ... e qualunque sforzato
> fu, era quivi in abito musorno;

> vedeanvisi le genti incatenate,
> porti di ferro e fortezze spezzate
>
> (VII, st. 36)

Whatever was won by force appeared there in sombre form; there were to be seen people in chains, iron gates, and shattered fortresses.

The stress is on quantity rather than specific quality—'ogni forza con gli aspetti elati', 'every kind of violence with elated looks ...' (st. 37); 'ognifedita', 'every kind of wound' (st. 37). The image of Mars appears 'everywhere', 'in ogni luogo'. Rarely, in Boccaccio's recital, are we stabbed with any special sense of the pity of violence as it erupts into the life of the individual, nor is our attention invited by the ugliness of death and destruction as it occurs in a personal, even domestic context:

> The shepne brennynge with the blake smoke;
> The tresoun of the mordrynge in the bedde ...
> The nayl ydryven in the shode a-nyght;
> The colde deeth, with mouth gapyng upright ...
>
> (ll. 2000-1, 2007-8)

Chaucer's inclusion of so many images of casual horror in this cavalcade dedicated to Mars—the dead hunter, the mauled child, the scalded cook—juxtaposing them with more conventional images of martial activity—the strewn battlefield, the ravaged city, the victorious tyrant—curiously webs the heroic with the pathetic. The general effect of the passage is to stress, once more, man's helplessness whether he win or lose in the service of Mars. Even the high accolade of triumph in battle may be succeeded by the accolade of death; conquest is always at risk—'With the sharpe swerd over his heed / Hangynge by a soutil twynes threed' (ll. 2029-30). There is, here, a sad and obvious reference to the coming fate of Arcite, who will conquer but die, and who has already expressed the peril of man's situation in a line which owes something to Boethius but much more to the poet's apprehension of a mystery,

> Infinite harmes been in this mateere
>
> (l. 1259)

Apart from this, there is the more general melancholy conclusion that this desperate review of human affairs, which lays much more stress upon the suffering of victims, is all that can be mustered 'in redoutynge of Mars and of his glorie' (l. 2050). It may be true, indeed, that Chaucer has decided to widen the scope of his Martian panorama by drawing upon the kind of incident associated with the 'children of Mars' in medieval astrological tradition as well as upon the detail of his Italian source.[11] The record of every-day disasters, the listing of the 'trades of Mars'—

> The barbour, and the bocher, and the smyth
> (l. 2025)

look forward to the live *genre*-scenes of fifteenth-century art, in which humanity, aggressive, oppressed, industrious, creative, acts out life as dictated by the power of the planetary deities.[12] But this does not explain, in any very simple way, why Chaucer felt the necessity to supplement Boccaccio, obscuring the heroic contours and shading in the misery of the inhabited landscape. Nor does it explain the precise and vivid language in which misery makes itself felt—

> The careyne in the busk, with throte ycorve ...
> (l. 2013)

nor the insistent probing of misery to come at its hidden fibres, its small, painful incongruities:

> The hunte strangled with the wilde beres;
> The sowe freten the child right in the cradel;
> The cook yscalded, for al his longe ladel.
> Noght was foryeten by the infortune of Marte
> The cartere overryden with his carte:
> Under the wheel ful lowe he lay adoun.
> (ll. 2018-23)

But it is quite evident, when the statue of Mars comes to be presented, in its full iconographic state—

> This god of armes was arrayed thus:
> A wolf ther stood biforn hym at his feet
> With eyen rede, and of a man he eet ...
> (ll. 2046-8)

that Chaucer felt the need to demonstrate, more strongly than Boccaccio had done, the unmotivated savagery which was an inevitable part of the glory of Mars. When Boccaccio mentions the images of Mars set about his temple, they are, it is true, of 'aspetto fiero', of 'fierce expression' (st. 37): even here, however, Chaucer builds upon the Italian, stressing the unbridled passion of the God—

> Armed, and looked grym as he were wood
> (l. 2042)

It is not surprising that the 'sweet sound' with which the armour of the altar-image of Mars eventually signalled victory to Boccaccio's Arcita—

> ... le cui armi risonaro
> tutte in sé mosse con dolce romore ...
> (*Teseida*, VII, st. 40)

Whose armour rang with a sweet sound as it moved

finds no place in the sinister reverberation of the English version:

> ... and atte laste
> The statue of Mars bigan his hauberk rynge;
> And with that soun he herde a murmurynge
> Ful lowe and dym, and seyde thus, 'Victorie!'
> (ll. 2430-3)

Even the different ordering of material may be significant here. In the *Teseida*, the prayers of Arcita, Palemone, and Emilia are made to Mars, Venus and Diana in that order, and the temple-descriptions follow suit. Only slight reference is made to the strife in heaven caused by the conflicting claims of the three human beings, and that reference is obscurely placed, between the account of the temple of Venus, and Emilia's sacrifice:

> e sì ne nacque in ciel novella lite
> intra Venere e Marte; ma trovata
> da lor fu via con maestrevol arte
> di far contenti i prieghi d'ogni parte
> (VII, st. 67)

and thus once more a new quarrel broke out in heaven between Venus and Mars; but with masterly skill they were to find a way of fulfilling the prayers of both parties

If there is irony in the Italian, it is faintly heard.

But the sequential changes made by Chaucer reveal more fully, and more ruthlessly, the ironies embedded in this narrative: the whole third section of his poem, dealing with the temples and the petitions, works to a crescendo of emotion, which does not reach its climax until the great concluding speech in heaven by 'pale Saturnus the colde ...' (l. 2443). Twice Chaucer alters Boccaccio's sequence of events. In the first place his account of the temples moves from the 'oratorie' of Venus to those of Mars and Diana, both of which, in their different ways, have the power to realize that violence which is only implied in the worship of love. Violence runs like a thread of variable thickness through the descriptions; if it is the subdued theme of the decorations in the place of love—

> Lo, alle thise folk so caught were in hir las,
> Til they for wo ful ofte seyde 'allas'!
>
> (ll. 1951-2)

it is openly displayed by the murals in the temples of Mars and Diana, the menacing god, the avenging goddess:

> Ther saugh I Attheon an hert ymaked,
> For vengeaunce that he saugh Diane al naked;
> I saugh how that his houndes have hym caught
> And freeten hym, for that they knewe hym naught ...
>
> (ll. 2065-8)

Then further, as if to intensify such a process, the three sacrifices to the gods are made in the order of Palamon to Venus, Emelye to Diana, and Arcite to Mars. The effect of this is to strengthen the impression of growing disaster, as the three human beings go about their votive rites only dimly conscious of how they illustrate the truth of Arcite's earlier comment—

> We witen nat what thing we preyen heere ...
>
> (l. 1260)

As they receive portents, they are pathetically unaware of the doubleness of their significance; only Emelye, now placed importantly between Palamon and Arcite, is given clear intimation that her suit cannot be granted. And whereas Boccaccio's heroine quickly becomes resigned to discovering which of the two knights she is destined to marry—

> e la mia volontà, ch'è ora mista,
> dell' una parte si farà parente!...
>
> (*Teseida*, VII, st. 87)

for my desire, which is undecided at the moment, will become fixed upon one of them!...

Chaucer's heroine is presented as a creature terrified before the signs of divine recognition. Drops of blood ooze from the wood on the altar-fires, with a strange whistling noise not mentioned by Boccaccio; the goddess herself appears, bow in hand, not delegating her message to her 'chorus of Virgins' as in the Italian (st. 88); her words, unlike theirs, are stern, unequivocal—

> Among the goddes hye it is affermed,
> And by eterne word writen and confermed,
> Thou shalt ben wedded ...
>
> (*K. T.*, ll. 2349-51)

And she vanishes, not to the sound of barking dogs and hunting-horns, but to the sound of clattering arrows—

> ... the arwes in the caas
> of the goddesse clateren faste and rynge,
> And forth she wente ...
>
> (ll. 2358-60)

The 'aventure of love' which she is promised, and which she does not desire, comes like a harsh conquest.

Conquest is, indeed what Arcite's prayer confirms; he and his god are to use force to win love:

> And wel I woot, er she me mercy heete,
> I moot with strengthe wynne hire in the place
>
> (ll. 2398-9)

The tension of the episode mounts when Arcite is granted his 'victorie', but in a context far more ominous than Boccaccio had thought necessary. The fact that the Theban does not now seem to suspect that anything but happiness may attend his victory, and goes to his lodging 'as fayn as fowel is of the brighte sonne' (l. 2437), gives no real relief to the situation; it is a grim comment upon the inability of man to deal with the secret workings of the gods, and serves as a tense introduction to the council in heaven which follows. And that council provides the definitive statement to which this whole section of the poem has been tending; Saturn is invoked to expound his nature and his powers in defence of his granddaughter, Venus:

> I am thyn aiel, redy at thy wille;
> Weep now namoore, I wol thy lust fulfille
>
> (ll. 2477-8)

And so, finally, departing radically from his Italian original, Chaucer shows us the goddess of love sponsored by forces quite as deadly as those appropriate to Mars, the 'stierne god army-potente' (l. 2441); no part of the divine plan, whatever god is concerned, operates without pain for humanity. Saturn, on behalf of Venus, is implacable:

> 'My deere doghter Venus', quod Saturne,
> 'My cours, that hath so wyde for to turne,
> Hath moore power than woot any man.
> Myn is the drenchyng in the see so wan;
> Myn is the prison in the derke cote
> Myn is the stranglyng and hangyng by the throte,
> The murmure and the cherles rebellyng,
> The groynynge, and the pryvee empoysonyng;
> I do vengeance and pleyn correccioun,
> Whil I dwelle in the signe of the leoun.
> Myn is the ruyne of the hye halles,
> The fallynge of the toures and of the walles
> Upon the mynour or the carpenter.
> I slow Sampsoun, shakynge the piler;
> And myne be the maladyes colde,
> The derke tresons, and the castes olde;
> My lookyng is the fader of pestilence. (ll. 2453-69)

The crucial positioning of this new speech, and the high finality of its poetic rhetoric make it extremely likely that Chaucer regarded it as the culmination of many processes of thought and action: it sums up, in relentless detail, what we may long have suspected—that the 'remedie' for strife will not depend upon any weighing of just dispensation, but only upon the superior craft and executive power of one god over another. Peace is to be restored to Mars and Venus by recourse to the old god Saturn, the purveyor of 'vengeance and pleyn correccioun', and it is already clear that peace will involve a kind of treachery—'the derke tresons and the castes olde ...'—and violent death—'I slow Sampsoun, shakynge the piler ...'. Nothing is admirable about Saturn's recitation of his activities; it is a fearful record of disastrous intervention in human affairs, which leaves out of account, completely, that more benevolent side of Saturn's influence, traditionally exerted upon agriculture and husbandry.[13] But for all that, his proposed solution is acceptable, not only to Mars and Venus, but to his son, Jupiter, who was anxious, it is said, to end the strife—'Juppiter was bisy it to stente' (l. 2442). The stage is now set, darkly, for the concluding section of the poem, which will illustrate the outmanoeuvring of human courage and magnanimity by divine ingenuity.

In many ways, the sweeping changes made by Chaucer in the replacement of Boccaccio's fierce and bloody battle by a tournament—his strict condensation of the Italian, his elimination of divine interference in the lists, and his removal, by edict of Theseus, of battle-to-death—all work towards producing Arcite's accident as a greater shock than it appears to be in the *Teseida*. His is the only fatality, and this insists, again, upon the way in which human compassion and care have no power against the prestige-struggles of the gods. In the *Teseida*, only Venus is responsible for sending an infernal fury to cause Arcita's horse to throw him: here, in the *Knight's Tale*, it is Saturn who operates on behalf of the unhappy Venus, chagrined to see the knight of Mars victor of the tournament—

> Weep now namoore, I wol thy lust fulfille
>
> (l. 2478)

The fact that Arcite's fall is arranged by Saturn, not Venus, gives his drawn-out sufferings a melancholy sense of inevitability; if he is under the influence of Saturn, already announced as dispenser of disease and death, there can be no hope for him. Moreover, as Chaucer's cold, precise analysis of his internal injuries makes quite certain, the manner of his death is particularly Saturnian: in his planetary role, Saturn

reigns over the retentive 'virtue', or force, in man's body, and
it is the domination of the retentive virtue over the expulsive
which finally prevents any relief of the 'venym and corrupcioun'
gathered in Arcite's shattered chest:

> Swelleth the brest of Arcite, and the soore
> Encreesseth at his herte moore and moore.
> The clothered blood, for any lechecraft,
> Corrupteth, and is in his bouk ylaft,
> That neither veyne-blood, ne ventusynge,
> Ne drynke of herbes may ben his helpynge.
> The vertu expulsif, or animal,
> Fro thilke vertu cleped natural
> Ne may the venym voyden ne expelle.
> The pipes of his longes gonne to swelle,
> And every lacerte in his brest adoun
> Is shent with venym and corrupcioun.
> Hym gayneth neither, for to gete his lif,
> Vomyt upward, ne dounward laxatif.
> Al is tobrosten thilke regioun;
>
> (ll. 2743-57)

In providing such clinical detail absent in the Italian, Chaucer
enriches his theme of the painfulness of life, and the ruthless-
ness of divine determination. The prettier triumph for Venus
may, indeed, be hinted at in Arcite's recommendation of
Palamon to Emelye—

> Foryet nat Palamon, the gentil man ...
>
> (l. 2797)

But her first dark triumph is the death-bed of Arcite, who ends,
as he has begun, in sharper bewilderment than Boccaccio's
Arcita at the unresolved enigma of existence:

> What is this world? What asketh men to have?
> Now with his love, now in his colde grave,
> Allone, withouten any compaignye
>
> (l. 2777-9)

It is not difficult to understand, at this point in the poem,
why Boccaccio's conduct of the last movements of the story was

not perfectly satisfying to Chaucer. The tracing of the ascent of Arcita's soul

> Ver la concavità del cielo ottava
>
> (*Teseida*, XI, st. 1)

towards the concavity of the eighth sphere

the austere judgement of the blindness and folly of those who still mourn upon earth

> e seco rise de' pianti dolenti
> della turba lernea, la vanitate
> forte dannando dell' umane genti,
> li quai, da tenebrosa cechitate ...
>
> (XI, st. 3)

And he smiled to himself at the dolorous plaints of all the Greeks, condemning the vanity of humankind, who live in dark and blind ignorance.

and the long-drawn-out practicalities of the consolatory speech made by Teseo (XII, st. 6) all presuppose a situation which demands swift acceptance on both narrative and thematic levels. As no great complexity of issue has arisen in the Italian, so no great ingenuity has to be expended upon the final settlement of causes and characters; reconciliations can be achieved with a certain briskness. Arcita is admitted to a heavenly perspective, regret dissolves as his history of suffering is recognized to be trivial; Teseo and his court are persuaded of the natural propriety, even the desirability of a death which can be seen as a victor's crown, an escape from old age, disgrace, infirmity. Who would hesitate when asked to choose one or the other—to be drawn

> ... o ad oscura
> vecchiezza piena d'infiniti guai,
> e questa poi da morte più sicura
> è terminata; overo a morte, essendo
> giovani ancora e più lieti vivendo ...
>
> (XII, st. 8)

... either from a dark old age full of an infinity of woes, finally terminated by a more certain death, or to death being still young, and living more joyfully ...

Order swiftly reasserts itself in attitudes of mind, and in rituals of mourning and marriage. Arcita's gesture of contempt as he passes 'nel loco che Mercurio li sortio' (XI, st. 3), Teseo's comforting and comfortable sermon on how to live happily with the certainty of death, are not unsuitable in their context; Boccaccio has never given the reader grounds for thinking that solutions such as these will not serve his purposes. But Chaucer may not have been content to minimize the final impression of human suffering by means of a plain rejection of the importance of worldly affairs: neither may he have been content to rest his case upon the kind of stoic argument put forward so confidently by Boccaccio's Teseo. His treatment of the poem had driven towards a serious confrontation of human and divine; his narrative had allowed the growth of a theme which could not so easily be disposed of—

> As flies to wanton boys are we to the gods:
> They kill us for their sport ...

The 'crueel goddes', against whose motives and actions Palamon early protests, are revealed as cruel over the course of the poem: that human protest, which should, according to the nature of its source-materials, have emerged as another example of man's 'tenebrosa cechitate', his 'dark blindness' (XI, st. 3), all too positively emerges as an example of man's sombre vision of reality. There is little in Palamon's words which the poem, with its new emphases, does not bear out. Even the bleak substitution of Mars for Mercury as the guide of Arcite's soul to its last home—'Arcite is coold, ther Mars his soule gye' (l. 2815)—reminds us as much of Palamon's first pessimistic comment upon life after death—

> But man after his deeth moot wepe and pleyne,
> Though in this world he have care and wo ...
>
> (ll. 1320-1)

as it does of the 'character' of the knightly narrator, brusquely discussing a difficult subject.[14]

In these circumstances, Chaucer may well have realized that his poem demanded more for its conclusion than Boccaccio's had done: as the gods and their intervention in human life had been strongly invoked, so that intervention must be ultimately justified. It would not be enough to show Arcite reconciled to his death: there must be some sense of an over-all coherence, of an over-riding divine purpose which might make all questions either answerable, or irrelevant. And it is, of course, the effort to rise to an occasion newly created by the adaptation of the Italian work which we must wholeheartedly admire in the ending of the *Knight's Tale*. This is not to say that we must admire the method of procedure or the finished product.

Chaucer's recognition of the difficulty of what lay before him, as he reached the death of Arcite, makes itself felt in various ways. Characteristically, he begins by taking some tentative steps towards a possible solution; Arcite's speech is full of unanswered questioning, but he does call twice upon Jupiter as the guide and receiver of his soul—

> And Juppiter so wys my soule gye ...
>
> (l. 2786)

> So Juppiter have of my soule part ...
>
> (l. 2792)

thus anticipating, but very lightly, what Theseus is to say in his final peroration of 'Juppiter the kyng / That is prince and cause of alle thyng' (ll. 3035-6). By contrast, the comment of the narrator upon the fate of Arcite's soul is not only laconic but inconsistent:

> ... ther Mars his soule gye ...
>
> (l. 2815)

The subsequent account of the grief of Emelye and the Athenians is a curious mixture of sentimental, almost absent-minded writing on the behaviour of bereaved women—

> For in swich cas wommen have swich sorwe,
> Whan that hir housbondes ben from hem ago,
> That for the moore part they sorwen so,
> Or ellis fallen in swich maladye,
> That at the laste certeinly they dye ...
>
> (ll. 2822-6)

and sharp, perhaps ironic, observation on a more practical feminine approach to death:

> Why woldestow be deed ...
> And haddest gold ynough, and Emelye?
>
> (ll. 2835-6)

The whole passage is left open to two kinds of interpretation: either Chaucer has decided, for the moment, to write 'in character', giving expression to attitudes typical of the knightly speaker (a mingling of sentiment and worldly appraisal would not be out of possibility), or he is marking time while preparing for a more ambitious undertaking. In the light of other similar occasions in Chaucer's poetry,[15] the second explanation seems more likely. Exploratory, too, may be the brief statement of consolation given to 'olde fader Egeus', which tries out a simple answer to Arcite's dying question, 'What is this world?'

> 'Right as ther dyed nevere man', quod he,
> 'That he ne lyvede in erthe in som degree,
> Right so ther lyvede never man', he seyde,
> 'In al this world, that som tyme he ne deyde.
> This world nys but a thurghfare ful of wo,
> And we been pilgrymes passynge to and fro.
>
> (ll. 2843-8)

This is the gist of one of Teseo's 'consolations' in his far longer speech from the *Teseida*:

> Così come alcun che mai non visse
> non morì mai, così si pò vedere
> ch'alcun non visse mai che non morisse.
>
> (XII, st. 6)

Just as a man who has never lived will never die, so we may see that no one who lives may escape death

And for all the melancholy grace imparted to it by Chaucer's amplification into the pilgrimage theme, nothing could possibly disguise the fact that it is quite inadequate to come to terms with the more thoughtful, more difficult English poem. The abstracting of the statement from its original context must certainly signal the poet's intention to do more than simply translate Teseo's final reconciling words.

Nothing could better mark the distance which by this time stretched between Chaucer's poem and Boccaccio's *Teseida* than the use of Boethius for the recasting of Teseo's speech. The provision of a new thirty-line preface and a later five-line insertion of material from the *Consolatio* is an act which surely registers the concern felt by Chaucer, at this stage of his work, to attempt a drawing-together of all the narrative and thematic threads of his new poetic fabric. And by beginning the speech on a high philosophic note, Chaucer encourages his readers, momentarily, to believe that, as he has engaged their interests in something more than Boccaccio's mannered tale of love and war, so he will satisfy their roused curiosity, their sense of being not simply observers but participants in a debate about the conduct of human life in a hostile universe. The first few lines seek to establish, in Boethian terms, the principle of cosmic order, the source and the nature of that force which infuses and binds all matter: the energy which drives the universe is divine love, and all is planned by divine wisdom:

> The Firste Moevere of the cause above,
> Whan he first made the faire cheyne of love,
> Greet was th' effect, and heigh was his entente
>
>   (ll. 2987-9)

But no restatement of the principle of divine order, love, and wisdom will be much help as a conclusion to this particular poem unless some attempt is made to relate it to those other 'divine principles' which seem to have been in full operation during the course of the narrative, and to those deities who have played so vivid a part in a drama principally of disorder. It is not long before it becomes clear that this will not be achieved. It gradually emerges that the speech will be in the nature of a substitution, a statement which will attempt to transcend difficulties, rather than to analyse and solve them. The brave words about 'heigh entente' and 'wise purveyaunce' are meant to redirect the reader's vision, away not only from the pain of the terrestrial drama, but also from the ignoble strife in heaven which has been, to a great extent, responsible for that pain.

Central in the process of redirection is the figure of Jupiter, who has appeared briefly in the poem—at his most prominent as the hopeful one-line peacemaker in the turbulent scenes in heaven,

> ... swich strif ther is bigonne ...
> Bitwixe Venus, the goddesse of love,
> And Mars ...
> That Juppiter was bisy it to stente.
>
> (ll. 2438-42)

Chaucer now begins to identify this figure with ultimate good, writing first of 'the firste moevere of the cause above', and then gradually revealing that the 'first mover' is Jupiter:

> What maketh this but Juppiter, the kyng,
> That is prince and cause of alle thyng,
> Convertynge al unto his propre welle
> From which it is dirryved, sooth to telle?
>
> (ll. 3035-8)

Indeed, Jupiter is the only member of that familiar pantheon who could possibly be brought forward to serve in such a role. But the attentive reader must surely remember that his anxiety to put an end to strife meant compliance with the dark counsels of his father Saturn, for Saturn's plans pleased everyone—

> he ful soone hath plesed every part ...
>
> (l. 2446)

This acceptance by Jupiter of Saturn's harsh executive solutions is no less a feature of Chaucer's poem than their acceptance by Venus. And if the goddess of love is strangely served by the god of violent retribution, so too is the god of highest wisdom and justice who is not only 'prince and cause of alle thynge', but also the maker of 'the faire cheyne of love'.

It is, in fact, one of the most interesting paradoxes of the *Knight's Tale* that the Boethian sections of Theseus's speech, by which Chaucer sought so strenuously to blur the outlines of a bleak story, worked to throw an even clearer light upon its bleak nature. More questions are raised than answered by the equation of Jupiter, the anxious but passive member of the council of heaven, with the Boethian principle of cosmic power and love. Why speak of the exercise of divine love in the design of this drama, when the narrative has so openly exposed no more than the exercise of divine power and resourcefulness?

It is here that the relationship between Boccaccio's Italian poem and Chaucer's English poem is finally revealed as an uneasy treaty between a work of elaborate surface but of simple import, and a work of much reduced decorative substance but of markedly, even dangerously, increased thematic content. Boccaccio's poem has little to answer for at this point in its progress: the death of Arcita has a causal connection with his dedication to Mars, just as the marriage of Palemone will eventually have with his dedication to Venus. The 'malice of the gods' has been raised formally by the two Thebans as an issue but has been given limited development. The speech of Teseo needs to deal, therefore, with a situation of limited emotional significance. It has only to find solace for the pity of sudden death in vigorous and triumphant youth. Expediency can be at the very heart of its message, though it may cushion its acceptance of mutability by restating the enduring power of heroic reputation:

> e noi che ora viviam, quando piacere
> sarà di quel che'l mondo circunscrisse,
> perciò morremo: adunque sostenere
> il piacer dell' iddii lieti dobbiamo,
> poi ch' ad esso resister non possiamo.
>
> (*Teseida*, XII, st. 6)

And we who are now alive will therefore die when it shall please him who encompasses the world. Therefore we should now joyfully uphold the will of the gods, since we may not resist it.

> cioè d'alcun la morte il cui valore
> fu tanto e tal, che grazioso frutto
> di fama s'ha lasciato dietro al fiore;
> il che se ben pensassomo, al postutto
> lasciar dovremmo il misero dolore,
> e intender a vita valorosa
> che ci acquistasse fama gloriosa
>
> (XII, st. 12)

... the death of one whose courage was so great that the gracious fruit of fame is left after the flower (fades). Thus, if we live in faith, we should leave behind wretched misery, and devote ourselves to a life of valour which will acquire glorious fame for us ...

Chaucer's poem, by contrast, has a great deal to answer for at this point: not only the pity but the justice of Arcite's death, not only the power but the motives of the gods. It is easy to see why he felt that Boccaccio's set-piece needed augmenting for a new occasion: it is not so easy to describe his methods of adjusting old and new material as both skilful and entirely scrupulous. The task of converting, through a retrospective philosophical haze, the ugly manoeuvres of the gods into dignified manifestations of a total beneficent purpose, was extremely ambitious; if Jupiter is credible in terms of the stark narrative, he is unlikely to be credible in terms of 'a thyng that parfit is and stable' (l. 3009). The pressure upon Chaucer to fresh composition is clearly felt, but the precise needs of the moment are hardly met. Having involved himself in matters far deeper than those suggested by his original, matters which required that the vision of evil, focused so particularly upon the terrible workings of Saturn, should be absorbed into a larger vision that all is ultimately good, Chaucer responds with a series of lesser statements, drawn from Boethius and Boccaccio, about the survival of the earthly generations 'by successiouns' (l. 3014), the necessity of resignation to death—

> Ther helpeth noght, al goth that ilke weye.
> Thanne may I seyn that al this thyng moot deye ...
>
> (ll. 3033-4)

and the impractical waste of emotion in lament—

> Why grucchen we? Why have we hevynesse?
>
> (l. 3058)

The solace offered by the poem is curiously thin and formal, considering its offer of unlimited pain: even the transition, in Theseus's speech, from the grand Boethian chords of 'Greet was th' effect, and heigh was his entente' (l. 2989) to the sharper Boccaccian notes of

> Thanne is it wysdom, as it thynketh me,
> To maken vertu of necessitee,
> And take it weel that we may nat eschue ...
>
> (l. 3041-3)

and to the brusquely phrased finale, also Boccaccian—

> Kan he hem thank? Nay, God woot, never a deel,
> That both his soule and eek hemself offende,
> And yet they mowe hir lustes nat amende ...
>
> (ll. 3064-6)

reinforces the sense of a narrowing-down, not an expansion of
the poem's issues. Suffering is answered, at best, by acceptance of the law of submission: no view of heaven, either
Christian or pagan, is glimpsed by the suppliant. The invitation to exchange sorrow for joy in the marriage of Palamon and
Emelye is a worldly argument for accepting a young hero's
death, and was not nearly ambitious enough. The content and
the tone of Teseo's speech, most of which Chaucer's Theseus
proceeds to render fairly accurately, are no better a sequel to
the events and issues of the English poem than Boethian philo-
sophizing—nor, I would suggest, do we pass from one to the
other with that sense of perfect artistic ease so often praised in
studies of the *Knight's Tale*.

Chaucer provided Theseus with a speech which is not, in
fact, a triumph of profound and integrated thought, and which
protects itself against the charge of being called a patchwork
affair by some impressive rhetorical phrasing:

> 'That same Prince and that Moevere', quod he,
> 'Hath stablissed in this wrecched world adoun
> Certeyne dayes and duracioun
> To al that is engendred in this place,
> Over the whiche day they may nat pace ...'
>
> (ll. 2994-8)

> 'And therefore, of his wyse purveiaunce,
> He hath so wel biset his ordinaunce,
> That speces of thynges and progressiouns
> Shullen enduren by successiouns'
>
> (ll. 3011-14)

accompanied by the invitation to 'thanken Juppiter of al his
grace' (l. 3069). But such is the memory of what has gone
before that the announcement of this long-delayed union
prompts relief rather than gratitude: the narrative, like the
poem, exhausts itself.

In Boccaccio's *Teseida*, Chaucer seems to have discovered
the material for a theme both sombre and dramatic—man's

confused encounter with the operation of destinal forces. Enriching that theme from his reading of Boethius and also, perhaps, from other later philosophers, he was still more strongly motivated by his feeling for the pathos of the human dilemma than by his conviction of that perfect ordering of the universe in which pathos should become irrelevant. If he was familiar with neo-platonic theory that the seemingly evil influences of planetary deities such as Saturn and Mars are only real in so far as they are brought into play by the imperfect, contradictory terrestrial world,[16] he did not allow that knowledge to dictate the emotional emphases of his poetry, nor to provide him with that great statement which might indeed have set the cruelties of the gods into a justifying context. As it is, those cruelties remain unjustified, unassimilated either into the narrative of the poem or into its stated philosophic system. For all the gravity of the language in which Theseus begins to attempt a reconciliation of suffering and happiness, Venus, Mars, and Saturn are never identifiable with the purposes of 'the Firste Moevere of the cause above' nor are their generally malignant influences properly subsumed into a benign law of life, administered by the creator of the 'faire cheyne of love', 'hym that al may gye'. Brought into harsh focus by the poet's vision of the pain for which they are responsible, they remain impressive, counselling nothing but obedience and endurance. Similarly no serenity, except perhaps that of 'all passion spent', is won through the unlikely metamorphosis, only acceptable on the most superficial verbal level, of Jupiter into 'cause of all thyng', the burning fountain of creation.

The lasting satisfactions of the poem do not lie in Chaucer's search for some formal ordering, of both art and concept, which will serve to control the rich, often contradictory materials assembled from his reading of romance, astrology, medicine, and philosophy. Comprehensible as that search is in an age which was dedicated to belief in ultimate and all-embracing order, it did not draw upon Chaucer's imaginative energies to the full. The *Knight's Tale*, at its most remarkable, is an uneven work of 'sad lucidity', presenting a view of a world in which there is 'nor certitude, nor peace, nor help for pain', and expressing best not the great orthodoxies of medieval faith, but the stubborn truths of human experience. The importance of this should not be underestimated. Only in certain limited contexts, and with limited emphases, did the medieval artist feel able to attend to those truths: when he did, he associated defiance, anger, despair, and doubt with a deficiency of moral strength and rarely with sensibility or intelligence. The medieval drama of protest is a religious drama, centred upon figures of unlawful rebellion and disbelief, from Lucifer to Cain, Noah's wife, Herod, and the unrepentant thief. The medieval Faustus is King Alexander, whose bid to defy his mortal destiny and scale the walls of Paradise was never more than an exemplum of vanquished pride. The *Knight's Tale* defends itself from criticism, to some extent, by preserving the form, if not the spirit, of a classical, non-Christian setting, and it comes, in the end, to rest upon conventional moral attitudes. But on the way to that ending, it allows its human beings a temporary freedom to act magnanimously and to speak movingly about their doubt of divine justice and benevolence. The fact that we can feel the power of what they say, and yet remain uncertain of Chaucer's over-all intention for his poem's meaning, still recommends the *Tale* as unusually well endowed with incentives to thought. Few other medieval poems offer us such a range of ironic reflection upon the confused nature of human affairs:

> Mind is a light which the Gods mock us with,
> To lead those false who trust it ...
> (Arnold, *Empedocles and Etna*)

Not only, then, for what it brings over into English of Italian pseudo-classical romance, but also for what it rejects and is stimulated to add, the *Knight's Tale* represents a major extension of the scope of medieval English poetry. Answering exactly to no particular literary genre of its time, either Italian or English, but indebted to many, it is an experimental poem of some distinction, in which we are able to see the making, not simply the confirming, of tradition.

Notes

CHAPTER 1

1. *Secular Lyrics of the XIVth and XVth Centuries*, ed. R. H. Robbins, 2nd edn. (Oxford, 1955), p. 106, no. 117.

2. *English Lyrics of the XIIIth Century*, ed. Carleton Brown (Oxford, 1932), p. 33. no. 23 (text somewhat regularized).

3. B-text, Passus V, ll. 560-84. Quotations from the B-text are from *Piers Plowman: the B Version*, ed. G. Kane and E. T. Donaldson (London, 1975), with modernization of ȝ and þ. Other quotations are from *The Vision of William Concerning Piers Plowman*, ed. W. W. Skeat (Oxford, 1886; revised J. A. W. Bennett, 1954).

4. The popular treatise known as the *Speculum Vitae*, written in the late fourteenth century, exists in two forms, verse and prose: 35 manuscripts of the poetic version, but only 3 manuscripts of the prose version remain. See W. Pantin, *The English Church in the Fourteenth Century* (Cambridge, 1955), pp. 228-9.

5. *The Minor Poems of John Lydgate*, ed. H. N. MacCracken, vol. 2: *Secular Poems*, EETS, OS 192 (1934), p. 723.

6. See Carleton Brown, 'Caiaphas as a Palm Sunday Prophet', in *Kittredge Anniversary Papers* (Boston, 1913), pp. 105-17; also R. Axton, 'Popular Modes in the Earliest Plays', in *Medieval Drama: Stratford-upon-Avon Studies 16*, ed. N. Denny (London, 1973), p. 30.

7. *European Literature and the Latin Middle Ages*, translated by W. R. Trask (London,1953), p. 392.

8. *English Lyrics of the XIIIth Century*, p. 14, no. 8: 'Birds in the trees, fish in the streams, and I am driven to despair. I wander sorrowful for the loveliest creature (on earth).'

9. *The Dance of Death* paintings, for instance, with their appropriate verses: see *The Dance of Death*, ed. F. Warren and B. White, EETS, OS 181 (1931), and Philippa Tristram, *Figures of Life and Death in Medieval English Literature* (London, 1976), pp. 167-73.

10. John Mirk, *Festial: A Collection of Homilies*, ed. Th. Erbe, EETS, ES 96 (1905), p. 171.

11. *English Lyrics of the XIIIth Century*, pp. 19-20, no. 13: 'If a man meditated inwardly and continuously how painful is the journey from bed to floor, how pitiful the removal from floor to pit, from pit to pain that nevermore shall end, I am sure no sin would win his heart.'

12. Ibid., p. 174.

13. See E. W. Tristram, *English Wall Painting of the Fourteenth Century* (London, 1955), pp. 112-14, 220. The *Three Living and the Three Dead* tableau is on the East wall of the tower.

14. *English Lyrics of the XIIIth Century*, p. 1, no. 1.
15. W. L. Renwick and H. Orton, *The Beginnings of English Literature to Skelton 1509*, 2nd edn. (London, 1952), Introduction, p. 60.
16. *English Lyrics of the XIIIth Century*, Introduction, p. xvi.
17. Ibid., p. 166. 'Do not marvel that I am brown and sunburnt, for the sun has discoloured me.'
18. See *Religious Lyrics of the XIVth Century*, ed. Carleton Brown (Oxford, 1924), 2nd edn. revised G. V. Smithers (Oxford, 1957), p. 45, no. 31 (ll. 22-3).
19. Jan Van Eyck's *Annunciation*, in the National Museum in Washington, or the *Annunciation* of the Hours of Isabella of Milan (Cambridge University Library, MS Additional 6689).
20. J. Speirs, *Medieval English Poetry: The Non-Chaucerian Tradition* (London, 1957), p. 47.
21. Ibid.
22. See 'The Hidden Struggle', by Henry Moore, *The Observer*, 24 Nov. 1957.
23. See, for instance, the St. Matthew portrait in the Dover Bible (Corpus Christi College, Cambridge, MSS 3-4) or the more extravagantly non-realistic evangelist portraits in the Mostyn Gospels (Pierpont Morgan Library MS 777): see T. S. R. Boase, *English Art 1100-1216* (Oxford, 1953), pp. 157, 167.
24. E. W. Tristram, *English Wall Painting*, p. 17.
25. The whalebone carving of the *Adoration of the Kings*, 11th-century English work, from the Victoria and Albert Museum, would be an excellent example. See Lawrence Stone, *Sculpture in Britain: The Middle Ages* (Pelican History of Art, 1955), pp. 64, 70, plate 41. Or see R. Hinks, *Carolingian Art* (London, 1935), plate xix, facing p. 188.
26. Georges Braque, 'The Power of Mystery', *The Observer*, 1 Dec. 1957.
27. Marshall McLuhan, *The Gutenberg Galaxy* (University of Toronto Press, 1964), p. 136.
28. See the *Rohan Book of Hours,* with an introduction and notes by Jean Porcher (London, 1959), plate 6, p.27.
29. J. Speirs, *Medieval English Poetry*, p. 47.
30. *Sir Gawain and the Green Knight*, ed. J. R. R. Tolkien and E. V. Gordon (Oxford, 1925), ll. 2000-6: 'But fierce storms arose in the world outside, clouds drove the cold sharply down to the earth, with bitter enough wind from the north to torment the naked; the snow showered down sharply,stinging the wild animals; the whistling wind blew strong from the heights, and filled each valley full of great drifts. The man listened hard as he lay in his bed.'
31. *The Book of the Duchess*, ll. 1308-10. All quotations from Chaucer are from the *Works*, ed. F. N. Robinson, 2nd edn. (Cambridge, Mass., 1957).
32. *Pearl*, ed. E. V. Gordon (Oxford, 1958), ll. 1093-6: 'Just as the mighty moon rises before the light of day all sinks down, even thus suddenly in a wondrous wise I became aware of a procession' (Gordon's translation, p. 84).

33. John Lawlor, 'The Pattern of Consolation in *The Book of the Duchess*', *Speculum* 31 (1956), 626-48.

34. Derek Pearsall, 'Rhetorical *Descriptio* in *Sir Gawain and the Green Knight*', *MLR* 50 (1955), 132.

35. Ibid.

36. Robert Frost, 'Tree at my Window'.

37. James Russell Lowell, essay on Chaucer in *My Study Windows*, as reprinted in *Chaucer: The Critical Heritage*, ed. D. Brewer, 2 vols. (London, 1978), ii. 132.

38. *Religious Lyrics of the XVth Century*, ed. Carleton Brown (Oxford, 1939), pp. 236-7, no. 149.

39. *Holy Sonnets*, no. VI.

40. Donne, 'A hymn to God the Father'. See also *Sonnet* no. 1, which ends, 'And thou like adamant draw mine iron heart'.

41. George Herbert, 'Affliction'.

42. *Pearl*, ll. 1167-71: 'Though I was rash and headstrong in my haste, I was promptly checked. For just as I hastened to the bank, that impetuous action startled me from my dream. Then I awoke in that beautiful arbour.'

43. See the comments of Henry Moore, in *The Observer*, 24 Nov. 1957, on the 'disturbing qualities' of all great art, and on the 'mixture of degrees of realism' in his work, and in certain primitive and medieval sculptural styles.

44. *Ratis Raving*, ed. J. R. Lumby, EETS, OS 43 (1870), p. 26, ll. 15-18.

45. *Religious Lyrics of the XVth Century*, pp. 269-72, no. 177.

46. *The Poems of John Audelay*, ed. E. K. Whiting, EETS, OS 184 (1931), p. 149.

47. Ibid., p. 211, no. 51, ll. 1-2, 7-9.

48. Ibid., p. 197, no. 41. We could compare the images of childhood used by the Yorkshire contemplative, Richard Rolle, always in a reductive context, e.g. 'But som er, þat lufes noght wysely, like til barnes, þat lufes mare an appel þan a castel', *Form of Living*, cap. 10, in *English Writings of Richard Rolle*, ed. Hope Emily Allen (Oxford, 1931), p. 113.

49. *The Poems of John Audelay*, p. 203, no. 44.

50. Ibid., p. 210, no. 50.

51. *Troilus and Criseyde*, iii. 1450-2.

CHAPTER 2

1. Laȝamon's *Brut*, ed. G. L. Brook and R. F. Leslie, EETS, 250 (1963), ll. 3058-64 (Caligula text). The punctuation has been modernized.

2. Only two MSS are extant: British Museum Caligula A.ix, and Otho C.xiii. The Otho MS is up to twenty years later than Caligula.

3. See J. S. P. Tatlock, *The Legendary History of Britain* (Berkeley and Los Angeles, 1950), pp. 6, 476.

4. See the edition by E. G. Stanley (Nelson's Medieval and Renaissance Library, London and Edinburgh, 1960), Introduction, pp. 25-33.

5. See M. Dominica Legge, *Anglo-Norman Literature and its Background* (Oxford, 1963), p. 94.

6. See R. W. Chambers, *On the Continuity of English Prose from Alfred to More and his School*, EETS, OS 191A (1932); R. M. Wilson, *Early Middle English Literature* (London, 1939), and 'English and French in England 1100-1300', *History*, 28 (1943), 37-60.

7. See M. Dominica Legge, *Anglo-Norman Literature*, p. 4, note 2: she quotes the chronicler Jocelyn of Brakelond, who testifies to the fact that by 1182 most country folk understood French.

8. Legge, *Anglo-Norman Literature*, pp. 362-7.

9. Legge, *Anglo-Norman Literature*, Chapter IX; W. A. Pantin, *The English Church in the Fourteenth Century* (Cambridge, 1955), Chapter X.

10. Her Lais were written for 'a king'—whether Henry II, the 'young King Henry', or for John is not clear. See Legge, *Anglo-Norman Literature*, p. 73. See also C. Bullock-Davies, *Professional Interpreters and the Matter of Britain* (Cardiff. 1966), pp. 14-17; id., 'Marie, Abbess of Shaftesbury, and her Brothers', *EHR* 80 (1965), 314-22.

11. See T. S. R. Boase, *English Art 1100-1216* (Oxford, 1953), pp. 190-2.

12. Ibid., pp. 78-91.

13. *Brut*, ed. cit. ll. 20-3 (Caligula text).

14. ed. A. S. Napier (Oxford, 1916).

15. *Floris and Blauncheflur*, ed. A. B. Taylor (Oxford, 1927).

16. It is necessary to stress this because so much of a vaguely sentimental nature has been written about medieval English literature intended for the 'peasant classes': no doubt their needs were taken into account in the simplest vernacular sermons, as in the simplest wall-paintings of medieval churches. But this should not be indiscriminately extended into the vernacular romance and lyric verses which remain to us, most of which were written for very different tastes and levels of perception.

17. Legge, *Anglo-Norman Literature*, p. 204.

18. Ibid., Chapters IV-VI, *passim.*

19. ed. (Corpus Christi College, Cambridge, MS 402) J. R. R. Tolkien, EETS 249 (1962); ed. (Parts Six and Seven) G. Shepherd (London and Edinburgh, 1959). For the original audience, see E. J. Dobson, *The Origins of Ancrene Wisse* (Oxford, 1976).

20. Dobson, *Origins*, p. 252.

21. The *Manuel* is edited by E. J. Arnould (Paris, 1940); Robert Mannyng's *Handlyng Synne* is edited by F. J. Furnivall, EETS, OS 119, 123 (1901, 1903).

22. Legge, *Anglo-Norman Literature*, p. 233.

23. Ibid., p. 236.

24. Ibid., p. 334.

25. See *English Lyrics of the XIIIth Century*, ed. C. Brown (Oxford, 1932), Introduction, pp. xxviii-xl.

26. Ibid., p. xxxiii.

27. *The Harley Lyrics*, ed. G. L. Brook (Manchester, 1948), p. 55, no. 19.

28. See R. Axton, 'Popular Modes in the Earliest Plays', in *Medieval Drama: Stratford-upon-Avon Studies 16* (London, 1973), 12-39 (p. 32).
29. Legge, *Anglo-Norman Literature*, pp. 235-6.
30. See the Preface to *Richard Cœur de Lion*, quoted above, p. 27.
31. See the unpublished Ph.D. Dissertation by J. Martin (Weiss) (Cambridge, 1967), 'Studies in some early middle English romances'.
32. See Legge, *Anglo-Norman Literature*, pp. 171-5. The sixteenth-century antiquary, John Leland, describes 'an old Englisch boke yn Ryme of the Gestes of Guarine' in such a way that the lost alliterative poem can sometimes be discerned. See *De Rebus Britannicis Collectanea* (London, 1770), I. 230 ff.
33. Alice Fitzwarren, for instance, the wife of Richard Whittington, Mayor of London (d. 1423), was 'the daughter of Sir Ivo Fitzwaryn, a knight of considerable landed property in the south-western counties, who on several occasions represented Dorset and Devon in parliament' and who also had interests in Hertfordshire and minor hereditary office under the Crown (see *DNB*, under *Whittington*).
34. From writers such as R. W. Chambers (see note 6, above) for instance, who gave their pioneer arguments for the 'continuity' of English literature throughout the Old and Middle English periods a semi-patriotic flavour.
35. V. H. Galbraith, 'Nationality and Language in Medieval England', *TRHS*, 4th Series, 23 (1941), 125.
36. See P. Brieger, *English Art 1216-1307* (Oxford, 1957), p. 154.
37. Ibid., p. 4.
38. *Opera Quaedam Inedita*, ed. J. S. Brewer (London, Rolls Series, 1859), p. 433. Bacon is asking that the new theologians should be competent in Greek, Hebrew, Arabic, and Chaldean, but not necessarily as fluent in them as if they were a mother tongue.
39. *Metrical Chronicle*, ed. W. A. Wright (London, Rolls Series, 1887), ll. 7544-5.
40. British Library MS Additional 46919, fo. 14b.
41. See W. Rothwell, 'The Teaching of French in Medieval England', *MLR* 63 (1968), p. 44; 'as time went on ... French even in its insular form became less and less a vernacular ...'.
42. Digby 86 is one of a number of manuscripts compiled by Friars—'the Golden Treasuries or Oxford Books of Verse of the thirteenth century' (*Secular Lyrics of the XIVth and XVth Centuries*, ed. R. H. Robbins, Oxford, 1955, p. xvii). Harley 2253 was also probably made up in some kind of religious setting: see below, text at note 63.
43. *Of Arthour and of Merlin*, ed. O. D. Macrae-Gibson, EETS 268 (1973), 279 (1979); *Richard Cœur de Lion*, ed. K. Brunner, Wiener Beiträge zur Englischen Philologie, Bd. 42 (Vienna, 1913).
44. See *Kyng Alisaunder*, ed. G. V. Smithers, EETS 237 (1957), Introduction, pp. 58-60.
45. Gwyn A. Williams, *Medieval London* (London, 1963), p. 196.
46. Quoted by B. Smalley, *English Friars and Antiquity in the Early Fourteenth Century* (Oxford, 1960), pp. 162-3.

47. ed. E. J. Arnould (Oxford, 1940), p. 239.

48. *Cursor Mundi* ed. R. Morris, EETS, OS 57, 59, 62, 66, 68, 99, 101 (1874-93), ll. 2-3.

49. Galbraith, 'Nationality and Language', p. 144.

50. For Holcot and Robert of Gloucester, see above, text at notes 39, 46; for Higden, see *Polychronicon*, ed. C. Babington and J. R. Lumby, Rolls Series, 9 vols. (1865-86), II.159; for the *Croyland Chronicle*, see *Ingulph's Chronicle of the Abbey of Croyland*, trans. H. T. Riley (London, 1854), p. 142, and Smalley, *English Friars*, p. 163.

51. M. McKisack, *The Fourteenth Century 1307-1399* (Oxford, 1959), p. 151. We should note, however, that this did not affect the Duke of Gloucester's enthusiasm for French and Anglo-French literature. See below, text at note 74.

52. *The Poems of Laurence Minot*, ed. J. Hall, 3rd edn. (Oxford, 1914), no. VIII, p. 27.

53. *Piers Plowman*, B.IX. 8.

54. *Cursor Mundi*, l. 235: see above, text at note 48.

55. See below, Chapter 3, note 105.

56. Advocates' MS 19.2.1, National Library of Scotland.

57. See L. H. Loomis, 'The Auchinleck Manuscript and a possible London bookshop of 1330-1340', *PMLA* 57 (1942), 595-627.

58. See S. L. Thrupp, *The Merchant Class of Medieval London 1300-1500* University of Chicago Press, 1948, Ann Arbor Paperbacks, 1962), Ch. VII, 'The Middle Strata of the Nation'.

59. Ibid., p. 311.

60. Williams, *Medieval London*, p. 98.

61. ed. ll. 77-8 from the extract (ll. 1-370) printed by J. Ullmann in *EStn* 7 (1884), 468-72.

62. *Harley Lyrics,* ed. Brook, p. 31, no. 3.

63. Adam of Orleton, Bishop of Hereford (1317-27), forbade the 'cantilenis inhonestis' of the monks at Wigmore—a house he disciplined. See N. R. Ker, Introduction to a *Facsimile of British Museum MS. Harley 2253*, EETS 255 (1965), p. xxiii; *Registrum Ade de Orleton*, ed. A. T. Bannister (Canterbury and York Society, vol. 5, 1908), p. 102.

64. Ker, Introduction, pp. xxii-xxiii.

65. *The Harrowing of Hell, Our Lady's Psalter, Sayings of St. Bernard, Ubi Sunt, The Thrush and Nightingale.*

66. In this connection, one might consider briefly the resemblances between the contents of Harley 2253 and those of some earlier Latin MSS of goliardic and erotic verse, such as the Benedictbeuern MS.

67. See L. H. Loomis, 'Chaucer and the Auchinleck MS', *Essays and Studies in Honor of Carleton Brown* (New York, 1940), pp. 111-28; 'Chaucer and the Breton Lays of the Auchinleck MS', *SP* 38 (1941), 14-33.

68. See D. S. Brewer, 'The Relationship of Chaucer to the English and European Traditions', in *Chaucer and Chaucerians* (London, 1966), pp. 1-38.

69. For Chaucer, see the essays by Loomis cited in note 67 above; for Langland, see E. Salter, *'Piers Plowman* and *The Simonie'*, *Archiv* 203 (1967), 241-54.

70. On Chaucer's middle-class origins, see V. B. and L. J. Redstone, 'The Heyrons of London', *Speculum* 12 (1937), 182-95; also *Chaucer Life Records*, ed. M. M. Crow and C. C. Olson (Oxford, 1966), pp. 1-12.

71. Smalley, *English Friars*, p. 26.

72. For Guy of Warwick's books, see M. Blaess, 'L'Abbaye de Bordesley et les Livres de Guy de Beauchamp', *Romania*, 78 (1957), 511-18, and E. Salter, 'The Alliterative Revival, I', *MP* 64 (1966), 148-9.

73. See *The Romans of Partenay*, ed. W. W. Skeat, EETS, OS 22 (1866), p. 231, ll. 108-12.

74. The 84 volumes, taken from his castle at Pleshy, are listed in the *Archaeological Journal*, 54 (1897), 300 ff. : a further collection seized 'within the city' by the Mayor of London, Richard Whittington, is listed in the *Calendar of Inquisitions Miscellaneous,* vi. 1392-9 (London, 1963), no. 372, p. 223.

75. See E. Rickert, 'King Richard II's Books', *The Library*, 13 (1933), 144-7.

76. See *Chronicles*, Bk. iv, trans. Lord Berners, ed. G. C. Macaulay (London, 1895), p. 430.

77. Rickert, 'King Richard II's Books', p. 146.

78. See J. Nichols, *Wills of the Kings and Queens of England* (London, 1780), pp. 181 ff.

79. The list can be found in British Museum Additional MS 25459-60. But see also M. V. Clarke, 'Forfeitures and Treason in 1388', *Fourteenth Century Studies,* ed. L. Sutherland and M. McKisack (Oxford, 1937), pp. 115-45.

80. See *The French Text of the Ancrene Riwle*, ed. J. A. Herbert, EETS, OS 219 (1944), Introduction, pp. xii-xiii. The elaborate Stonyhurst MS of the *Livre de Seyntz Medicines* belonged to Humphrey of Gloucester, who was the author's great-grandson, through Blanche of Lancaster: see Legge, *Anglo-Norman Literature*, p. 218; also E. J. Arnould, *Etude sur le Livre des Saintes Médecines* (Paris, 1948), p. lxix.

81. Thrupp, *Merchant Class*, p. 162.

82. Williams, *Medieval London*, p. 299.

83. *Mirror of Justices*, ed. W. J. Whittaker (Selden Society, vol. 7, London, 1895).

84. Helen Suggett, 'The use of French in England in the later Middle Ages', *TRHS* 28 (1946), 78.

85. In 1362 Parliament was first opened in English; in the same year it was laid down that all law-suits should be conducted in English; and in 1385 Trevisa tells his familiar story of the change-over to English as the language of instruction in English grammar-schools. See A. C. Baugh, *A History of the English Language* (New York, 1957), pp. 171-9.

86. Suggett, 'The use of French', pp. 78, 79.

87. See 'William of Kingsmill—a Fifteenth Century Teacher of French in Oxford', by M. Dominica Legge, in *Studies in French Language and Medieval Literature Presented to M. K. Pope* (Manchester, 1939), pp. 241-6.

88. See N. F. Blake, 'The Vocabulary in French and English Printed by William Caxton', *ELN* 3 (1965), 7-15.
89. *Catalogue of Wills Proved and Enrolled in the Court of Hustings, London,* ed. R. R. Sharpe, (London, 1889), i. 234.
90. See E. Rickert, 'Chaucer at School', *MP* 29 (1932), 257-74, for a suggestion that a list of eighty-four books bequeathed to St. Paul's Almonry School in 1358 (mainly classical and post-classical Latin works) provides an interesting background to Chaucer's own reading, evidenced in his poetry.
91. *Catalogue of Wills,* ed. Sharpe, i. 606-7.
92. Ibid., i. 344.
93. Ibid., i. 681. Left by William le Peyntour, notary, in 1354.
94. Ibid., i. 557.
95. Ibid., i. 649, 588.
96. Ibid., i. 363. This may have been Rolle's version of the *Psalter.*
97. See M. Deanesley, 'Vernacular Books in England in the Fourteenth and Fifteenth Centuries', *MLR* 15 (1920), 352-6.
98. See J. A. F. Thomson, *The Later Lollards* (Oxford, 1965), p. 119: a group in Essex were 'alleged to read English books in secret.'
99. For a list of Carpenter's books, see T. Brewer, *Memoirs of the Life and Times of John Carpenter* (London, 1856), p. 130.
100. See W. F. Schirmer, *John Lydgate* (1952; trans. Ann E. Keep, London, 1961), pp. 128 and 144.
101. *Hoccleve's Works: The Minor Poems,* ed. F. J. Furnivall and I. Gollancz, EETS, ES 61 (1892), 73 (1925), p. 63.
102. See Thrupp, *Merchant Class,* Ch. VI, 'Trade and Gentility'. Sir Thomas Urswyck, for example, married the daughter of a mercer, Richard Rich.
103. For the Pastons and their origins, see H. S. Bennett, *The Pastons and their England* (Cambridge, 1922).
104. A complete list of John Paston's books is given in *The Paston Letters,* ed. J. Gairdner (London, 1910), iii. 300-1, item 869.
105. See Thrupp, *Merchant Class,* p. 248. It is interesting that a Robert Urswyck was King's Esquire, in company with Chaucer: the family was in those days in the employ of John of Gaunt.
106. See *Lincoln Diocese Documents 1450-1544,* ed. A. Clark, EETS, OS 149 (1914), pp. 48-9.
107. See Thrupp, *Merchant Class,* p. 248.
108. Ibid., p. 248.
109. See R. J. Dean, 'An Essay in Anglo-Norman Palaeography', *Studies Presented to M. K. Pope* (see note 87, above), pp. 84-5.
110. See N. F. Blake, 'Caxton and Chaucer', *Leeds Studies in English,* n.s. 1 (1967), p. 22; N. F. Blake, *Caxton and his World* (London, 1969), pp. 102-3.
111. *The Prologues and Epilogues of William Caxton,* ed. W. J. B. Crotch, EETS, OS 186 (London, 1928), p. 27.
112. N. F. Blake, 'Investigations into the Prologues and Epilogues by William Caxton', *BJRL* 49 (1966-7), 27.

113. N. F. Blake, *Caxton's Own Prose* (London, 1973), p.61.
114. *Troy Book*, ed. H. Bergen, EETS, ES 97, 103, 106, 126 (1906-35), iii. 4238, 4240.
115. N. F. Blake, in 'Caxton and Courtly Style', *Essays and Studies* 21 (1968), 37, suggests that 'Caxton must have meant the alliterative poems': I think this is rather a limited interpretation, for reasons which are set out below, in the first part of Chapter 4.
116. D. Brewer, 'Relationship' (note 68, above), pp. 4-15, stresses the indebtedness of Chaucer to romances of the Auchinleck type: *Sir Thopas,* however, remains a strikingly malicious comment by a professional upon the inferior work of amateurs.
117. D. Pearsall, 'The Development of Middle English Romance', *MS* 27 (1965), 91-2.
118. See Williams, *Medieval London*, pp. 313-14.
119. See the tables in Appendix I of W. H. Schofield's *English Literature from the Norman Conquest to Chaucer* (London, 1906), which show quite clearly the importance of the period 1275-1325 for translation of all kinds.
120. See above, note 69.
121. See E. Rickert, 'King Richard II's Books' (note 75, above).
122. *Chronicles* (see note 76, above).
123. See H. Braddy, *Chaucer and the French Poet Graunson* (Louisiana State University Press, 1947), Chaps. I, III, IV.
124. For Clanvowe and his work, see V. J. Scattergood, *Sir John Clanvowe: Works* (Cambridge, 1975), and below, text at note 137.
125. For Halsham's *Balade* see *Religious Lyrics of the XVth Century,* ed. C. Brown (Oxford, 1939), no. 171, p. 262, and below, Chapter 3, text at note 85.
126. See D. Brewer, 'Relationship', (note 68 above), p. 15.
127. This particular copy is now in the British Library MS Royal 19.B.xiii. For Sir Richard Sturry see K. B. McFarlane, *Lancastrian Kings and Lollard Knights* (Oxford, 1972), p. 184.
128. See McFarlane, *Lancastrian Kings,* p. 180.
129. K. B. McFarlane, in *The Nobility of Later Medieval England* (Oxford, 1973), pp. 43, 243-6, quotes an interesting series of examples.
130. For John Montacute, see the *DNB*, xiii. 652-3, and M. Boirin, *Vie de Christine de Pisan, Collection des Meilleurs Ouvrages Francois,* ed. de Keralio (Paris, 1787), ii. 118.
131. See *Archaeologia,* 20 (1824), 1-442 for translation and text of this *Chronicle* which is variously supposed to have been written by a French knight, Creton, or by a Bishop Trevor of St. Asaph.
132. *Archaeologia,* 20 (1824), 71.
133. See E. Salter, 'The Alliterative Revival', *MP* 64 (1966), 149. [Note that 'the west country' is used, here and elsewhere, to designate the area of the south-west midlands, Gloucestershire, Herefordshire, etc.—D.P.]
134. See *William of Palerne,* ed. W. W. Skeat, EETS, ES 1 (1867), ll. 5529-33.

135. *The Gest Hystoriale of the Destruction of Troy*, ed. G. A. Panton and D. Donaldson, EETS, OS 39, 56 (1869, 1874), p. lxx.

136. See Salter, 'The Alliterative Revival', pp. 149-50.

137. For Sir John Clanvowe and his poem, see Scattergood, *Clanvowe* (note 124 above).

138. See J. R. L. Highfield, 'The Green Squire', *MAE* 22 (1953), 18-23, and Salter, 'The Alliterative Revival', pp. 233-7.

139. J. H. Fisher, *John Gower: Moral Philosopher and Friend of Chaucer* (New York, 1964), p. 41.

140. This is from Gower's own colophon, composed about 1390, as translated by Fisher, *John Gower*, pp. 88-9. See *English Works*, ed. G. C. Macaulay, EETS, ES 82 (1901), pp. 479-80.

141. *Confessio Amantis*, in *Works*, ed. G. C. Macaulay, EETS, ES 81 (1900), Prologue, l. 39.

142. See J. H. Fisher, *John Gower*, p. 78, and Williams, *Medieval London*, p. 23.

143. D. Pearsall, 'Gower's Narrative Art', *PMLA* 81 (1966), 475.

144. M. Dominica Legge, *Anglo-Norman Literature*, p. 364.

145. See C. A. Luttrell, 'Three North-West Midland Manuscripts', *Neophilologus* 42 (1958), 38-50.

146. See above, text at notes 99-112.

147. See J. Burrow, 'The Audience of *Piers Plowman*', *Anglia* 75 (1957), 373-84.

148. See above, p. 45.

149. *Piers Plowman*, C.I.8.

150. See J. Burrow, 'Audience of *Piers Plowman*', p. 381.

151. See *Piers Plowman*, ed. E. Salter and D. Pearsall (London, 1967), p. 55.

152. Ibid., pp. 51-8.

153. Burrow, 'Audience', p. 377.

154. See E. P. Hammond, *English Verse between Chaucer and Surrey* (Durham, N. Ca., 1927), pp. 214 ff.

155. For Henry V, while still Prince, Hoccleve wrote his *Regement of Princes;* his poems in Durham University Library MS V.iii.9 were written and presented to the Countess of Westmorland. Lydgate dedicated his *Fall of Princes* to Humphrey, Duke of Gloucester, younger brother of Henry V, and wrote for many other patrons: see D. Pearsall, *John Lydgate* (London, 1970), pp. 1, 125, 161-88.

156. See H. S. Bennett, *The Pastons and their England*, p. 111.

157. See above, note 72.

158. By Stephen Scrope: edited by C. F. Bühler, EETS, OS 211 (1941).

159. For William of Worcester, see T. D. Kendrick, *British Antiquity* (London, 1950), pp. 29 ff.

160. See *Archaeologia*, 66 (1870), 275 ff.

CHAPTER 3

1. *The Canterbury Tales, Parson's Prologue*, ll. 42-3, in *Works*, ed. F. N. Robinson, 2nd edn. (Cambridge, Mass., 1957).
2. *Wynnere and Wastoure*, ed. I. Gollancz (London, 1930), ll. 8-9: 'No westerner dare ever send his son south, on any sort of business, for fear of his remaining there, while his father grows old.'
3. fo. 197b. See E. Salter, *Nicholas Love's 'Myrrour of the Blessed Lyf of Jesu Christ'*, Analecta Cartusiana 10 (Salzburg, 1974), 13.
4. fo. 1a. Ibid., p. 11. 'Be careful with these words: "gude" for "gode", also "hir" for "heere" in the plural.'
5. Higden, *Polychronicon*, as excerpted in K. Sisam, *Fourteenth Century Verse and Prose* (Oxford, 1921), p. 149.
6. The first thorough-going localization of the tail-rhyme romances (using a distinctive stanza-form, made up of couplets and short rhyming lines) was proposed by A. McI. Trounce, 'The English Tail-Rhyme Romances', a series of articles in *MAE* 1, 2, 3 (1932-4). The exclusively western tradition of alliterative poetry received much earlier attention, but was probably stated most authoritatively by R. W. Chambers, in his monograph *On the Continuity of English Prose from Alfred to More and his School* (from the Introduction to EETS, OS 191A, 1932), which argued for the continuity of English literature on the evidence of western alliterative poetry and prose.
7. J. R. Hulbert, 'A Hypothesis Concerning the Alliterative Revival', *MP* 28 (1931), 405-22. For detailed argument against this hypothesis, see E. Salter, 'The Alliterative Revival'.
8. See A. McI. Trounce, ed. *Athelston*, EETS, OS 224 (1951), Introduction, p. 43.
9. J. A. Burrow, 'The Audience of *Piers Plowman*', *Anglia* 75 (1957), 373.
10. *Pearl, Cleanness, Patience, Sir Gawain and the Green Knight*, ed. A. C. Cawley and J. J. Anderson (London, 1976: *Pearl* and *Gawain* from the edition of 1962), p. viii.
11. For criticism of Trounce's hypothesis, see G. Taylor, 'Notes on *Athelston*', *Leeds Studies in English* 4 (1935), 47-57; A. R. Dunlap, 'The Vocabulary of the Middle English Romances in Tail-Rhyme Stanza', *Delaware Notes* (1941).
12. Sir Frank Stenton, 'The Roads of the Gough Map', in *The Map of Great Britain circa AD 1360 known as the Gough Map*, facsimile, with Introduction by E. J. S. Parsons (Oxford, 1958), p. 15.
13. Ibid., p. 16.
14. Thrupp, *The Merchant Class of Medieval London*, p. 208.
15. See R. Ekwall, *Studies on the Population of Medieval London* (Stockholm, 1956).
16. Williams, *Medieval London*, pp. 131 ff.
17. Ibid., p. 140.
18. Ibid., p. 101.
19. See E. L. G. Stones, 'Sir Geoffrey le Scrope (*c.*1285-1340), Chief Justice of the King's Bench', *EHR* 69 (1954), 3, for reference to the

personal wealth of Henry, first Lord Scrope of Masham, at his death in 1391. For the library of Henry, the third Lord Scrope, executed in 1415, see McFarlane, *Nobility*, p. 237.

20. See Fisher, *John Gower*, pp. 39 ff.
21. Williams, *Medieval London*, p. 109.
22. Ibid., p. 138.
23. Ibid., p. 140.
24. Thrupp, *Merchant Class*, pp. 211, 369.
25. Ibid., p. 332. See also p. 349 for John de Heylesdon, mercer, alderman in the 1370s, and citizen of Norwich.
26. See note 70 to Chapter 2, above.
27. M. L. Samuels, 'Some Applications of Middle English Dialectology', *ES* 44 (1963), 81-4.
28. See M. L. Samuels, 'Some Applications', p. 85, note 5. The MSS concerned are: Bodley MSS Laud. Misc. 448, Bodley 592, and British Library MS Harley 2415.
29. Trounce, 'The English Tail-Rhyme Romances', *MAE* 1 (1932), 88-9.
30. Ibid., *MAE* 3 (1934), 31.
31. Ibid., *MAE* 2 (1933), 35, 42.
32. Ibid., *MAE* 3 (1933), 49-50.
33. The so-called *Chronicle* of Créton: British Library MS Harley 1319. See above, Chapter 2, note 131, and for further examples of tail-rhyme in Anglo-Norman, see M. Dominica Legge, *Anglo-Norman Literature*, pp. 180, 182, 230, 275, 335, 353.
34. The poem 'Lenten ys come wiþ love to toune', for instance: see *Harley Lyrics*, ed. G. L. Brook (Manchester, 1948), no. 11, p. 43.
35. See above, Chapter 2, note 57.
36. Trounce places it firmly in Norfolk: *MAE* 2 (1933), 45.
37. Ibid., *MAE* 1 (1932), 94.
38. The first four occur in Lincoln Cathedral MS 91 and the last two in British Library MS Additional 31042. Trounce refers to the poems in the Lincoln MS as 'Lincoln versions', and to both MSS as 'Lincoln MSS' (*MAE* 1. 95), which is misleading if it associates the poems with the Lincoln area. In fact, the Lincoln Cathedral MS had no connection with Lincoln until the nineteenth century. See below, note 139.
39. For Thomas Chestre, see *Sir Launfal*, ed. A. J. Bliss, Nelson's Medieval and Renaissance Library (London and Edinburgh, 1960), and *DNB*.
40. Trounce, *MAE* 3 (1934), 41-2, argues for the north-east Midlands; earlier critics had favoured the north-west. The Anglo-French original was certainly composed in the west country, for a western patron—the Lord of Monmouth. See M. Dominica Legge, *Anglo-Norman Literature*, pp. 86 ff.
41. See *Athelston*, ed. Trounce, pp. 38-9.
42. The alliterative *St. Erkenwald*, for instance: see below, text at note 121.
43. The Peterborough Psalter, Corpus Christi College, Cambridge, MS 53, which may have been illuminated in Peterborough or Norwich.
44. The Ormesby Psalter, Bodleian MS Douce 366, which was given by a monk of Norwich, Robert of Ormesby, to Norwich Cathedral in 1325.

45. The St. Omer Psalter, British Library MS Additional 39810, begun *c*.1330 for the St. Omer family of Mulbarton, Norfolk; the Luttrell Psalter, British Library MS Additional 42130, made for Sir Geoffrey Luttrell of Irmingham, Norfolk, *c*.1340.

46. Exemplified by the styles of the Westminster Psalter, British Library MS Royal 2.A.xxii and of the Douce Apocalypse, Bodleian MS Douce 180.

47. A Psalter in the Glazier Collection, New York, MS G.50.

48. See M. Rickert, *Painting in Britain in the Middle Ages* (Pelican History of Art, 1954), p. 148.

49. Fitzwilliam Museum of Art, Cambridge, MS 242.

50. New York Public Library, Spencer Collection, MS 26.

51. Munich, Bayerische Staatsbib. Cod. gall. 16.

52. See D. D. Egbert, 'The Grey FitzPayne Hours', *The Art Bulletin*, 18 (1936), 527 ff.

53. See H. Johnstone, 'Isabella, the She-Wolf of France', *History*, 21 (1936), 208-18.

54. See G. A. Holmes, *The Estates of the Higher Nobility in Fourteenth Century England* (Cambridge, 1957), pp. 9-59.

55. S. Armitage-Smith, *John of Gaunt* (London, 1904), p. 207.

56. See K. B. McFarlane, *The Nobility of Later Medieval England* (Oxford, 1973), p. 56.

57. See E. L. G. Stones, 'Sir Geoffrey le Scrope', (note 19 above), Appendix b, 'List of Scrope's diplomatic Missions'.

58. McKisack, *The Fourteenth Century*, p. 20.

59. Ibid., p. 259.

60. See the evidence for this in Gaunt's *Register 1379-1383*, ed. E. C. Lodge and K. Somerville, Camden Society (London, 1937). K. B. McFarlane comments upon Gaunt's file of warrants to his Chancellor as leaving us 'in no doubt who was the mainspring of his vast administration' (*Nobility*, p. 47).

61. See G. L. Kittredge, 'Chaucer and Some of his Friends', *MP* 1 (1903), 4-5.

62. J. R. L. Highfield, 'The Green Squire', *MAE* 22 (1953), 18-23.

63. Gaunt's *Register, 1379-1383*, i. 698, pp. 225-6.

64. See Salter, 'The Alliterative Revival', p. 234.

65. See R. H. Robbins, 'A Gawain Epigone', *MLN* 58 (1943), 361-6, and 'The poems of Humfrey Newton, Esquire, 1466-1536', *PMLA* 65 (1950), 249-81.

66. See W. T. Waugh, 'The Lollard Knights', *Scottish Historical Review*, 11 (1913), 55-92 (p. 81).

67. Ibid., pp. 75-6; see also K. B. McFarlane, *Lancastrian Kings and Lollard Knights* (Oxford, 1972), p. 189.

68. Waugh, 'Lollard Knights', p. 66; McFarlane, *Lancastrian Kings*, p. 188.

69. Waugh, 'Lollard Knights', p. 70; McFarlane, *Lancastrian Kings*, pp. 184-5.

70. See above, Chapter 2, note 128.

71. See *The Complete Peerage*, ed. G. H. White (London, 1953), xii. 247-8.
72. See *Chaucer: A Bibliographical Manual*, by E. P. Hammond (New York, 1908), pp. 333-4, who concludes that 'this codex ... was apparently executed for a Lord Stanley by a well-trained scribe ...'. [See now J. Norton-Smith's Introduction to the Scolar Press *Facsimile of MS Fairfax 16* (London, 1979), and E. Wilson, '*Sir Gawain and the Green Knight* and the Stanley family of Stanley, Storeton, and Hooton', *RES*, n.s. 30 (1979), 308-16.]
73. See C. A. Luttrell, 'Three North-west Midland manuscripts', *Neoph.* 42 (1958), 38-50.
74. Ed. J. P. Oakden, Chetham Society Miscellanies 94 (Manchester, 1935).
75. See G. H. Gerould, 'The Legend of St. Christina by William Paris', *MLN* 29 (1914), 129-33.
76. Ibid., p. 129.
77. Ibid., p. 133.
78. *Religious Lyrics of the XVth Century*, ed. C. Brown, no. 172, p. 263. Compare Chaucer's early *ABC* poem, which uses a stanza similar to that of Parys, but a line which runs to a five-stress pattern.
79. See *Calendar of Patent Rolls*, Richard II, v. 1391-6 (London, 1905), p. 426, in which John Parys of London is given protection 'as going on the king's service to Picardy'.
80. *Calendar of Patent Rolls*, Richard II, ii. 1381-5 (London, 1897), p. 267.
81. Ibid., p. 541.
82. *Calendar of Patent Rolls*, Richard II, iv. 1388-92 (London, 1902), p. 182.
83. He was executed in 1388, by order of the Merciless Parliament: see *The Complete Peerage*, i. 45-6, and McKisack, *The Fourteenth Century*, p. 458.
84. McKisack, *Fourteenth Century*, p. 346.
85. See H. P. South, 'The Question of Halsam', *PMLA* 50 (1935), 362-71.
86. A fine brass in memory of Philippa (d. 1395) remains in West Grinstead Church in Sussex (South, op. cit., p. 368).
87. *Religious Lyrics of the XVth Century*, ed. C. Brown, no. 171, p. 262.
88. Bodleian MS Fairfax 16 (see above, note 72) contains Halsham's *Balade*, and also twenty English poems identified by MacCracken as the work of the Duke of Suffolk. See H. N. MacCracken, 'An English Friend of Charles of Orléans', *PMLA* 26 (1911), 142-80.
89. 'Though I fly free, I am held on a hawk-leash.'
90. See *The Minor Poems of John Lydgate*, ed. H. N. MacCracken, EETS, OS 192 (1934), pp. 730, 734, and 832. It is interesting that in the last example Lydgate weakened Halsham's image, by substituting 'lyne' for 'lune'.
91. See T. F. Tout, 'The English Civil Service in the Fourteenth Century', *John Rylands Library Bulletin*, 3 (1916-17), 185 ff.
92. Williams, *Medieval London*, p. 98.
93. Holmes, *Estates of the Higher Nobility*, pp. 64-5.
94. Printed in E. H. Wilkins, *Was John Wycliffe a Negligent Pluralist?* Also, *John de Trevisa, his Life and Work* (London, 1915), p. 94.
95. Highfield, 'The Green Squire', p. 23.

96. Burrow, 'The Audience of *Piers Plowman*', p. 376.
97. See *Piers Plowman: The A Version*, ed. G. Kane (London, 1960), Introduction, p. 7.
98. *Testamenta Eboracensia* (Surtees Society, 1836-1902), i. 209; ii. 34.
99. See the arguments put forward by Burrow, 'Audience', pp. 378 ff.
100. A map of the distribution of *Piers Plowman* manuscripts provided by Professor M. L. Samuels (see note 27 above) raises interesting speculations: the A texts have an almost totally provincial circulation; the B texts spread from London to Worcestershire; and the C texts are curiously clustered in Herefordshire and Worcestershire.
101. Richard Maidstone, the Carmelite Friar who was a prominent anti-Lollard writer, and Confessor to John of Gaunt. His *Seven Penitential Psalms* in English exist in many manuscripts, one of which (British Library MS Addition 39574) was edited for the Early English Text Society (OS 155, 1921) by M. Day, *The Wheatley Manuscript*, pp. 19-59. See also E. Salter, 'The Alliterative Revival', p. 237, for reminiscences of Chaucer in Maidstone's Latin poetry.
102. *Amis and Amiloun*, ed. MacEdward Leach, EETS, OS 203 (1937), ll. 457-67.
103. See A. McIntosh, 'The Textual Transmission of the Alliterative *Morte Arthure*', *English and Medieval Studies presented to J. R. R. Tolkien*, ed. N. Davis and C. L. Wrenn (London, 1962), p. 240: 'it must be said that a West Midland origin has not been satisfactorily proven.'
104. Ibid., pp. 237-8.
105. Ed. T. Wright, *The Political Songs of England* (Camden Society, vi, 1839), pp. 323-45. See E. Salter, *'Piers Plowman* and *The Simonie'*, *Archiv* 203 (1966-7), 241-54.
106. The Auchinleck MS, National Library of Scotland, Advocates' MS 19.2.1, and Peterhouse, Cambridge, MS 104. The Auchinleck has an accepted London origin, and the Peterhouse MS belonged to Thomas of Exeter, buried at Bury St. Edmunds in 1418.
107. The sole manuscript of the poem is British Library Cotton Caligula A.ii. The standard edition is by H. H. Gibbs, EETS, ES 6 (1868). I have been able to consult and use the edition by Miss E. G. Williams, as yet unpublished (University of London, MA thesis, 1963).
108. 'Mede and Muche Thank', from Bodleian MS Digby 102, an interesting fifteenth-century collection which contains several important poems written in the South or South-East—a C-text of *Piers Plowman* and Richard Maidstone's metrical version of the Psalms. See *Twenty-Six Political and other Poems,* from Digby MS 102, etc., ed. J. Kail, EETS, OS 124 (1904).
109. Ed. J. E. Wülfing, EETS, OS 121-2 (1902-3).
110. K. Sisam, *Fourteenth Century Verse and Prose,* pp. 169-70. [For an extended discussion of this poem in its literary and historical context, see now E. Salter, *'A Complaint against Blacksmiths'*, *Literature and History* 5 (1979), 194-215.
111. 'gnacchen', 1.9, is not recorded in Middle English until the fifteenth century: see *MED*.

112. *Canterbury Tales*, I. 3760 ff.
113. See E. P. Kuhl, 'Daun Gerveys', *MLN* 29 (1914), 156.
114. See N. R. Ker, 'Medieval manuscripts from Norwich Cathedral Priory', *Transactions of the Cambridge Bibliographical Society,* I (1949-53), 1-8.
115. Henry Howard, sixth Duke of Norfolk (1628-84), divided his manuscripts between the Royal Society (who sold them to the British Musuem in 1830) and the College of Arms by his gift of 1681. Lord William Howard (1563-1640) spent his early years in Essex and near London. See *DNB*, x. 32, 81; *Catalogue of the Manuscripts of the British Museum: The Arundel Manuscripts* (London, 1834), Preface, pp. i-ii.
116. *Calendar of Close Rolls of the Reign of Henry III, AD 1251-53* (London, 1927), pp. 216-17.
117. The only distinctive western dialectal form is 'flunderys', 1.12 (cf. Norw. *flindra*), in 'fere-flunderys', 'sparks of fire'.
118. Although the collocation 'den ... dyntes' seems to be uncommon in alliterative poetry, 'deth ... dyntes' is very frequently found. See J. P. Oakden, *Alliterative Poetry in Middle English,* 2 vols. (Manchester, 1930, 1935), ii. 277.
119. See Oakden, ibid. ii. 304.
120. See *OED* and *MED* under 'cammede' and 'kongons'.
121. Ed. I. Gollancz (Oxford, 1922).
122. Ibid., p. xxvi.
123. Ibid., p. lviii.
124. Ibid., pp. vi-vii; Luttrell, 'Three North-west Midland Manuscripts', p. 39.
125. See the edition by H. L. Savage (New Haven, 1926), p. lii. But cf. L. D. Benson's argument against common authorship in *JEGP* 64 (1965), 393-405.
126. See *Piers Plowman*, C-text, Passus VI, l. 1.
127. E. Salter, 'The Alliterative Revival', p. 237.
128. See *Winner and Waster*, ed. Gollancz, l. 317: 'and Scharshull it wiste', a reference to William de Shareshull, Head of the Court of the King's Bench, 1350-7. See Gollancz, op. cit., Preface. [For an extended discussion of this poem in its literary and historical context, see now E. Salter, 'The Timeliness of *Wynnere and Wastoure*', *MAE* 47 (1978), 40-65.]
129. *Richard the Redeles*, ed. W. W. Skeat, *The Vision of William Concerning Piers the Plowman*, pp. 603 ff.; also edited as part of *Mum and Sothsegger*, ed. M. Day and R. Steele, EETS, OS 199 (1936).
130. The fifteenth-century MS Chetham 6709 abstracts two of the *Canterbury Tales* to make up a volume of Saints' Lives and Miracles of the Virgin—ignoring their context, form, and authorship. For this and similar examples, see D. S. Silvia, 'Some Fifteenth-Century Manuscripts of the *Canterbury Tales*', *Chaucer and Middle English Studies in Honour of R. H. Robbins,* ed. B. Rowland (London, 1974), pp. 153-63.
131. For discussion of the provenance of the MS, see A. I. Doyle, 'The

Shaping of the Vernon and Simeon Manuscripts', in *Robbins Studies* (cited in previous note), pp. 328-41.

132. Vernon MS (Bodleian MS Eng. Poet. a.l., *c.*1380-1400), fo. l^r. See 'The Index of the Vernon Manuscript' by M. Serjeantson, *MLR* 32 (1937), 222-61 (p. 227).

133. Ed. F. J. Amours, *Scottish Alliterative Poems*, STS, 1st Series, 27, 38 (1892, 1897).

134. See the facsimile edition by N. Ker, EETS 255 (1965), Introduction, pp. ix-xvi.

135. For the King's College MS, see *William of Palerne*, ed. W. W. Skeat, EETS, ES 1 (1867), p. vi; for the Lincoln's Inn MS, see *Kyng Alisaunder*, ed. G. V. Smithers, EETS 237 (1957), p. 3.

136. Nos. 2, 3, and 5 in Kail's edition (note 108, above).

137. British Library MS Additional 31042 and Lincoln Cathedral MS 91 (A.5.2).

138. E. Rickert, in her Introduction to *Emaré* (EETS, ES 99, 1906), p. xi, points to the 'marked religious and didactic element' in the poems of this MS: we may find the unifying principle here.

139. The name occurs on fo. 213a of the Additional MS: a Robert Thornton was lord of East-Newton, in Ryedale, by 1418. The Lincoln Cathedral MS seems to have remained in the possession of the Thornton family until the sixteenth century. See M. S. Ogden, *Liber de Diversis Medicinis* (EETS, OS 207, 1938), Introduction, pp. viii-xv.

140. Rickert, Introduction to *Emaré*, p. xi.

141. Sir Robert Cotton had the manuscript bound up between two Latin manuscripts to form the present MS Cotton Nero A.X.

142. Luttrell, 'Three North-west Midland Manuscripts', p. 42.

143. Ibid., pp. 42 ff.

144. See above, note 73.

145. See D. S. Brewer, 'An Unpublished Late Alliterative Poem', *English Philological Studies*, 9 (1965), 84-8.

146. Ibid., p. 84.

147. Ed. I. Gollancz (London, 1930).

148. *Winner and Waster*, ll. 31-2.

149. *Religious Lyrics of the XIVth Century*, ed. C. Brown (Oxford, 1924; rev. edn. 1957), no. 95, p. 125 ('... proud beasts roamed the country').

150. *Harley Lyrics*, ed. G. L. Brook, no. 25, p. 63: 'When the Nyhtegale singes ...'.

151. See above, Chapter 2, note 103.

152. See above, Chapter 2, note 106.

153. The list is printed from Bodleian MS Fairfax 10 by R. J. Dean, 'An essay in Anglo-Norman Palaeography', *Studies Presented to M. K. Pope* (Manchester, 1939), pp. 84-5, and commented upon by A. I. Doyle in 'A New Chaucer Manuscript', *PMLA* 83 (1968), 25, n. 26.

154. The Coventry manuscript, described by A. I. Doyle, as cited in note 153.

155. Anthony Wood's *Athenae Oxonienses*, ed. P. Bliss (London, 1815), ii, cols. 201-2, 203. Savile's dates are 1568-1617. For a comprehensive

study of Savile, see A. G. Watson, *The Manuscripts of Henry Savile of Banke* (London, 1969). For Banke, or Blaidroyd, his Yorkshire house, see J. Watson, *The History and Antiquities of the Parish of Halifax* (London, 1775), pp. 365-6.

156. See J. P. Gilson, 'The Library of Henry Savile of Banke', *Transactions of the Bibliographical Society*, 9 (1908), 127-210, now largely superseded by A. G. Watson's monograph.

157. The Catalogue notes the MS as 'paper': the Cotton MS is, of course, vellum. But A. G. Watson (*Manuscripts of Henry Savile* p. 68) notes that the reference to 'paper' is a mistake derived from a misreading of *pay*.

158. See C. E. Wright, 'The Elizabethan Society of Antiquaries and the Formation of the Cottonian Library', in *The English Library before 1700*, ed. F. Wormald and C. E. Wright (London, 1958), p. 199.

159. See C. E. Wright, 'The Dispersal of the Libraries in the Sixteenth Century', in *English Library before 1700*, pp. 157-8; A. G. Watson, *Manuscripts*, pp. 7-9.

160. See A. G. Watson, *Manuscripts*, pp. 4, 8.

161. Borthwick Institute of Historical Research, York, Prerog. and Excheq. Court of York, vol. xiii, fol. 1031; vol. xvii, fol. 501.

162. See Wright, 'Dispersal of Libraries', p. 173, n. 25, and A. G. Watson, *Manuscripts*, p. 8.

163. A. McIntosh, 'A New Approach to Middle English Dialectology', *English Studies* 44 (1963), 1-11 (p. 5).

164. A. G. Watson, *Manuscripts*, pp. 4-5.

165. British Museum MS Cotton Julius F.vi, fo. 316a; Watson, *Manuscripts*, p. 5.

166. The 'Mr. Savel of the Middle Temple', who was present with Cotton at a meeting of the Society of Antiquaries in 1590 (see C. E. Wright, in *The English Library before 1700*, p. 183) was probably John Savile, Master of the Bench, who died in 1607. But Henry Savile was certainly well acquainted with that learned and gentlemanly circle of men.

167. *Archdeaconry of Surrey, Register of Wills*, Calendar 1595-1630, fo. 142a: see Watson, *Manuscripts*, p. 8.

CHAPTER 4

1. G. T. Shepherd, 'The nature of alliterative poetry in late medieval England', *PBA* 56 (1970), 57-76 (pp. 68, 62, 72).

2. A. C. Spearing, *The Gawain-Poet* (Cambridge, 1970), p. 18.

3. See above, pp. 68-77.

4. J. A. Burrow, *Ricardian Poetry* (London, 1971), p. 4.

5. *Canterbury Tales*, X. 42-3.

6. *Destruction of Troy*, ed. G. A. Panton and D. Donaldson, EETS, OS 39, 56 (1869-74), 8053-4. For the Latin of the *Historia Destructionis Troiae*, see the edition by N. E. Griffin (Cambridge, Mass., 1936).

7. See C. David Benson, 'A Chaucerian Allusion and the Date of the Alliterative *Destruction of Troy*', *NQ* 219, n.s. 21 (1974), 206-7.

8. See C. A. Luttrell, 'Three North-west Midland Manuscripts', *Neoph.* 42 (1958), 38-50 (p. 42).

9. Boccaccio, *Filostrato*, viii. 29-30. Translation from *Chaucer's Boccaccio: Sources of Troilus and the Knight's and Franklin's Tales*, ed. and trans. N. R. Havely, Chaucer Studies III (Cambridge, 1980).

10. Shepherd, 'The nature of alliterative poetry', p. 72.

11. Ibid., p. 65.

12. *The Laud Troy Book*, ed. J. Ernst Wülfing, EETS, OS 121-2 (1902-3), ll. 11-14.

13. *Cligés*, ed. W. Foerster (Halle, 1888), ll. 22-9.

14. *Gui de Warewic*, ed. Alfred Ewert, Classiques français du Moyen Age, 2 vols. (Paris, 1932-3), ll. 13-16.

15. *Life of the Black Prince*, ed. Mildred K. Pope and Eleanor C. Lodge (Oxford, 1910), ll. 29-38. Translation from same edition, p. 135.

16. *English Works of John Gower*, ed. G. C. Macaulay, EETS, ES 81-2 (1900-1), *Conf. Am.*, Prol., ll. 40-4.

17. Lydgate, *Fall of Princes*, ed. H. Bergen, EETS, ES 121-4 (1924-7), iv. 22-8.

18. Shepherd, 'The nature of alliterative poetry', pp. 64-5.

19. *Winner and Waster*, ll. 20-7.

20. *Erec*, ed. W. Foerster (Halle, 1896), ll. 19-22. Translation by W. W. Comfort, *Chrétien de Troyes, Arthurian Romances* (London, 1914; reissued with Introduction and Notes by D. D. R. Owen, 1975), p. 1.

21. [I have tried to find the source of this quotation, but have not been successful.—D.P.]

22. *Life of the Black Prince*, ed. cit., ll. 1-7, 15-23.

23. Shepherd, 'The nature of alliterative poetry', p. 69.

24. Gower, *Vox Clamantis*, II. 367-8, 371-3, in *The Complete Works of John Gower*, ed. G. C. Macaulay, vol. 4: *The Latin Works* (Oxford, 1902), p. 94. Translation from E. W. Stockton, *The Major Latin Works of John Gower* (Seattle, 1962), p. 106. See also *Piers Plowman: the B Version*, ed. George Kane and E. Talbot Donaldson (London, 1975), B. XVII. 206-47; *The Siege of Jerusalem*, ed. E. Kölbing and Mabel Day, EETS, OS 188 (1932), 97-120; *Joseph of Arimathie*, ed. W. W. Skeat, EETS, OS 44 (1871), 121-46, 336-44.

25. *Vox Clamantis*, ed. cit., II. 3-6; translation from Stockton, *Major Latin Works*, p. 96.

26. *Destruction of Troy*, ed. cit., ll. 1-4; *Morte Arthure*, ed. E. Brock, EETS, OS 8 (1865; a new edition, 1871), ll. 1-11.

27. *Mum and the Sothsegger*, ed. Mabel Day and Robert Steele, EETS, OS 199 (1936), i. 1-2.

28. *Mum and the Sothsegger*, Fragment M, ll. 206-7, 211-12. Note the view, now generally accepted, of Dan Embree, '"Richard the Redeless" and "Mum and the Sothsegger": A Case of Mistaken Identity', *NQ* 220, n.s. 22 (1975), 4-12, that Fragment M is from a poem originally distinct.

29. *O Deus Immense*, ll. 21-2, in *Latin Works*, ed. cit., p. 362.

30. Gower, *Cronica Tripertita*, III. 472-5, in *Latin Works*, ed. cit., p. 342; translation from Stockton, *Major Latin Works*, p. 325.

31. *The Battle of Lewes*, ll. 285-6, 297-9, in *The Political Songs of England from the Reign of John to that of Edward II*, ed. Thomas Wright, Camden Society, 1st Series, no. 6 (1839), p. 86.

32. *On the Truce of 1347*, in *Political Poems and Songs*, ed. Thomas Wright, Rolls Series 14 (London, 1859), I. 57.

33. See Elizabeth Salter, 'Alliterative Modes and Affiliations in the Fourteenth Century', *NM* 79 (1978), 25-35.

34. *De Ortu Waluuanii*, ed. J. D. Bruce, *PMLA* 13 (1898), 365-456; *Vita Meriadoci*, ed. J. D. Bruce, *PMLA* 15 (1900), 327-414. Bruce later brought out an edition of the two romances together, *Historia Meriadoci and De Ortu Waluuanii*, Hesperia, Heft 2 (Göttingen, 1913), with revised Introduction.

35. For Arthur's Snowdonian campaign, see *Historia Meriadoci* (edn. of 1913), pp. 14-17; for comparisons between the Arthur of the *Morte Arthure* and Edward III, see William Matthews, *The Tragedy of Arthur: A Study of the Alliterative 'Morte Arthure'* (Berkeley and Los Angeles, 1960), pp. 184-92.

36. William Vantuono, 'The Structure and Sources of *Patience*', *MS* 34 (1972), 401-21 (esp. pp. 413-15).

37. See þe *Wohunge of Ure Lauerd*, ed. W. Meredith Thompson, EETS, OS 241 (1958), p. xvi.

38. Ed. in Migne, *PL* 171: columns 1687-92.

39. See Gabriel M. Liegey, 'The *Canticum Amoris* of Richard Rolle', *Traditio* 12 (1956), 369-91.

40. See M. Dominica Legge, *Anglo-Norman Literature*, pp. 75-81.

41. See E. Salter, 'Alliterative Modes and Affiliations' (cited in note 33, above); also 'Langland and the Contexts of *Piers Plowman*', *E & S* 32 (1979), 19-25.

42. See S. S. Hussey, 'Langland's reading of alliterative poetry', *MLR* 60 (1965), 163-70.

43. *Pierce the Ploughmans Crede*, ed. W. W. Skeat, EETS, OS 30 (1867), ll. 425-7.

44. *Dives and Pauper*, ed. Priscilla Heath Barnum, EETS 275 (1976), p. 57. (introductory dialogue on 'Holy Poverty', cap. iv).

45. A sermon of Bishop Brunton, quoted in G. R. Owst, *Literature and Pulpit in Medieval England* (Cambridge, 1933), pp. 560-1.

46. Gordon Leff, 'Heresy and the Decline of the Medieval Church', *Past and Present 20* (1961), 36-51 (pp. 50-1).

47. See above, note 15.

48. R. H. Hilton, *The English Peasantry in the Later Middle Ages* (Oxford, 1975), p. 18. The reference to Marx's 'historic process of dissolution' follows on p. 19.

49. See G.H. Russell, 'The Salvation of the Heathen. The Exploitation of a Theme in *Piers Plowman*', *JWCI 29* (1966), 101-16; also M. D. Knowles, 'The Censured Opinions of Uthred of Boldon', *PBA* 37 (1951), 305-42.

50. Walter L. Wakefield, 'Some Unorthodox Popular Ideas of the Thirteenth Century', *Medievalia et Humanistica*, n.s. 4 (1973), 25-35 (p. 33).
51. K. B. McFarlane, *Lancastrian Kings and Lollard Knights* (Oxford, 1972), p. 225.
52. Richard Crashaw, 'The Flaming Heart', l. 82, in *Poems*, ed. L. C. Martin (Oxford, 1927), p. 326. [Crashaw actually has '*crowd* of loues and martyrdomes', but the misquotation is a very happy one.—D.P.]
53. Charles Muscatine, *Poetry and Crisis in the Age of Chaucer* (Notre Dame, 1972), p. 22.
54. *The Rohan Book of Hours*, with an introduction and notes by Jean Porcher (London, 1959); *The Rohan Book of Hours*, with introductions by Millard Meiss and Marcel Thomas, trans. Katharine W. Carson (London, 1973).
55. Kenneth Clark, *The Nude: A Study of Ideal Art* (London, 1956), p. 249.
56. [This passage, like that referred to in note 60 below, is certainly inspired by Rilke's *Letters to a Young Poet*, but I have not been able to find the exact source of the quoted translation.—D.P.]
57. Muscatine, *Poetry and Crisis*, p. 107.
58. Gerard Manley Hopkins, 'As kingfishers draw fire', in *Poems*, ed. W. H. Gardner and N. H. Mackenzie (4th edn., London, 1967), p. 90.
59. Priscilla Jenkins, 'Conscience: the Frustration of Allegory', in *Piers Plowman: Critical Approaches*, ed. S. S. Hussey (London, 1969), pp. 125-42 (p. 140). It is Barbara Palmer, 'The Guide Convention in *Piers Plowman*', *LSE* n.s. 5 (1971), 13-27, who sees Langland's handling of allegory as confused and inept.
60. See above, note 56.
61. See especially *The Goad of Love* (his translation of the pseudo-Bonaventuran *Stimulus Amoris*), ed. Clare Kirchberger (London, 1952).
62. See Elizabeth Salter, Introduction to *Piers Plowman*, selections from the C-text (London, 1967), pp. 9-20, 28-51.
63. See Priscilla Jenkins, 'Conscience' (note 59, above).
64. Charles Muscatine, 'Locus of Action in Medieval Narrative', *Romance Philology*, 17 (1963), 115-22.
65. *The Cloud of Unknowing*, Chap. 68. For the original Middle English, see the edition of *The Cloud* by Phyllis Hodgson, EETS, OS 218 (1944), p. 121.
66. *Epistola ad Solitarium*, trans. Joy Russell-Smith, *The Way* (1966), pp. 230-41.
67. *The Goad of Love*, ed. Kirchberger, Chap. 16, p. 126.
68. Richard of Saint-Victor, *De Quattuor Gradibus Violentae Caritatis*, ed. Gervais Dumeige, Textes Philosophiques du Moyen Age, III (Paris, 1955), caps. 28-9, 45-6. See also 'Of the Four Degrees of Passionate Charity', in *Richard of Saint-Victor: Selected Writings on Contemplation*, translated with an Introduction and Notes by Clare Kirchberger (London, 1957), pp. 228-33.

CHAPTER 5

1.   For discussion of Chaucer's possible reading of Langland, see J. A. W. Bennett, 'Chaucer's Contemporary', in *Piers Plowman: Critical Approaches,* ed. S. S. Hussey (London, 1969), pp. 310-24; Jill Mann, *Chaucer and Medieval Estates Satire* (Cambridge, 1973), pp. 207-12.

2.   *Piers Plowman,* ed. Skeat, A. VIII. 1-8.

3.   Clanvowe, *Works,* ed. V. J. Scattergood (Cambridge, 1975).

4.   See Mann, *Chaucer and Medieval Estates Satire,* esp. pp. 37-54; Arnold Williams, 'Chaucer and the Friars', *Speculum* 28 (1953), 499-513.

5.   See above, Chapter 3, note 101.

6.   See especially J. A. Burrow, *Ricardian Poetry* (London, 1971).

7.   See above, p. 21.

8.   See P. M. Kean, *Chaucer and the Making of English Poetry,* 2 vols. (London, 1972), vol. 2: *The Art of Narrative,* pp. 210-39.

9.   See M. R. James, *The Bohun Manuscripts,* Roxburghe Club (Oxford, 1936); Otto Pächt, 'A Giottesque Episode in English Medieval Art', *JWCI* 6 (1943), 51-70.

10. *A Lament over the Passion,* l. 17, in *Religious Lyrics of the XIVth Century,* ed. Carleton Brown (Oxford, 1924; 2nd edn., revised G. V. Smithers, 1952), p. 95.

11. See A. C. Spearing, *The Gawain-Poet* (Cambridge, 1970), pp. 15-18.

12. *Sir Gawain and the Green Knight,* ll. 2505-12. See A. C. Spearing, *The Gawain-Poet,* p. 230; J. A. Burrow, *A Reading of Sir Gawain and the Green Knight* (London, 1965), p. 155.

13. *Gawain,* ll. 2138-9, 2158-9, 2208-11.

14. *Pearl,* ed. E. V. Gordon (Oxford, 1953), ll. 51-2, 55-6, 1189-1200.

15. See above, pp. 26 ff.

16. See Gervase Mathew, *The Court of Richard II* (London, 1968), pp. 1-11.

17. See above, pp. 96 ff.

18. See D. S. Brewer, 'The relationship of Chaucer to the English and European traditions', in *Chaucer and Chaucerians: Critical Studies in Middle English Literature,* ed. D. S. Brewer (London and Edinburgh, 1966), pp. 1-38 (pp. 1-15).

19. See J. S. P. Tatlock, 'The Epilog of Chaucer's *Troilus*', *MP* 18 (1921), 625-59.

20. For a brief account of the sources and development of the medieval Troy-Story, see R. K. Root's edition of *Troilus and Criseyde* (Princeton, 1926), Introduction, pp. xx-xlviii.

21. *Teseida delle Nozze di Emilia* is quoted from Giovanni Boccaccio, *Tutte le Opere,* ed. Vittore Branca, 6 vols. (I Classici Mondadori, 1964), vol. 2. The translations are the author's.

22. In the last stanza of *Troilus* (v. 1863-9), ll. 1863-5 are imitated from Dante, *Paradiso,* xiv. 28-30.

23. *The Parlement of Foulys,* ed. D. S. Brewer, Nelson's Medieval and Renaissance Library (London and Edinburgh, 1960), Introduction, pp. 31, 44.

24.   That is, the *Commentary* by Macrobius on the *Dream of Scipio* attributed
      To Cicero. There is a translation by W. H. Stahl (New York, 1952).

25.   Dante, *Inferno*, v. 25-45.

26.   For some account of Chaucer's handling of his sources here, see
      Parlement of Foulys, ed. Brewer, Introduction, pp. 38-46; J. A. W.
      Bennett, *The Parlement of Foules: An Interpretation* (Oxford, 1957),
      pp. 70-106.

27.   The matter is different with the *Chiose*, the commentary added by
      Boccaccio to particular passages of the *Teseida* (e.g. to Mars and Venus,
      Teseida, VII, st. 30, 50), where the glossing is explicitly interpretative.

28.   *Roman de la Rose*, ed. E. Langlois, SATF, 5 vols. (Paris, 1914-24),
      ll. 961-8: Orguiauz, Vilanie, Honte, Desesperance, Noviaus Pensers.

29.   *Roman de la Rose*, ll. 938-49; Biautex, Simplece, Franchise, Com-
      paignie, Biaus Semblanz.

30.   The *Pèlerinage de Vie Humaine*, as translated by Lydgate, *The Pilgrimage of
      the Life of Man*, ed. F. J. Furnivall and K. B. Locock, EETS, ES 77, 83,
      92 (1899-1904), ll. 13089-102.

31.   *Reson and Sensuallyte*, ed. E. Sieper, EETS, ES 84 (1901), ll. 1538-78.

32.   By contrast, again, there is much that is explicitly interpretative in the
      Chiose, e.g. 'Per la belleza di Venere, la quale sappiamo essere cosa
      labile e caduca, intende il falso giudicio de' voluttuosi, il quale da
      verissime ragioni leggierissimamente si convince e mostrasi vano'
      ('Through Venus's beauty, which we know to be a fleeting and tran-
      sient thing, he intends to be understood the false judgement of those
      who seek mere pleasure, a judgement which can readily be shown by
      true reason to be empty and vain').

33.   E. H. Gombrich, 'Botticelli's Mythologies: A Study in the Neoplatonic
      Symbolism of his Circle', *JWCI* 8 (1945), 7-60 (p. 43).

34.   Contrast the remarks of D. S. Brewer: 'In both texts there is an impli-
      cation of disapproval' (*Parlement of Foulys,* Notes, p. 108); and of
      J. A. W. Bennett: 'the atmosphere of the scene ... grows ... more
      sultry, more sinister' (*Parlement of Foules,* p. 91).

35.   e.g. Chaucer, *Merchant's Tale,* where Priapus is spoken of as 'god of
      gardyns' (*Canterbury Tales,* IV. 2035).

36.   Bacchus and Ceres are said to represent *gulosità*, 'gluttony', by
      Boccaccio in the *Chiose*.

37.   'Che partorì il bel Partenopeo, / nepore al calidonio Oeneo' (VII, st.
      61). D. S. Brewer (*Parlement of Foulys,* Notes, p. 111) claims that this
      second Atalanta (Chaucer mentions only one, without specifying
      detail) was introduced by Boccaccio because of a discreditable episode
      in her life mentioned by Ovid; but Boccaccio makes no allusion to this
      episode, neither in the text nor in the *Chiose*.

38.   J. A. W. Bennett (*Parlement of Foules*, p. 105) also alludes to Keats's
      Ode to Melancholy, but draws very different conclusions.

39.   Contrast the remarks of Bennett (*Parlement of Foules,* p. 93), who
      suggests that the atmosphere of the scene 'is, if anything, still more
      wanton, more erotic than Boccaccio implies'.

40. See Antonio Morassi, 'Una "camera d'amore" nel Castel di Avio', *Festschrift für Julius Schlosser zum 60. Geburtstage*, ed. A. Weixlgärtner and L. Planiscig (Vienna, 1927), pp. 99-103.

41. For Bennett (*Parlement of Foules*, p. 105), the relationship is very significant: 'Chaucer, for whom the temple in the last resort signifies sultriness and sorrow, suddenly takes us outside again to the temperate air, green grass, pellucid streams ... we escape to breathe again the freshness of the open park.'

42. See Derek Pearsall and Elizabeth Salter, *Landscapes and Seasons of the Medieval World* (London, 1973), Chap. 4, pp. 76-118 (esp. pp. 116-17).

43. e.g. that of *Le Roman de la Rose*, ll. 631 ff.

44. e.g. D. S. Brewer (*Parlement of Foulys*, Introduction, p. 25): 'A complex whole of related thoughts, feelings, and experiences has been created ... a place for many things in an organised whole ...'; J. A. W. Bennett (*Parlement of Foules*, pp. 15-16): 'if we assume that it has no organic unity ... then we had better close our Chaucer and open our *Reader's Digest.*'

CHAPTER 6

1. For discussion of this possibility, and of the general nature of Chaucer's adaptation of the *Teseida* in the *Knight's Tale*, see Robinson's edition of Chaucer's *Works*, 2nd edn., pp. 669-70.

2. Chaucer's *Treatise on the Astrolabe*, II.4, ll. 33-8 (*Works*, ed. Robinson, p. 551).

3. Chaucer's *Boece* (his translation of Boethius *De Consolatione Philosophiae*), Bk IV, pr. 7, ll. 12-14 (*Works*, ed. Robinson, p. 371).

4. As thus by J. A. W. Bennett, in his edition of *The Knight's Tale*, Harrap's English Classics (London, 1954), Notes, p. 118.

5. *Teseida*, Bk. IV, st. 13-14, 17, 82, 84-5.

6. See above, Chapter 5.

7. For a thorough discussion of this change, see Meg Twycross, *The Medieval Anadyomene: A Study in Chaucer's Mythography*, Medium Ævum monographs, n.s. I (Oxford, 1972).

8. e.g. J. A. W. Bennett, in his edition of *The Knight's Tale*, Notes, p. 131.

9. Statius, *Thebaid*, VII. 55-62; text and translation from the Loeb edition by J. H. Mozley, 2 vols. (London, 1928).

10. See Bennett's edn. of *Knight's Tale*, Notes, pp. 131-3; Walter Clyde Curry, *Chaucer and the Mediaeval Sciences* (Oxford, 1926; 2nd revised edn., New York, 1960), pp. 119-63 (esp. 121-4).

11. See Curry, *Chaucer and the Mediaeval Sciences*, pp. 123-4. For the 'children of Mars' and the incidents associated with them, see Raymond Klibansky, Erwin Panofsky, and Fritz Saxl, *Saturn and Melancholy: Studies in the history of natural philosophy, religion, and art* (London and Edinburgh, 1964), pp. 204-5.

12. See Klibansky, Panofsky, and Saxl, *Saturn and Melancholy*, pp. 205-7; also, F. Saxl, 'The Literary Sources of the "Finiguerra Planets"', *JW(C)I* 2 (1938), 72-4.

13. See Klibansky, Panofsky, and Saxl, *Saturn and Melancholy*, pp. 173-95.
14. An explanation suggested by Bennett, in his edition of *The Knight's Tale*, Notes, p. 144.
15. e.g. the preparation for the ending of *Troilus and Criseyde*, Bk. V, ll. 1765-1806.
16. See Dorothy Bethurum, 'Saturn in Chaucer's *Knight's Tale'*, in *Chaucer und seine Zeit: Symposion für Walter F. Schirmer,* Buchreihe der Anglia Zeitschrift für Englische Philologie, vol. 14 (Tübingen: Niemeyer, 1968), pp. 149-61. See also, E. H. Gombrich, 'Botticelli's Mythologies: A Study in the Neoplatonic Symbolism of his Circle', *JWCI* 8 (1945), 7-60; Jean Seznec, *La Survivance des dieux antiques*, Studies of the Warburg Institute, XI (London, 1940).

Select Bibliography

PRIMARY SOURCES

Amis and Amiloun, ed. MacEdward Leach, EETS, OS 203 (1937).

Ancrene Wisse, ed. J. R. R. Tolkien (Corpus Christi College, Cambridge MS 402), EETS, OS 249 (1962); Parts Six and Seven, ed. G. T. Shepherd, Nelson's Medieval and Renaissance Library (London and Edinburgh, 1959).

Of Arthour and of Merlin, ed. O. D. Macrae-Gibson, EETS, OS 268 (1973).

Athelston, ed. A. McI. Trounce, EETS, OS 224 (1951).

Audelay, John, *Poems*, ed. E. K. Whiting, EETS, OS 184 (1931).

Boccaccio, Giovanni, *Tutte le Opere*, ed. V. Branca, 6 vols. (I Classici Mondadori, 1964).

Caxton, William, *Prologues and Epilogues*, ed. W. J. B. Crotch, EETS, OS 176 (1928).

Chaucer, Geoffrey, *Works*, ed. F. N. Robinson (1933; 2nd edition, Cambridge, Mass, 1957).

Chestre, Thomas, *Sir Launfal*, ed. A. J. Bliss, Nelson's Medieval and Renaissance Library (London and Edinburgh, 1960).

Chevelere Assigne, ed. H. H. Gibbs, EETS, ES 6 (1898); unpublished edition by Elizabeth G. Williams, Univ. of London M. A. thesis (1963).

Chrétien de Troyes, *Cligés*, ed. W. Foerster (Halle, 1888).

Chrétien de Troyes, *Erec*, ed. W. Foerster (Halle, 1896).

Chronicle of the Deposition and Death of Richard II, ed. J. Webb, in *Archaeologia*, 20 (1824), 1-442.

Clanvowe, Sir John, *Works*, ed. V. J. Scattergood (Cambridge, 1975).

The Cloud of Unknowing, ed. Phyllis Hodgson, EETS, OS 218 (1944).

Cursor Mundi, ed. R. Morris, EETS, OS 57, 59, 62, 66, 68, 99, 101 (1874-93).

Death and Life, ed. I. Gollancz (London, 1930).

Dives and Pauper, ed. Priscilla H. Barnum, EETS, OS 275 (1976).

English Lyrics of the XIIIth Century, ed. Carleton Brown (Oxford, (1932).

Floris and Blauncheflur, ed. A. B. Taylor (Oxford, 1927).

Sir Gawain and the Green Knight, ed. J. R. R. Tolkien and E. V. Gordon (Oxford, 1925); ed. R. A. Waldron, York Medieval Texts (London, 1970).

The Gest Hystoriale of the Destruction of Troy, ed. G. A. Panton and D. Donaldson, EETS, OS 39, 56 (1869, 1874).

Gower, John, *Confessio Amantis*, in *Works*, ed. G. C. Macaulay, EETS, ES 81-2 (1900, 1901).

Gower, John, *Vox Clamantis*, in *Works*, ed. G. C. Macaulay, vol. 4: *The Latin Works* (Oxford, 1902).

Gui de Warewic, ed. Alfred Ewert, Classiques français du Moyen Age, 2 vols. (Paris, 1932-3).

The Harley Lyrics, ed. G. L. Brook (Manchester, 1948).

Henry of Lancaster, *Livre de Seyntz Medicines*, ed. E. J. Arnould (Oxford, 1940).

Historia Meriadoci and De Ortu Walwanii, ed. J. D. Bruce, Hesperia, 2 (Göttingen, 1913).

Hoccleve, Thomas, *Works: The Minor Poems*, ed. F. J. Furnivall and I. Gollancz, EETS, ES 61, 73 (1892, 1925).

Joseph of Arimathie, ed. W. W. Skeat, EETS, OS 44 (1871).

Kyng Alisaunder, ed G. V. Smithers, EETS, OS 237 (1957).

Langland, William, *Piers Plowman*, ed. W. W. Skeat, in three parallel texts, 2 vols. (Oxford, 1886).

Langland, William, *Piers Plowman: The B Version*, ed. G. Kane and E. T. Donaldson (London, 1975).

The Laud Troy Book, ed. J. E. Wülfing, EETS, OS 121-2 (1902-3).

Laȝamon, *Brut*, ed. G. L. Brook and R. F. Leslie, EETS, OS 250 (1963).

The Life of the Black Prince, ed. M. K. Pope and E. C. Lodge (Oxford, 1910).

Lydgate, John, *The Dance of Death*, ed. Florence Warren and Beatrice White, EETS, OS 181 (1931).

Lydgate, John, *The Fall of Princes*, ed. H. Bergen, EETS, ES 121-4 (1924-7).

Lydgate, John, *Minor Poems*, ed. H. N. MacCracken, vol. 2: Secular Poems, EETS, OS 192 (1934).

Lydgate, John, *The Pilgrimage of the Life of Man*, ed. F. J. Furnivall and K. B. Locock, EETS, ES 77, 83, 92 (1899, 1901, 1904).

Lydgate, John, *Reson and Sensuallyte*, ed. E. Sieper, EETS, ES 84 (1901).

Lydgate, John, *Troy Book*, ed. H. Bergen, EETS, ES 97, 103, 106, 126 (1906-35).

Macrobius, *Commentary on the Dream of Scipio*, trans. W. H. Stahl (New York, 1952).

Maidstone, Richard, 'The Seven Penitential Psalms', in *The Wheatley*

Manuscript, ed. Mabel Day, EETS, OS 155 (1921).

Mannyng, Robert, *Handlyng Synne*, ed. F. J. Furnivall, EETS, OS 119, 123 (1901, 1903).

Minot, Laurence, *Poems*, ed. J. Hall, 3rd edn. (Oxford, 1914).

Mirk, John, *Festial: A Collection of Homilies*, ed. T. Erbe, EETS, ES 96 (1905).

Morte Arthure, ed. E. Brock, EETS, OS 8 (1865, revised 1871).

Mum and Sothsegger, ed. Mabel Day and R. Steele, EETS, OS 199 (1936).

The Owl and the Nightingale, ed. E. G. Stanley, Nelson's Medieval and Renaissance Library (London and Edinburgh, 1960).

Pearl, ed. E. V. Gordon (Oxford, 1958).

Pierce the Ploughmans Crede, ed. W. W. Skeat, EETS, OS 30 (1867).

Political Poems and Songs, ed. T. Wright, Rolls series (London, 1859).

The Political Songs of England, ed. T. Wright, Camden Society, 6 (1839).

Ratis Raving, ed. J. R. Lumby, EETS, OS 43 (1870).

Religious Lyrics of the XIVth century, ed. Carleton Brown (1924; 2nd edn., revised by G. V. Smithers, Oxford, 1952).

Religious Lyrics of the XVth Century, ed. Carleton Brown (Oxford, 1939).

Richard Coeur de Lion, ed. K. Brunner, Wiener Beiträge zur Englischen Philologie, 42 (Vienna, 1913).

Richard the Redeles, ed. W. W. Skeat, with Langland, *Piers Plowman*.

Robert of Gloucester, *Metrical Chronicle*, ed. W. A. Wright, Rolls Series (London, 1887).

Rolle, Richard, *English Writings*, ed. Hope Emily Allen (Oxford, 1931).

Roman de la Rose, ed. E. Langlois, *SATF*, 5 vols, (Paris, 1914-24).

The Romans of Partenay, ed. W. W. Skeat, EETS, OS 22 (1866).

Saint Erkenwald, ed. I. Gollancz (1922); ed. H. L. Savage (New Haven, 1926).

Scottish Alliterative Poems, ed. F. J. Amours, Scottish Text Society, 1st series, 27, 38 (1892, 1897).

Scottish Field, ed. J. P. Oakden, Chetham Society Miscellanies, 94 (Manchester, 1935).

Secular Lyrics of the XIVth and XVth Centuries, ed. R. H. Robbins, 2nd edn. (Oxford, 1955).

The Siege of Jerusalem, ed. E. Kölbing and M. Day, EETS, OS 188 (1932).

Twenty-six Political and other Poems, ed. J. Kail, EETS OS 124 (1904).

William of Palerne, ed. W. W. Skeat, EETS, ES 1 (1867).

The Wohunge of Ure Laverd, ed. W. Meredith Thompson, EETS, OS 241 (1958).

Wynnere and Wastoure, ed. I. Gollancz (London, 1930).

SECONDARY SOURCES

Arnould, E. J., *Étude sur le Livre des Saintes Médecines* (Paris, 1948).

Axton, Richard, 'Popular Modes in the Earliest Plays', in *Medieval Drama: Stratford-upon-Avon Studies, 16,* ed. N. Denny (London, 1973), pp. 12-39.

Bennett, J. A. W. (ed.), *The Knight's Tale* (London, 1954).

Bennett, J. A. W., *The Parlement of Foules: An Interpretation* (Oxford, 1957).

Bennett, J. A. W., 'Chaucer's Contemporary', in *Piers Plowman: Critical Approaches,* ed. S. S. Hussey (London, 1969), pp. 310-24.

Bethurum, Dorothy, 'Saturn in Chaucer's *Knight's Tale*', in *Chaucer und seine Zeit: Symposion für Walter F. Schirmer* (Tübingen, 1968), pp. 149-61.

Blaess, Madeleine, 'L'Abbaye de Bordesley et les Livres de Guy de Beauchamp', *Romania,* 78 (1957), 511-18.

Blake, N. F., 'Caxton and Chaucer', *LSE,* n.s. 1 (1967), 19-36.

Blake, N. F., 'Caxton and Courtly Style', *E & S* 21 (1968), 29-45.

Blake, N. F., *Caxton and his World* (London, 1969).

Braddy, Haldeen, *Chaucer and the French Poet Graunson* (Louisiana State Univ. Press, 1947).

Brewer, D. S. (ed.), Chaucer's *Parlement of Foulys* (London and Edinburgh, 1960), Introduction.

Brewer, D. S., 'The Relationship of Chaucer to the English and European Traditions', in *Chaucer and Chaucerians,* ed. D. S. Brewer (London, 1966), pp. 1-38.

Brieger, P., *English Art 1216-1307* (Oxford, 1957).

Bullock-Davies, Constance, *Professional Interpreters and the Matter of Britain* (Cardiff, 1966).

Burrow, J. A., 'The Audience of *Piers Plowman*', *Anglia,* 75 (1957), 373-84.

Burrow, J. A., *A Reading of Sir Gawain and the Green Knight* (London, 1965).

Burrow, J. A., *Ricardian Poetry* (London, 1971).

Chambers, R. W., *On the Continuity of English Prose from Alfred to More and his School,* EETS, OS 191A (1932).

Clarke, M. V., *Fourteenth Century Studies* (Oxford, 1937).

Crow, M. M., and C. C. Olson (ed.), *Chaucer Life Records* (Oxford, 1966).

Curry, Walter C., *Chaucer and the Mediaeval Sciences* (1926; 2nd revised edn., New York, 1960).

Curtius, E. R., *European Literature and the Latin Middle Ages,* trans. W. R. Trask (London, 1953).

Deanesley, Margaret, 'Vernacular Books in England in the Fourteenth and Fifteenth Centuries', *MLR* 15 (1920), 352-6.

Dobson, E. J., *The Origins of Ancrene Wisse* (Oxford, 1976).

Doyle, A. I., 'The Shaping of the Vernon and Simeon Manuscripts', in *Chaucer and Middle English Studies in Honour of R. H. Robbins,* ed. Beryl Rowland (London, 1974), 328-41.

Dunlap, A. R., 'The Vocabulary of the Middle English Romances in Tail-Rhyme Stanza', *Delaware Notes* (1941).

Embree, Dan, ' "Richard the Redeless" and "Mum and the Sothsegger" ': A Case of Mistaken Identity', *NQ* 220 (1975), 4-12.

Fisher, J. H., *John Gower, Moral Philosopher and Friend of Chaucer* (New York, 1964).

Galbraith, V. H., 'Nationality and Language in Medieval England', *TRHS*, 4th series, 23 (1914), 113-28.

Gerould, G. H., 'The Legend of St. Christina by William Parys', *MLN* 29 (1914), 129-33.

Hammond, Eleanor P., *Chaucer: A Bibliographical Manual* (New York, 1908).

Hammond, Eleanor P., *English Verse between Chaucer and Surrey* (Durham, N. Ca., 1927).

Highfield, J. R. L., 'The Green Squire', *MAE* 22 (1953), 18-23.

Hilton, R. H., *The English Peasantry in the Later Middle Ages* (Oxford, 1975).

Hinks, Roger, *Carolingian Art* (London, 1935).

Holmes, G. A., *The Estates of the Higher Nobility in Fourteenth Century England* (Cambridge, 1957).

Hulbert, J. R., 'A Hypothesis concerning the Alliterative Revival', *MP* 28 (1931), 405-22.

Hussey, S. S., 'Langland's reading of Alliterative poetry', *MLR* 60 (1965), 163-70.

James, M. R., *The Bohun Manuscripts*, Roxburghe Club (Oxford, 1936).

Jenkins, Priscilla, 'Conscience: the Frustration of Allegory', in *Piers Plowman: Critical Approaches*, ed. S. S. Hussey (London, 1969), pp. 125-42.

Kean, P. M., *Chaucer and the Making of English Poetry*, 2 vols. (London, 1972).

Kendrick, T. D., *British Antiquity* (London, 1950).

Kirchberger, Clare (ed.), *Richard of Saint-Victor: Selected Writings on Contemplation* (London, 1957).

Kittredge, G. L., 'Chaucer and some of his Friends', *MP* 1 (1903), 1-18.

Klibansky, Raymond, Erwin Panofsky, and Fritz Saxl, *Saturn and Melancholy: Studies in the history of natural philosophy, religion and art* (London and Edinburgh, 1964).

Lawlor, John, 'The Pattern of Consolation in *The Book of the Duchess*', *Speculum*, 31 (1956), 626-48.

Leff, Gordon, 'Heresy and the Decline of the Medieval Church', *Past and Present*, 20 (1961), 36-51.

Legge, M. Dominica, 'William of Kingsmill—a Fifteenth Century Teacher of French in Oxford', in *Studies in French Language and Medieval Literature presented to M. K. Pope* (Manchester, 1939), pp. 241-6.

Legge, M. Dominica *Anglo-Norman Literature and its Background* (Oxford, 1963).

Liegey, Gabriel, 'The *Canticum Amoris* of Richard Rolle', *Traditio*, 12 (1956), 369-91.

Loomis, Laura H., 'The Auchinleck Manuscript and a possible London bookshop of 1330-1340', *PMLA* 57 (1942), 595-627.

Loomis, Laura H., 'Chaucer and the Auchinleck MS', *Essays and Studies in Honor of Carleton Brown* (New York, 1940), pp. 111-28.

Loomis, Laura H., 'Chaucer and the Breton Lays of the Auchinleck MS', *SP* 38 (1941), 14-33.

Luttrell, C. A., 'Three North-West Midland Manuscripts', *Neoph.* 42 (1958), 38-50.

MacCracken, H. N., 'An English Friend of Charles of Orleans', *PMLA* 26 (1911), 142-80.

Mann, Jill, *Chaucer and Medieval Estates Satire* (Cambridge, 1973).

Martin (Weiss), Judith, 'Studies in some early Middle English romances', Cambridge Ph.D. dissertation (1967), unpublished.

Mathew, Gervase, *The Court of Richard II* (London, 1968).

Matthews, William, *The Tragedy of Arthur: A Study of the Alliterative 'Morte Arthure'* (Berkeley and Los Angeles, 1960).

McFarlane, K. B., *Lancastrian Kings and Lollard Knights* (Oxford, 1972).

McFarlane, K. B., *The Nobility of Later Medieval England* (Oxford, 1973).

McIntosh, Angus, 'The Textual Transmission of the Alliterative *Morte Arthure*', in *English and Medieval Studies presented to J.R.R. Tolkien*, ed. N. Davis and C. L. Wrenn (London, 1962), pp. 231-40.

McIntosh, Angus, 'A New Approach to Middle English Dialectology', *ES* 44 (1963), 1-11.

McKisack, May, *The Fourteenth Century 1307-1399* (Oxford, 1959).

Muscatine, Charles, 'Locus of Action in Medieval Narrative', *Romance Philology*, 17 (1963), 115-22.

Muscatine, Charles, *Poetry and Crisis in the Age of Chaucer* (Notre Dame, Ind., 1972).

Oakden, J.P., *Alliterative Poetry in Middle English*, 2 vols. (Manchester, 1930, 1935).

Owst, G. R., *Literature and Pulpit in Medieval England* (Cambridge, 1933).

Pächt, Otto, 'A Giottesque Episode in English Medieval Art', *JWCI* 6 (1943), 51-70.

Palmer, Barbara, 'The Guide Convention in *Piers Plowman* ', *LSE*, n.s. 5 (1971), 13-27.

Pantin, W., *The English Church in the Fourteenth Century* (Cambridge, 1955).

Pearsall, Derek, 'Rhetorical *Descriptio* in *Sir Gawain and the Green Knight*', *MLR* 50 (1955), 129-34.

Pearsall, Derek, 'The Development of Middle English Romance', *MS* 27 (1965), 91-116.

Pearsall, Derek, 'Gower's Narrative Art', *PMLA* 81 (1966), 475-84.

Pearsall, Derek, *John Lydgate* (London, 1970).

Pearsall, Derek, and Elizabeth Salter, *Landscapes and Seasons of the Medieval World* (London, 1973).

Rickert, Edith, 'Chaucer at School', *MP* 29 (1932), 257-74.

Rickert, Edith, 'King Richard II's Books', *Library*, 13 (1933), 144-7.

Rickert, Margaret, *Painting in Britain. The Middle Ages* (Pelican History of Art, 1954).

Robbins, R. H., 'A Gawain Epigone', *MLN* 58 (1943), 361-6.

Robbins, R. H., 'The Poems of Humfrey Newton, Esquire, 1466-1536', *PMLA* 65 (1950), 249-81.

Russell, G. H., 'The Salvation of the Heathen: The Exploitation of a Theme in *Piers Plowman*', *JWCI* 29 (1966), 101-16.

Salter, Elizabeth, *Chaucer: the Knight's Tale and the Clerk's Tale*, Studies in English Literature 5, (London: Edward Arnold, 1962).

Salter, Elizabeth, *Piers Plowman: an Introduction*, (Oxford: Blackwell, 1962).

Salter, Elizabeth, 'The Alliterative Revival', *MP* 64 (1966), 146-50, 233-7.

Salter, Elizabeth, 'Piers Plowman and "The Simonie"', *Archiv* 203 (1967), 241-54.

Salter, Elizabeth, ed. (with Derek Pearsall), *Piers Plowman*, selections from the C-text, York Medieval Texts (London: Edward Arnold, 1967).

Salter, Elizabeth, *Nicholas Love's Myrrour of the Blessed Lyf of Jesu Christ*, Analecta Cartusiana 10 (Salzburg: Institut für Englische Sprache und Literatur, Universität Salzburg, 1974).

Salter, Elizabeth, 'The Timeliness of *Wynnere and Wastoure*', *MAE* 47 (1978), 40-65.

Salter, Elizabeth, 'Alliterative Modes and Affiliations in the Four-teenth Century', *NM* 79 (1978), 25-35.

Salter, Elizabeth, 'Langland and the Contexts of *Piers Plowman*', *E & S* 32 (1979), 19-25.

Salter, Elizabeth, 'A Complaint against Blacksmiths', *Literature and History* 5 (1979), 194-215.

Samuels, M. L., 'Some Applications of Middle English Dialec-tology', *ES* 44 (1963), 81-94.

Schirmer, W. F., *John Lydgate* (1952; trans. Ann E. Keep, London, 1961).

Serjeantson, Mary, 'The Index of the Vernon Manuscript', *MLR* 32 (1937), 222-61.

Shepherd, G. T., 'The nature of alliterative poetry in late medieval England', *PBA* 56 (1970), 57-76.

Silvia, D. S., 'Some Fifteenth-Century Manuscripts of the *Canter-bury Tales*', in *Chaucer and Middle English Studies in Honour of R. H. Robbins*, ed. Beryl Rowland (London, 1974), pp. 153-63.

Smalley, Beryl, *English Friars and Antiquity in the Early Fourteenth Century* (Oxford, 1960).

South, Helen P., 'The Question of Halsam', *PMLA* 50 (1935), 362-71.

Spearing, A. C., *The Gawain-Poet* (Cambridge, 1970).

Stenton, Sir Frank, 'The Roads of the Gough Map', in *The Map of Great Britain circa AD 1360 known as the Gough Map*, facsimile, with Introduction by E. J. S. Parsons (Oxford, 1958).

Stone, Lawrence, *Sculpture in Britain: The Middle Ages* (Pelican History of Art, 1955).

Suggett, Helen, 'The use of French in England in the later Middle Ages', *TRHS*, 28 (1946), 61-83.

Tatlock, J. S. P., *The Legendary History of Britain* (Berkeley and Los Angeles, 1950).

Taylor, G., 'Notes on Athelston', *LSE* 4 (1935), 47-57.

Thrupp, Sylvia L., *The Merchant Class of Medieval London 1300-1500* (Univ. of Chicago Press, 1948).

Tout, T. F., 'The English Civil Service in the Fourteenth Century', *John Rylands Library Bulletin*, 3 (1916-17), 185-214.

Tristram, E. W., *English Wall Painting of the Fourteenth Century* (London, 1955).

Tristram, Philippa, *Figures of Life and Death in Medieval English Litera-ture* (London, 1976).

Trounce, A. McI., 'The English Tail-Rhyme Romances', *MAE* 1, 2, 3 (1932-4).

Twycross, Meg, *The Medieval Anadyomene: A Study in Chaucer's Mytho-graphy*, Medium Ævum Monographs, n.s. I (Oxford, 1972).

Watson, A. G., *The Manuscripts of Henry Savile of Banke* (London, 1969).

Waugh, W. T., 'The Lollard Knights', *Scottish Historical Review,* 11 (1913), 55-92.

Williams, Gwyn A., *Medieval London* (London, 1963).

Wilson, R. M., *Early Middle English Literature* (London, 1939).

Wilson, R. M., 'English and French in England 1100-1300', *History,* 28 (1943), 37-60.

Wormald F., and C. E. Wright (ed.), *The English Library before 1700* (London, 1958).

SUPPLEMENTARY BIBLIOGRAPHY OF BOOKS AND ARTICLES MORE RECENTLY PUBLISHED

Aers, David, *Chaucer, Langland and the Creative Imagination* (London, 1980).

Bennett, Michael J., '*Sir Gawain and the Green Knight* and the literary achievement of the north-west Midlands: the historical background', *Journal of Medieval History,* 5 (1979), 63-88.

Boitani, Piero, *Chaucer and Boccaccio*, Medium Ævum Monographs, n.s. VIII (1977).

Brewer, Derek, 'The Social Context of Medieval English Literature', in *The New Pelican Guide to English Literature,* ed. Boris Ford, vol. i, *Medieval Literature,* Part One: *Chaucer and the Alliterative Tradition* (Penguin Books, 1982), pp. 15-40.

Burrow, J. A., *Medieval Writers and their Work: Middle English Literature and its Background 1100-1500* (Oxford, 1982).

Clanchy, M. T., *From Memory to Written Record* (London, 1979).

Coleman, Janet, *English Literature in History 1350-1400: Medieval Readers and Writers* (London, 1981).

Coleman, Janet, *Piers Plowman and the Moderni,* Letture di Pensiero e d'Arte, 58 (Rome, 1981).

Green, Richard F., 'Richard II's Books revisited', *Library* 31 (1976), 235-9.

Green, Richard F., *Poets and Princepleasers: Literature and the English Court in the late Middle Ages* (Toronto, 1980).

Havely, N. R., *Chaucer's Boccaccio*, Chaucer Studies, v (Cambridge, 1980).

Lawton, David A., '*Scottish Field:* Alliterative Verse and Stanley Encomium in the Percy folio', *LSE* 10 (1978), 42-57.

Martin, Priscilla, *The Field and the Tower* (London, 1979).

Medcalf, Stephen (ed.), *The Context of English Literature: The Later Middle Ages* (London, 1981).

Middleton, Anne, 'The Idea of Public Poetry in the Reign of Richard II', *Speculum,* 53 (1978), 94-114.

Pearsall, Derek, *Old English and Middle English Poetry*, Routledge History of English Poetry, vol. I (London, 1977).

Pearsall, Derek, 'The Origins of the Alliterative Revival', in *The Alliterative Tradition in the Fourteenth Century*, ed. B. S. Levy and P. E. Szarmach (Kent State Univ. Press, 1981), pp. 1-24.

Turville-Petre, Thorlac, *The Alliterative Revival* (Cambridge, 1977).

Vale, Juliet, 'Law and Diplomacy in the alliterative *Morte Arthure*', *Nottingham Medieval Studies*, 23 (1979), 31-46.

Wilson, Edward, *The Gawain-Poet* (Leiden, 1976).

Wilson, Edward, '*Sir Gawain and the Green Knight* and the Stanley family of Stanley, Storeton, and Hooton', *RES* 30 (1979), 308-16.

Windeatt, B. A., *Chaucer's Dream Poetry: Sources and Analogues*, Chaucer Studies vii (Cambridge, 1982).

Index

Figures in bold type indicate major references